The Paranormal

The Paranormal

Research and the Quest for Meaning

ERIC CARLTON

Ashgate

Aldershot • Burlington USA • Singapore • Sydney

#429530025

© Eric Carlton, 2000

Published by
Ashgate Publishing Limited
Gower House
Croft Road
Aldershot
Hants GU11 3HR
England

Ashgate Publishing Company
131 Main Street
Burlington
Vermont 05401–5600
USA

Ashgate website: http://www.ashgate.com

British Library Cataloguing in Publication Data

Eric Carlton.
   The Paranormal: Research and the Quest for Meaning.
   1. Parapsychology.
   I. Title.
   133

Library of Congress Catalog Card Number: 99–69505

ISBN 0 7546 0170 6

This book is printed on acid free paper

Typeset in Sabon by Manton Typesetters, Louth, Lincolnshire
Printed and bound by Athenaeum Press, Ltd.,
Gateshead, Tyne & Wear.

Contents

List of Abbreviations

BMJ	*British Medical Journal*
BUFORA	British UFO Research Association
CIA	Central Intelligence Agency
CNS	central nervous system
CSAR	Centre for Scientific Anomalies Research
CSETI	Centre for the Study of Extraterrestrial Intelligence
CSICOP	Committee for Scientific Investigation in Claims of the Paranormal
EEG	electroencephalogram
ESP	extrasensory perception
JSPR	*Journal of the Society for Psychical Research*
NASA	National Aeronautics and Space Administration
NDE	near death experience
OBE	out-of-body experience
PK	psychokinesis
SETI	Search for Extraterrestrial Intelligence
SPR	Society for Psychical Research
TM	transcendental meditation
UFO	unidentified flying object

'I have yet to see any problem, however complicated, which, when looked at the right way, did not become still more complicated.'

Poul Anderson

Introduction:
Meanings and Methods

We hardly need to be reminded that in a number of instances the scientific truths of yesterday are the relics of today. With scientific advances, theories, assumptions and 'facts' that were once unquestioningly accepted have come to be seen as erroneous and misleading, and it is the contention of those concerned with the study of the paranormal (parapsychologists) that there are – or may be – levels of complexity about the world and about human experience that we are now only just beginning to fathom. Parapsychologists insist that there are all kinds of anomalous data such as telepathy, clairvoyance, precognition, distance imaging, psychokenesis (the ability to move/affect objects by thought only) and the like, that are not susceptible to 'normal' scientific explanations.

Unsurprisingly, not everyone believes such things are possible, and they are therefore inclined either to regard the whole thing with acute scepticism or – on a more generous assessment – are likely to accept that people do have unusual experiences, but that these can be explained naturalistically. The view here is that people are notoriously credulous and are liable to make mistaken observations or misinterpretations, or – failing that – are possibly deceived by downright fraud. Believers, on the other hand, are more liable to attribute these phenomena to causes outside the normal range of human experience. They argue that such experiences are just not yet understood and deserve further careful investigation. Hence the discipline of parapsychology which, if the British Society for Psychical Research is anything to go by, is becoming more experimental and rigorous in its procedures.

Parapsychology, as a discipline, welcomes conventional scientific explanations of the phenomena in question if this is possible (for example, it is generally accepted that perhaps up to 90 per cent of unidentified flying object (UFO) sightings can be explained without recourse to alien visitors). This clears the way for other possible interpretations. What parapsychologists deplore is the tendency of extremists and sensationalists to mislead the public with facile and exaggerated claims that will not stand up to close scrutiny.

Parapsychology, therefore, is concerned with the apparent human capacity for paranormal experiences (PSI) and involves the study of a wide variety of phenomena which are not amenable to normal scientific investigation. Where attempts are made to establish the reality of paranormal phenomena, it is disputable whether the usual scientific canons of evidentiality are even appropriate. The key problem is that paranormal phenomena rarely conform to regular patterns. They are often spontaneous, and occur without prior planning or preparation for observational control. Even experimentation is of doubtful use in many cases because repeatability and predictability are by no means certain. It is only after all the evidence has been documented and analysed, and all normal explanations rejected, that any particular phenomenon can be reasonably categorized as paranormal. It follows that, because claims to have had a paranormal experience are so unusual, the evidential support has to be virtually incontestable before others will accept its plausibility (see Carlton: 1995, p. 66ff.).

It is not the task of this text to verify or otherwise the truth of such claims, but to look in some detail at the nature of acceptance. It is not so much the belief that is in question, as the *nature of believing*. Parapsychology is not, therefore, entirely outside the province of psychology, indeed, in institutional areas the departments of study are sometimes linked. It is rather on the 'unexplored borders' of psychology (and, for that matter, of sociology) that parapsychology may arguably have a place.

Any mention of paranormal experiences raises certain images in the public mind. So it is as well to clarify some of the issues involved. At the outset, it should be made clear that the paranormal should not be equated with what is generally understood as the occult. Or to be more specific, the occult could be subsumed under the broad heading of the paranormal, but paranormal is strictly a more specialized term and does not have to connote some of the more bizarre features that we tend to associate with the idea of the occult. So what is the occult? Having alluded to it, we should perhaps look at it a little more closely so as to avoid any kind of confusion. The occult usually connotes the idea of esoteric knowledge which is revealed only to initiates; a privileged kind of gnosis which is only vouchsafed to a few. It includes a belief in supernatural powers which may therefore be at the disposal of human beings; a set of special techniques which are only available to chosen or trained practitioners. Note that this might also be said to be true of religion generally, but a distinction should be made between supplicative beliefs and practices (religion) and manipulative beliefs and practices (occult). This may seem a slightly forced or artificial distinction, but it is a useful one.

The occult may be seen as an arcane or secret science, an idea that is implicit in certain forms of witchcraft. Such notions can also be found in atavistic teachings about the 'Old Religion' of ancient Britain with its marked fertility emphasis. In modern times this has been revitalized by some 'natural living' environmentalists who wish to protect the 'old ways', and is thus given a patina of respectability. It has also been taken up by some feminists who repudiate patriarchal religion, and have turned their attentions to the traditional mother goddess for matriarchal comfort.

The paranormal is therefore technically the special province of the – admittedly – ill-defined subject of parapsychology. So, at the risk of unnecessary reiteration, we can say that the main concerns of parapsychology are those phenomena whose mechanisms cannot be explained in terms of currently acceptable science. It is felt, however, that the phenomena in question cannot be lightly dismissed, yet it is conceded that the hypotheses that are held to account for them must take their place among an assortment of contenders for meaning and explanation. Parapsychologists can easily feel intimidated by the overarching claims of scientific orthodoxy compared with which their 'science' is relegated to the sidelines, if, indeed, it is recognized at all. One parapsychologist, deploring the state of affairs says 'so long as the pursuit of psychical research is given neither the economic resources nor the basic academic respect that any field of knowledge needs in order to flourish, it cannot possibly ... develop' (Gregory: 1983b).

Parapsychologists are not only on the defensive in relation to the accepted science disciplines, they are also wary of the behavioural sciences with which they might be thought to share more common ground. Their interests overlap at certain points, but what work has been done is seen by some devotees as little more than mere trivializing, if not downright condescending (Grattan-Guinness: 1985).

The entire issue is vitiated by the problem of knowledge. How is knowledge derived, fashioned and authenticated? Presumably it must derive from experiment and experience, but what *counts* as knowledge is very much a social construct. The climate of opinion will be conditioned by the intellectual ethos of the culture concerned. This will determine what is and what is not to be regarded as 'proper knowledge', and how that knowledge is to be legitimated. Inevitably there will be a problem of conflicting rationalities. Different theorists present us with seemingly irreconcilable paradigms, yet each may have their own distinctive merits. Parapsychology may thus be seen as a discrete knowledge system which constitutes an additional avenue to understanding and explanation.

A further issue which should be clarified is that of the relationship between religion and the paranormal, something we have already anticipated and which crops up again in further discussion. At its most basic level religion, by its very nature, is concerned with another order of reality. It treats of the supramundane; it imputes a quality of sacredness to otherworldly beings who may be associated with the fundamental structure of the universe. To this extent, religion, by definition, comes under the heading of the paranormal. But what is usually assumed by the paranormal is not rehearsed in rituals and has no ritual functionaries (unless we include – as perhaps we should – the highly contentious 'ritual' of the seance, sometimes conducted by professional mediums or mystics). Furthermore, it is not normally believed that an interest in the paranormal necessarily involves some ethical dimension. No behavioural imperatives flow from a belief in extrasensory perception, precognition, telekinesis and so forth, although a number of people do claim to have had their lives changed quite fundamentally by out-of-body experiences.

Religion is very much a communal activity, but it also has very important *subjective* implications. Religions, and this very much concerns the 'high' or universal religions, tend to lay considerable stress on mysticism and the religious experience, and many believers would try to distinguish these from 'altered states' of consciousness which can result from drugs, fasting and even solitude, and which, they might argue, had only a psychological significance. Also, the religious experience often involves a *claim to revelation*, a special knowledge which is held to be quite unlike any artificially induced experiences.

The paranormal, as it is usually conceived is similar but different. One of the main characteristics of the paranormal is that it deals with *dissonant and contradictory claims to knowledge* (Truzzi: 1974). These claims are concerned with the dissonance between empirical 'truth' and non-empirically validated 'truth', and are either related to *anomalous objects*, that is, things which are out of the ordinary such as Loch Ness Monsters, fairies, UFOs and suchlike, or *anomalous processes*, for example, belief in/claims that 'curses' and 'spells' (as in witchcraft) can affect human experience, and constitute a kind of 'fate'. It is even possible to integrate these into a fully developed system, as in astrology, though bearing in mind what Carl Jung called the problem of 'synchronicity' (coincidence).

As these systems lay claim to knowledge, certain questions must be asked:

1. What is it that is alleged to be known? What is the *nature* of the information or the claim that has been made?
2. Who claims to know it? What is the *source* of the information or claim?

3. How or why do they know it? Under what *conditions* did they learn or experience this?
4. How is this belief sustained? Does it/has it been modified or lessened by time, or 'neutralized' by discussion?
5. Has this knowledge or experience changed the subject's world view in any significant way? For example, some people who claim to have had an out-of-body experience (OBE) maintain that they no longer fear death.
6. Does this world view fit or integrate with any known or accepted world view/ideology or belief system, for example, visions or apparitions which may confirm religious beliefs?

As we shall see when we look at the history and development of studies of the paranormal (Chapter 1), the 'raw materials' of such studies have been reported from time immemorial and include a whole spectrum of strange and inexplicable phenomena. These range from unusual dreams which turn out to have some special significance, to extraordinary 'cures' for seemingly intractable conditions. It follows, therefore, that the armoury of research techniques available to the investigator is both limited and uncertain. Attempts have been made to refine these techniques so as to produce fail-safe experiments and yield valid results, but – by and large – they still do not satisfy the demanding criteria advocated by most orthodox scientists.

We have already noted that many instances of the paranormal or psychic experience are spontaneous and non-recurrent. There are many case histories of these, but the problem is that they cannot subsequently be replicated. It hardly needs to be emphasized, therefore, that the evidential status of such personal experiences which are obviously so real to the subject, is considered doubtful and is consequently treated with some reserve by investigators. Personal conviction does not have to be convincing to others. And even where statistics are used to test the validity of a number of experiences of a similar kind, for example, reported instances of telepathy, it is extraordinarily difficult to rule out the possibility of coincidence. On the other hand, there are case collections which are really quite impressive, especially the data which have been evaluated by several independent groups of researchers. Where experiences are recurrent, such as those where people have claimed repeated instances of seeing the same apparition or of hearing ghostly noises, attempts have been made to check the details with other independent observers or by setting up experimental conditions with experienced researchers. Again, this has often been done with interesting results, as in the study by Gauld and Cornell (1979) who examined

500 cases of hauntings. But, as even the 'trade' admits, reported instances of hauntings are rarely taken that seriously. The media may make something of them, but critics are inclined to attribute such experiences either to fraud or to unexplained – possibly drug-induced – hallucination.

The parapsychologist, Robert Morris, admits that there is an endless variety to the strategies for being misled about the psychic skills (gifts?) that we believe we possess or others appear to display. We can so easily deceive ourselves and, in turn, be deceived by many competent fraudsters. Both experienced researchers and lay people can be – and have been – led astray by clever charlatans. M.L. Keene (1976) has written in some detail about his life as a fake medium and of his time as head of a spiritualist church. He has described the various techniques that he and others have employed to fool the unwary. Almost any mediumistic phenomena from plaintive voices to ethereal apparitions could be reproduced by technical means. Quite unscrupulously these were used to considerable effect upon those – often only recently bereaved – who desperately wanted to believe the truth of the 'psychic message'. The potentially exploitable were always fair game, especially if they were wealthy.

In order to guard against possible accusations of fakery, parapsychologists have tried to perfect their own research methodology. This, they feel, will not only help them to detect fraud in others, but also enable them to make what they believe to be 'true' statements about certain paranormal phenomena to the public at large. For them it is of fundamental importance to decide on the genuineness of the reported experience, and then to decide whether this can really be regarded as evidence of PSI quality in the subject concerned. Spontaneous incidents such as premonitions are very difficult to assess. (There were 17 known cases before the sinking of the *Titanic* in 1912, but could this be regarded as *proof* of precognition?) But if a particular experience is set up, such as a card-guessing game, and a subject scores significantly higher than could be expected by chance (something which is mathematically calculable), can this be regarded as valid evidence of some strange precognitive skill?

Suppose parapsychologists want to test for ESP (extrasensory perception) and they use the well-tried card sequence method. What does it actually tell them? They might be able to rule out alternative interpretations based on sensory cues and non-random target sequences, but would this demonstrate that ESP really exists? What they would know is that some form of perception – as yet to be explained – had led to the acquisition of a particular kind of knowledge. In other words, they have discovered an *anomaly*, and the term ESP is nothing more than a label that is used to express the presence of this anomaly. They have learned a curious fact, but nobody is that much wiser. It is generally true to say that the challenge of modern PSI research is to try to discover what such anomalies mean.

Experimental parapsychologists employ a whole battery of tests in their work to elicit different kinds of response. After eliminating, as far as possible, the various sources of error, statistical analysis is used to test for the relevant degree of significance. A particularly popular test with a number of experimentalists is the Automated Ganzfeld System in which the 'receiver' (of the telepathic message) is seated in a soundproofed room with headphones playing 'white noise' (a soft hiss), and halved table tennis balls taped over the eyes. A strong light is shone on the receiver's face, incidentally to keep him alert, but primarily to create the Ganzfeld effect, that of a featureless red void. These conditions are intended to produce 'cortical arousal', an altered state of consciousness in which the receiver is deprived of sensory stimuli without being put to sleep. In another soundproofed room, a 'sender' looks at slides or videotapes containing a number of vivid images which he attempts to transmit telepathically to the receiver. Each image is randomly selected by computer from a group of four, and the receiver, using a microphone, tells the sender what impressions he is having. Afterwards, all four slides/videos are shown to the receiver and he is asked which most corresponds with image(s) he 'saw'. This is then compared with the spoken responses at the time of the test, and evaluated by the researchers.

According to the late Charles Honorton, a reputable American parapsychologist, this test works best – for some reason or another – with extroverted, artistic people. He reported particularly good results from students at the Juilliard School of Music and Drama in New York, and insisted that critics had no alternative but to accept them, whatever they might mean. He certainly did not think that they could be easily explained in terms of coincidence. In this sense, Ganzfeld results are rather like those obtained from intelligence testing: when the tests have been carried out and the results evaluated, what do they mean? What exactly has been tested? We are still not sure what intelligence *is*. Perhaps – as some critics have argued – it is simply what intelligence tests measure, whatever that is.

Testing for the paranormal, then, has become more and more sophisticated. But, as in the subject of psychology, there has been something of a backlash from the humanistic lobby within the discipline. There are those who have serious doubts about results gleaned from artificially contrived experimental situations, and applaud the 'simple' approach of accepting at face value the testimony of rational and reliable witnesses. It is conceded that experimental methods have a place in the investigation of the paranormal, but it is vigorously argued that the stated experiences of reputable people should not be disparaged or discredited. Renee Haynes, a respected member of the Society for Psychical Research, says that her own preference is for spontaneous cases arising from conviction, and adds that paranormal faculties are best studied in context, the natural setting of time and place and circumstances, rather than in the laboratory (Haynes: 1982, pp. viii–ix). It probably is useless to assume that paranormal faculties or experiences can be generated to order. And it is known that in testing procedures one can get different results with the same person doing the same test at different times; there are often too many variables to take into account. Perhaps there should be some scepticism about such things as ectoplasm, materialization, levitation and the like. Maybe these should be given a wide berth. But this still leaves a whole host of phenomena which are so well attested that they deserve careful and serious investigation.

CHAPTER ONE

The Development of Ideas about the Paranormal

As far as we know, there never was a time when people did not have – or claim to have – 'psychic' experiences and/or 'psychic' powers. The evidence we have suggests that such ideas go back into remote antiquity. The belief, for example, in an evil or daemonic power which is thought to exist as a potent unseen force, or as a quality possessed by certain individuals seems to be ubiquitous. Such ideas and beliefs have a universal distribution and can be found in every kind of society. There are many variations to the forms this evil takes, although there is a remarkable similarity about the essentials. One common cultural form is that of witch beliefs which today would be classified as a feature of the occult. These comprise a constellation of ideas and practices that can be found in preliterate tribal society, in developed medieval society and – especially in its 'white witch' form – in modern society as well. It is estimated that the Inquisition burned some 30 000 witches, and that perhaps as many as 200 000 suffered in Europe between c. 1450 and c. 1750 (Robbins: 1964). It is surprising to learn that the last witch to be burned in the UK was in Scotland in 1727, and that the final repeal of the Witchcraft Act which concerned not only the practice but also the *pretence* to practise witchcraft did not take place until as recently as 1951.

The witch 'experience' is said to have strong moral connotations in so far as it recognizes an opposition of moral values and a reversal of the norms of society (Mayer: 1970). Modern 'white' witches, on the other hand, claim that what they do with the aid of nature-spirits is positively beneficial to society. This power is often believed to be specifically located, and it may be held – as it is in a number of African societies – that it can be identified by various oracular practices (Evans-Pritchard: 1937). Witches are also said to possess peculiar characteristics (for example, the ability to take werewolf form among the Navaho) as well as exercise uncanny powers. Needless to say, it is – and always has been – impossible to demonstrate empirically any connection between those said to possess these powers and the effects (often misfortune) they are supposed to have caused (Carlton: 1994, pp. 178–85).

From remotest times, various cultures had traditions concerning the paranormal; stories of miraculous healings, telepathic communication,

divination and revelation, besides a fairly full quota of evil omens and
daemonic possession. We are not, of course, able to test the reliability of
these traditions or always to make sense of exactly what took place, but
in so far as there is an enduring and consistent pattern of experience it
deserves some respect.

If we look briefly at the two archaic cultures of ancient Mesopotamia
and its contemporary ancient Egypt we find ample evidence of belief in
paranormal experiences. In the earliest developed Mesopotamian society, that of the Sumerians, there was a vast pantheon of gods (the
Sumerians themselves gave the almost certainly inflated figure of 3 600)
together with an unseen assembly of daemons. The gods were seen as a
hierarchy of divine beings ranging from family deities to tutelary or
city-state deities. The casting of spells was commonplace, especially
when it was feared that the gods had handed a person over to evil
spirits, in which case yet more magic was required. For magic to be
effective, purification (by bathing) and sometimes exclusion were required. The Sumerians and the later Babylonians believed themselves to
be continually at the mercy of evil powers. The daemons/evil spirits that
caused misfortune were rarely documented in case they might be used
against those who were casting the spell. There were also good spirits
that were susceptible to white magic and could be invoked for protection against the depredations of the evil spirits which could be summoned
by the esoteric use of black magic. Daemons could be of either sex, and
it was held that they even existed in the Underworld to plague the dead.
Priests were often requested to help combat the forces of evil. But it is
intimated in the texts that incantations may not have been enough to
ward them off, and that the only solution was for the 'witches' who
were believed to be guilty of sorcery to be identified and symbolically
tried and burned (von Soden: 1994, pp. 198–201).

The Egyptians present a similar case. Spells to counter the malevolent
activities of evil beings were well known, whether their victims were the
living or the dead. The Egyptian Book of the Dead contains spells for
the deceased who were often afraid that the evil ones might deprive
them of some vital organ of the body, especially the heart which was
believed to be the seat of consciousness. Innumerable serpents and
crocodiles were also thought to lay in wait for the departed, and powerful magic was needed to keep them at bay. Indeed, the entire passage to
the Other World was fraught with dangers from fierce demons who
would do everything they could to prevent the dead from reaching their
destination. Naturally, this called for the recitation of the appropriate
spells in order to neutralize their attacks. Only then would the deceased
be able to pass through the 14 districts to reach the Other World in

safety (Shorter: 1978, pp. 67–8). Magical protection for the deceased was increased by the inclusion of grave goods such as figurines and the like. Even the texts themselves are believed to have been arranged in a certain order so as to enhance the potency of the magic. This was particularly the practice for rulers and members of the royal family.

Rulers had periodic 'jubilees' during their lifetime, ostensibly to restore magically their waning powers. By the time of the Old Kingdom (c. 2680–c. 2180 BC) magical substitution probably took the place of human sacrifice (a known ritual in many relatively modern African tribes such as nineteenth-century Uganda). Magic and religion were practically inseparable. When a ruler died, his Ka, his spirit or life force, had to be insured against violation, and this meant that the appropriate magical rituals had to be performed. Tombs existed to protect the physical body (plundering of tombs was a capital offence) and there were incantations to ward off the evil spirits. All illness had a cause, and not unusually it was attributed to some kind of 'devil' which could be invoked by those who were bent on causing harm. For instance, towards the end of the New Kingdom (c. 1570–c. 1080 BC) there was a conspiracy between certain high officials and the women of the harem to do away with the king, Rameses III, which was foiled. It failed not only because it was betrayed, but because the method the conspirators employed was nothing more lethal than the writing of magic spells (David: 1982).

It has to be said that in many societies there was a healthy concern about purveyors of the occult. Some philosophers – especially the Greek sophists – treated various omens with disdain, and Thucydides in his classic account of the Peloponnesian War between Sparta and Athens (431–404 BC), openly ridicules the soothsayers who were trying to exploit the plague that raged in Athens during the early part of the war. But not everyone was so sceptical. Interestingly, the turning-point of the war was the defeat of the Athenian invasion of Syracuse (415–413 BC) when the Athenian general, Nikias, refused to evacuate his troops until he had received the right omens – and then it was too late to save the destruction of his army.

In the ancient world people high and low were fascinated by oracles. In antiquity, divination was considered to be an official institution. In Egypt and Mesopotamia, and even in Israel, and later in Greece and Rome, it was obligatory for political and military leaders to consult an oracle, to take the 'auspices', before embarking upon any enterprise. If they failed to do so, it was regarded as the height of irresponsibility. And if the enterprise failed, it was seen as a punishment by the gods who felt slighted that they had not been suitably consulted (Flaceliere:

1965). The Greeks, whose intellectuals tended to take a more rationalistic approach to these matters, could also be extremely susceptible to such ideas. Before the Syracusan expedition, the gods were affronted by the thoughtless vandalism of certain high-spirited individuals who had damaged some religious images by knocking off their phalluses. This was held by some to be the real reason for the expedition's failure.

Even Socrates was not immune, and advised people to consult oracles. After all, it was the oracle of Apollo at Delphi which had proclaimed him the wisest of men. This oracle whose medium was the Pythia, or priestess, was actually manned by priests through whom the consultation was made. Her prophecy or pronouncement was given while in a state of ecstasy possibly induced by a drug of some kind (laurel leaves have been suggested). However paranormal the process was thought to be, it is known that it was possible to influence the oracle – or, more accurately, its functionaries – to give answers/advice that was politically advantageous to the 'customers', especially if they were highly placed or wealthy officials.

It is notable that the Greeks not only recognized the gods (*theoi*) but also what were sometimes referred to as 'The Stronger Ones' which included the *daimones* (from which we – somewhat misleadingly – derive our word daemons). In the ancient world this term was ill-defined but, broadly speaking, it represents a kind of occult power, a force that impels people which they do not understand and yet find it difficult to resist. A daemon had no image and no cult; according to one classicist, 'daimon is the veiled countenance of divine activity' (Burkert: 1985, p. 180). The daemons were not the only uncanny powers in the over-crowded realms of the supernatural, but very generally speaking they were the 'spirits' which were thought to have evil characteristics – a view possibly fostered by Plato. (Interestingly, in some Greek rituals it was believed that evil spirits could be banished by telling lewd jokes; see Kirk: 1974, p. 199.) For example, in the fifth century BC, the zenith of Greek achievement, a doctor is known to have attributed the suicides of neurotic women and girls to imaginary apparitions, to 'evil daimones'. It is ironic, however, that Plato's mentor Socrates, at his trial on a highly disputable charge of atheism spoke about his unique inner experience as his 'daimon'. And it cost him his life (399 BC).

A special knowledge of daemons was claimed by the sect known as the Pythagoreans who insisted that they could see and hear them, and were surprised that others did not share their experience. The Pythagoreans were ascetics who lived by strict dietary and sexual rules (*akousmata*) which had to be scrupulously observed. Their communities were considered élitist. Their assumed 'holier-than-thou' attitudes came to be regarded as an affront to the wider society, and in due course they were unjustly persecuted and suffered the most fearful massacres.

Many Greek ideas about the supernatural found their counterparts in Rome. The gods – though under different titles – were very similar, and in some cases were virtually identical. But with the success of Roman arms in western Europe, North Africa and Asia Minor came an influx of foreign, 'mystery' religions. Many gravitated towards these more exotic faiths which emanated mainly from Egypt and Asia Minor, areas that had much older civilizations than Rome, and which were therefore held in some awe by the parvenu culture that had now conquered much of the known world. Their devotees felt that at last there was an alternative to the avowedly State religion of Rome. In these cults they found an explanation for the world and possible answers to the problems of evil and death. Ordinary citizens apparently regarded these oriental cults with some ambivalence. By no means everyone was seduced by them, especially the more sceptical intellectuals. The satirist, Juvenal, for instance, wrote of the Orontes pouring her muddy floods of superstition into the Tiber, and deplored the ways in which gullible people were taken in by those he regarded as rogues and charlatans.

Juvenal was quite indiscriminate in his criticisms, and perhaps unjustifiably caustic in some of his comments, but he and others were understandably cynical about divination (long practised in Rome and not peculiar to the newer cults) and the prognostications of the astrologers. Petronius also cites a character whose guests dine round a table designed with the signs of the zodiac, and who listened credulously to stories of werewolves and vampires, and is in fear of evil omens. Pliny too speaks cuttingly of occultism and magic-mongering, although he admits that at least some people are helped by them (Carcopino: 1970, pp. 128–35). By contrast, Cicero, the aristocrat lawyer-statesman, whom many would associate with a more rationalist turn of mind, encouraged the use of divination. He writes of 'fauns who have been heard speaking in battles', and he reminds his readers that in times of disturbance 'voices speaking the truth are said to have come forth from the unseen' (*ex occulto*). And in support he cites voices that had been heard from the 'grove of Vesta' during an invasion by the Gauls, and 'the temple of Juno during an earthquake' (quoted by Grant: 1957, p. 39).

Nothing we have said so far about ancient societies is really that unusual. Paranormal phenomena of various kinds have been reported in widely different cultures over time and have given rise to all sorts of esoteric movements. The Magi and Mithraism in early Iran, the Kabalah and Gnostic (secret knowledge) sects in Judaism, fairy myths and the like in Celtic culture, magic and oracles associated with Buddhism in China and Tibet, and so forth. Islam, a fervently monotheistic religion was itself not free from the taint of magic and superstition. The very fact that the Koran (Qur'ān) inveighs against occult practices is ample proof that such practices existed. From its inception in the seventh century AD, arising as it did in a polytheistic environment, Islam accepted that its adherents might protect themselves from the malevolence of evil spirits by the wearing of charms and amulets. The medieval period in Western civilization was no less affected with similar underlying ideas. The Church at this time found itself having to deal with reported cases of hauntings and poltergeists, many of which were attributed to daemonic possession, and some – more especially apparitions – to divine revelation. One has only to think of the scepticism of the ecclesiastical authorities when faced with Joan of Arc's insistence that she was guided by divine voices or, at a more unintentionally comic level, of Martin Luther, the scourge of the Catholic hierarchy in the sixteenth century, throwing an inkwell at what he held to be the Devil. In the following century, the Church had to deal with the mysterious organization known as the Rosicrucians, one of whose members was the author and archaeologist, Elias Ashmole, whose antiquities became the basis of the Ashmolean Museum at Oxford. The Rosicrucians had a keen interest in the occult, and even attracted the attention of noted rationalist philosophers such as Descartes, Spinoza, and Leibniz who was an association secretary of the Rosicrucians in his early years (Crow: 1972).

In the eighteenth century, Prospero Lambertini (later Pope Benedict XIV) initiated a study of reported paranormal phenomena which is still regarded as something of a landmark today. His conclusions were liberal – one might almost say, humanistic – in nature, especially his view that many of these phenomena need not be attributed to either divine or demonic agencies but to certain little understood innate characteristics or capacities of the persons concerned. As Joseph Rush puts it, 'Thus within the spiritistic orientation of the Church we find a precociously naturalistic interpretation of psi phenomena' (Rush: 1986b, p. 12).

As early as the sixteenth century, the physician, Paracelsus (who also recorded the 'experiences' of those who reported meetings with otherwordly 'Elementals') advocated the use of magnets as an aid to communication with other-worldly bodies, and in the eighteenth century, we find the radical Dr Franz Mesmer in Paris employing similar techniques to induce all manner of hysterical states in patients, many of whom went on to claim some improvement in their ailments. Some entered a hypnotic or trancelike state – that is, a state of heightened suggestibility – and apparently displayed a propensity for supranormal cognition. Again – though all rather mystical – there is a departure from the notion of spirits, and a willingness to entertain the possibility of a rational explanation for these unusual occurrences.

It is somewhat surprising to note that during the whole of these periods there were intriguing reports of what some now assume to be extraterrestrial phenomena. These traditions are not confined to the archaic societies of Egypt and Mesopotamia, but in various forms can be found in writings from the seminal societies of Israel and Greece, as well as numerous Far Eastern cultures. Jacques Vallee a critical investigator of UFO phenomena, cites the example of medieval Japan where in August AD 989, during a period of great social unrest, some round objects of 'unusual brilliance' were observed. There was a tendency to associate disruptive social movements and revolutionary activity with celestial apparitions as 'signs from heaven'. In September AD 1271, for instance, when a questioning priest was about to be beheaded at Kamakura, an object like a full moon appeared in the sky. The officials panicked and the execution was not carried out. In the following centuries, there were further instances of bright, flying objects being reported in the sky, and many people – especially the nobility – saw them as omens and portents (Vallee: 1977, pp. 12–13).

We cannot say – certainly not as this stage – just how authentic any of these accounts of the paranormal are. We know only the *reported experiences* of others, although the testimony that has been given in many cases does come from what most of us would regard as honest and reliable witnesses. The case obviously becomes both weaker and stronger the more up to date the incidents reported happen to be: weaker, in that more technology makes charlatanism that much easier, and stronger in that it is obviously simpler to check the facts of contemporary claims to paranormal experiences.

If we, therefore, now concentrate on the development of research into such claims from the nineteenth century onwards, we find a much more critical ethos prevailing, and this accords with the growing ascendancy of the physical sciences. In different ages the experience of paranormal phenomena tends to take different forms. From the middle of the twentieth century, with the first intrepid beginnings of space travel, minds have been exercised by reports of UFO sightings and the possibility of tentative exploratory visits by extraterrestrials. It was quite different in the middle of the nineteenth century. Then the issue was survival after death, and this gave rise to the spiritualist movements which actually had their beginnings in Sweden and Germany, and spread to the USA, Britain and Western Europe generally (Nelson: 1969). Early cultures, especially those which practised ancestor worship, had long believed that spirits affected and even interfered in human affairs. It was also held that certain privileged individuals, quasi-divine rulers, prophets, shamen and the like were in occasional touch with the spirits. But the idea that by the use of *special techniques*, usually by entering an hypnotic or trance-like state, certain gifted people could effectively communicate with the 'other world' *as a matter of routine* or ritual, had not so far been extensively exploited. The movements expanded, and their seances were not confined to the traditional esoteric group holding hands in a dark room. Mediums became famous for their *public* demonstrations. For many in their audiences they unquestionably satisfied an urgent longing to know that such spirits existed and that they, too, would one day join them. Spiritualism flourished on the apparent resolution of doubt, and became so popular that one book on the subject went through 34 editions in 30 years.

As time went on, the 'gift' of mediumship appeared to become universalized. More and more people found themselves able to exercise the same powers. Demand stimulated supply; the phenomena proliferated. Table tipping, automatic writing sometimes on slates, levitation, clairvoyant diagnoses of illnesses, and even materializations (sometimes partial and sometimes whole human figures), besides speaking with trance-induced spirit voices, became almost commonplace (Rush: 1986c, pp. 13–17). With such widespread interest, the unscrupulous quickly sensed that there was money to be made from the new 'craze'. The experts began to charge for their services, and trickery and fraud soon made an appearance and eventually brought the movement into disrepute. In some cases, however, even seasoned investigators were still not able to sort the wheat from the chaff. Many frauds were quickly exposed, but some phenomena have not been satisfactorily explained to this day. The American medium, Daniel Home, was a case in point. He was able to display an impressive repertoire of effects almost like an illusionist, but was never caught out (John Beloff quoted in Rush: 1986c, p. 16). Strange as it may seem, this sometimes applied to the tricksters themselves. They produced effects which were shown to be false, but there were others which even *they* could not explain, almost as though they were working 'magic' in spite of themselves (note the case of the Italian woman, Eusapia Palladino – a particularly controversial medium).

These phenomena attracted many eminent people, both as devotees and as critics, from the arts and from the sciences. The possibility of ESP had profound implications, and it is not surprising that certain academic philosophers such as Henry Sidgwick, Frederic Myers and

William James began to take a keen interest in what was happening. In Britain, the Society for Psychical Research (SPR) was founded in February 1882 with Professor Sidgwick as its president. In its early years, the Society boasted several Fellows of the Royal Society, two Prime Ministers and a number of professors among its members. The emphasis, though still very much concerned with the question of survival, shifted somewhat to questions concerning the possible unrealized capacities of the human personality such as clairvoyance, telepathy, telekinesis, and the ubiquitous phenomena of hauntings and poltergeists.

Divisions soon began to appear among the PSI-minded fraternity. There were differences of opinion between the spiritualists and those with broader interests, and between those who were unalterably convinced about the 'truth' of the paranormal, and those who took an uncompromisingly rational approach to such phenomena. The 'rationalists' effectively won the day, and the scientific study of the paranormal became well established. Work on the Continent took a little longer to get going, but by the end of the century, experiments were under way both there and in the USA.

Despite these promising beginnings, the pace slackened in the early years of the twentieth century. Why? We are not quite certain. One would have thought it might have been otherwise in the aftermath of the carnage of the First World War. We know that this occasioned increased questioning about the accepted religious truths but, at the same time, the bereaved wanted to believe that their husbands, sons and brothers had not departed for ever. This happened in the case of the eminent Oliver Lodge, who was drawn to the Society for Psychical Research after the wartime death of his son. Mediumistic activity should have come into its own, but fakery and charlatanism had brought an understandable degree of disillusionment among would-be converts. In 1923, Margery Crandon, the wife of a well-known Boston lawyer, held seances that were attended by many famous people including the illusionist and escapologist, Harry Houdini, but she too was shown to be a fraud. Professional investigators became very hesitant about the whole seance procedure. There was often a great deal of ambiguity and obscurity in the 'messages', and all in all the entire display was found difficult to evaluate. Similar problems obtained over the matter of survival. Investigators found it virtually impossible to tell whether the seance experience had a paranormal dimension (i.e. a spirit 'guide') or whether there was just some kind of inexplicable telepathic communication taking place between the medium and the enquirer (Roll: 1974).

The dissatisfaction that was felt led investigators to develop (one can hardly say perfect) more refined techniques for testing various manifestations of what they saw as PSI. Controlled experiments with sets of cards had been employed as early as the 1880s, but were modified and the results given greater credence by the use of sophisticated statistical evaluations. The work of J.B. Rhine and his wife Louisa at Duke University, North Carolina, from 1930 onwards is one of the most important landmarks in the history of the discipline. They were both keen to test recurrent paranormal phenomena although neither (and this is especially true of Louisa Rhine) were averse to giving considerable respect to well-attested reports of non-recurrent phenomena. Their speciality was ESP card tests for telepathy, clairvoyance and precognition (25 cards in sets of five symbols), but they also used dice for the same purpose. These tests and their purported results excited a lot of interest elsewhere, but other experimenters were not able to reproduce such good results as the Rhines. As is all too common – and to some extent necessary – among academics, the Rhines came in for a great deal of criticism from a number of their fellows, mainly on the grounds of imprecise statistical procedures and the experimental conditions in which the tests were conducted. The Rhines did their best to refute these allegations, but inevitably the criticisms took a little of the gilt off the gingerbread.

Meanwhile, other experimenters, for example, in France, were taking a more psychological approach and subjecting select groups of subjects to analysis in terms of personality characteristics. One particularly novel feature here was the assumption that ESP ability might actually improve with 'training', whereas the Rhines' tests, if anything, indicated that the scores of their subjects tended to suggest a gradual deterioration of ESP ability. In the Soviet Union too, various testing techniques were being developed, although here there were no underlying spiritistic assumptions – not surprising really considering the basic tenets of Marxist materialism. In the USA, it may be that one reason for the growing popularity for studies of the paranormal, was that it might act as a philosophical counterweight to the implications of the prevailing cult of Behaviourism, besides being a useful adjunct to religious belief. But in the Soviet Union, where – following the work of Pavlov – Behaviourism also held sway, parapsychology could be seen as a companion discipline in so far as it held out further possibilities for personality control.

Regardless of the criticisms that continued from the traditional scientific establishment, the Duke University experiments in particular spawned kindred movements elsewhere. The USA was – and still is – very much in the forefront of the work on parapsychology, where enthusiasts founded the American Society for Psychical Research. During the Second World War in Europe when academic institutions – like everything else – were greatly affected, in the USA studies went on pretty much as usual. And in 1957 American academics established a professional society known by the logically incorrect title of the Para-psychological Association. In general, the movement continued to move away from spiritist, seance-oriented experiments to laboratory-based recurrent testings using increasingly sophisticated techniques. However, interesting as some of these have been, they have not really contributed that much to our understanding of the PSI phenomenon.

It must seem to the observer that what modern experimenters are doing in effect, is to try to show that *the paranormal is actually normal*, that PSI is a natural endowment that is not generally recognized. It is therefore little wonder that the entire pursuit has been under attack from all sides. There is now a professional organization of sceptics known as the Committee for the Scientific Investigation of Claims of the Paranormal. This organization was actually an offshoot of the American Humanist Association, and in the first editorial of their jour-nal *The Zetetic* (later renamed *The Skeptical Enquirer*) the editor insisted that although most of their results would be likely to prove negative, the main purpose of their organization was not that of debunking claims concerning the paranormal or to close discussions on the subject. Instead it was intended to open up the paranormal to serious rational debate. Has the organization lived up to its high intentions? The prob-lem has been that in its attempt to eliminate rash claims, hoaxes, exhibitionism and outright fraud, it has found it perilously easy to slip over into ridicule.

An even more open-minded innovation has been the founding of the Society for Scientific Exploration. This began in 1981 when a group of scientists representing various disciplines in the USA decided that a new initiative in scientific research was necessary. They were only too aware that a number of phenomena or apparent phenomena had not been taken that seriously by the scientific community. Yet, if 'real', these phenomena would inevitably challenge accepted scientific beliefs. The underlying assumption was that these phenomena were on the fringes of acceptance although, as yet, the evidence was inconclusive. The result was that the Founding Committee organized the first meeting of the Society in 1982, and thereafter they published a semi-annual news-letter, the *Explorer*. Interest was such that in 1987 they were able to bring out their *Journal of Scientific Exploration* in which various anoma-lous phenomena are critically examined. Knowledge, after all, is structured in a particular way, and as one of the founding members put it, 'the fact that certain topics may be curious and even bizarre, does not mean that these topics should be ignored' (Sturrock: 1987).

In the UK, the most interesting venture in parapsychology in recent years has been the establishment of a Parapsychology Unit in the Department of Psychology at the University of Edinburgh. This was set up in 1985 with the help of a bequest from the late Arthur Koestler who died in 1983. Koestler, a highly respected author, claimed to have had out-of-body experiences when he was languishing in a Spanish prison under sentence of death during the Spanish Civil War. After this he had a consuming interest in the paranormal, and published several books on the subject. It was almost as though this had become his religion; the atheist-cum-Communist did an intellectual (and spiritual?) volte-face and thereafter the pursuit of the paranormal became something of a quest. Reviewing the literature on the study of the paranormal, one suspects that this is also true of its devotees who see their task almost as a mission.

CHAPTER TWO

The Paranormal as a Form of Social Compensation

If we ask the question why it is that the whole subject of the paranormal is so popular, and why it gets so much coverage in the media, there are obviously several answers. Immediately one thinks of the fascination with the unusual and the bizarre but then, if we push the issue a little further and ask why it is that the public are so intrigued by the unusual and bizarre, we might hypothesize that it was rather more than just mere curiosity. In fact, we might suppose that such interests, to some extent at least, might arise from a sense of deprivation. This is not as odd as it sounds. For most people life is about how to survive – admittedly in as much comfort as they can afford. Deprivation – or, as social scientists would prefer, *relative* deprivation – has strong economic connotations but there are, of course, other kinds of deprivation: physical deprivation due to some infirmity or another, social and status deprivation deriving from a lack – or *sensed* lack – of esteem, and cognitive, emotional and intellectual deprivation which often still exist when economic needs have been met. For any one, or all, of these conditions, the paranormal – the suspicion or hope that there are more things in heaven and earth than are dreamed of in our philosophies – may serve as a kind of psychological compensation.

We could look at the economic dimension first. For the past century we have been living in an age of abnormal abundance. Despite two world wars, and innumerable other social disasters, the dazzling achievements of science and technology allowed us the dream of endless material growth. Politicians and scientists and the earlier social philosophers such as John Locke and Adam Smith who, with some exceptions, gave the West its political directions, assumed that there was always going to be more. Whether it was the philosophy of progressive capitalism or radical communism, the message was the same, given the will and determination, men could forge a greater and better destiny.

This was really an abnormal age, and its abnormality gave rise to an unjustified optimism. Scarcity is the normal condition of humankind, something we are just beginning to rediscover. Predictably, the response to scarcity has been conflict – wars to control resources, to acquire land, or otherwise to maintain inequalities of wealth. The link between scarcity and oppression is well attested in every kind of society, and it hardly needs to be reiterated that in the modern world this has been exacerbated by the kindred problems of ecological pollution and over-population. As William Ophuls was keen to point out some years ago, the scarcity problem poses a classic dilemma. It may be possible to avoid crashing into physical limits, but only by adopting radical and unpalatable measures that, paradoxically, are little different from the dire predictions of the most pessimistic soothsayers. In giving scientists power over nature, the more power we give to their political masters; it is 'farewell to the free lunch – and to freedom as an infinite resource' (Ophuls: 1975).

At the macro level, Marx was well aware, in principle, of the dimensions of deprivation, although he could not foresee them in their present form. He maintained that given the nature of human beings and the range of possible solutions to their economic dilemmas, then social development would take predictable forms. Furthermore, he argued that until society underwent a radical change, the exploiters (bourgeoisie) would continue to deprive the exploited (proletariat). Economic power is inextricably linked to political domination and this is facilitated by the instrumentality of ideology – persuading the unthinking masses to be resigned to their lot. But there will always be a residual sense of alienation which will increase as the masses, or significant sections of them, become more politically aware and begin to question their situation. Meanwhile, for most people, work is unconducive to self-fulfilment. It is non-creative, merely a means to material reward, and neither the striving nor the rewards are really satisfying. People feel as though they are at the mercy of irrational market forces which relentlessly affect exploited and exploiters alike – both do what they have to do in the same structural situation. Thus the masses feel alienated from competing classes, from their products, from one another and, ultimately, from themselves.

It is contended that one of the most important factors in resigning people to their lot is religious ideology, in effect, one 'manifestation' of the paranormal. Marx was ambivalent about religion. He regarded it as an illusion, a distortion of reality and a perversion of historical 'truth' which leads to misconceptions of the human condition. It encourages a 'false consciousness' and a sense of mystification which help to justify and legitimate the domination of the ruling classes. As a humanly produced ideology it acts as a tool of subordination and encourages compliance and resignation. Essentially, following Feuerbach, he argued that religion is mere compensation for the human sense of inadequacy (in this case specifically to achieve self-realization in a capitalist society).

The gods are simply a reification of the ideal self, and this now constrains us by artificial (humanly constructed) behavioural imperatives. At the same time, however, it may function as an 'opiate', a social analgesic, which eases the pain produced by exploitation and oppression. To this extent, it gives some measure of comfort to those victims of society who believe in its tenets.

For Marx, therefore, religion was an active force in society, contra, say, the neo-Marxist, C. Wright Mills, who insisted that it was merely *re*active in relation to the other facets of the social complex. The truth is that religion can be what Marx said it was. It can be an instrument of oppression, but it can also be a means of cushioning oppression. Furthermore, it can also divert attention from the real source of oppression, and even justify that oppression. What is not always considered in these arguments are the additional beneficial effects of religion. Besides providing hope and consolation, religion provides a counter-ideology. It often challenges oppression, and questions subordination, and where possible tries to alleviate them. This has certainly been true of some Marxian-inspired Communist societies where it is noteworthy that the behavioural manifestations of alienation (for example, the incidence of suicide) are just as common as in capitalist societies.

The genius of Marx was that he cleverly extended Feuerbach's psychological inadequacy arguments to the problems of social inadequacy. And he refashioned the gods-as-objectified-self-consciousness argument so as to include such things as the state, monarchy, capital and so forth, which are also human constructions but which, like religion, continue in a reified way to exercise dominion over us. But he was also ready to suppose that with enlightenment the need for religion would be rendered unnecessary. He would no doubt have endorsed Lenin's prediction that religion would cease to exist when the conditions which support it disappear. Yet it has not done so. And although there is undoubtedly increased secularization in the modern world, especially in Western society, there has been a notable revitalization of religion elsewhere, particularly in Islamic society. Furthermore, it can be persuasively argued that with more knowledge and education, the sense of human inadequacy actually increases. We become increasingly aware that there is so much we do not know, and how much more there is to know. It is hardly to be supposed that in some future, hypothesized Utopia there will be such a treasury of wisdom and expertise that all the perennial problems will be solved. It tends to be overlooked that true creativity is often not born of leisure and liberty, but out of struggle and adversity.

Is it accurate therefore to suppose that preoccupation with the paranormal (or perhaps *supra*normal if we are to include religion) can be explained in terms of compensatory day-dreaming? Do some people turn to what they believe to be psychic experiences and/or events merely as a diversion? Are they simply consoling themselves with the hope of other-wordly 'rewards'? This was not only the general contention of Marx, it was also very much that of Freud who maintained that the strength of religion (and here again we might well substitute the word paranormal) derives from the power of the wishes it reflects. As we shall see when we examine the issue of religion and parapsychology specifically (Chapter 8), those involved with paranormal issues often display a kind of religious zeal, and many obviously *want to believe* that the 'indicators' (for example, out-of-body experiences, hauntings and poltergeists) give evidential support of the supernatural. For Freud and his psychoanalytical school, these ideas constituted an 'illusionary shield against the terrors of fate'; their function was thus primarily to exorcise the terrors of nature and reconcile us to its inexplicable cruelties, and to make amends for the privations and suffering of 'communal life' – in short, to give protection and consolation.

Fundamental to Freud's thinking are the twin concepts of *illusion* and *alienation*. The desire for wish fulfilment is seen as a fantasy which is characteristic of the ignorant. Belief in the supernatural is no more than a 'necessary illusion' (reminiscent of Plato's 'noble lie' and the anthropologist, Bronislau Malinowski's 'pragmatic fiction'). Freud went even further: it was a collective obsessional neurosis that only time and rationality might heal. Needless to say, he never tries to prove any of these highly generalized assertions scientifically. These are mere assumptions on his part. Perhaps the desire to see things this way is also nothing more than a wish – but in the mind of the analyst. Freud's dismissive approach, which has been often and ably criticized (for example, Stafford-Clark: 1967), is not unlike the cavalier way in which many still treat any mention of the supernatural/paranormal.

Regarding alienation, Freud never abandoned the idea that the norms of society were, in a sense, unnatural, and that social conformity was based on renunciation and coercion. However, he saw such norms as necessary because they helped to contain the individual's naturally destructive tendencies. In fact, he argued that the principal task of culture was guarding against nature. Belief in the supernatural – and especially the possibility of supernatural sanctions – can be a useful adjunct in this respect, but he still thought it 'dangerous' because it sanctified bad institutions, dulled critical enquiry and permitted morality to rest on uncertain (i.e. unscientific) foundations.

Many neo-Freudians, needless to say, have tended to stray from the paths of truth as established by their mentor. Erich Fromm, for instance, has argued that the desire to fulfil wishes is not necessarily bad. Most discoveries have been made in trying to verify that something was true. If, for example, we take the attempts to communicate with possible extraterrestrial intelligences by probing possible signals from space (including the famous Search for Extraterrestrial Intelligence – SETI – programme) we have to admit that the chances of detecting anything are very slim. After all, the number of possible sources together with the possible permutations of frequencies make success rather doubtful. But when it is considered that our own radio 'leakage' may fill a sphere some 160 light years across, perhaps something will eventually be detected. To date, results have been negligible. Project Ozma, for instance, which was set up in 1960 at the National Radio Observatory in the USA 'listened' to the stars Tau Ceti (12 light years away) and Epsilon Eridani (10.7 light years away) in the hope of finding hydrogen-based life forms, but found nothing. However, further projects are planned, including Project Cyclops using 1 000 radiotelescopes. To some all this may seem completely ludicrous and a senseless waste of time and money – in effect, another effort at wish-fulfilment – but the wish *in itself* does not invalidate the investigation or the evidence – only the bias of interpretation.

The need/desire for a belief in certain aspects of what is construed as the paranormal may be necessary for those who feel themselves to be victims of circumstance. Yet others will argue that circumstances do not always have to govern our lives, and that if the *will* is there, life can be made to conform more closely to our wishes. The concept of will is interesting, yet psychologists have yet to define it satisfactorily. Will is said to be a matter of *proactivity* and *reactivity*. Proactive people, we are told, resist habit and custom, and believe in making their own futures, whereas reactive people behave in a more socially determined fashion, responding to rather than initiating events. The Psychoanalytical school has traditionally insisted that we are largely at the mercy of unconscious determinants, and presumably what we cannot govern, we cannot be entirely responsible for. The Behaviourists, on the other hand, who, in general, are at loggerheads with the Psychodynamic theorists, are also deterministic in that they hold that human behaviour is mainly conditioned by the circumstances in which it operates. B.F. Skinner, for example, the doyen of Behaviourism, maintains that people must move beyond fictitious concepts such as 'freedom' and 'dignity', and abolish the idea of the autonomous person who initiates – or wills – action because the real causes of human behaviour are to be found in the environment.

However, it is significant that even the natural, i.e. physical, sciences have moved away from purely deterministic models. The apparent indeterminacies that scientists have found in the nature of matter, especially at the quantum level, have tended to undermine the earlier notions of a clockwork universe. Anyway, who is to say that human behaviour must follow patterns similar to those of atomic particles? In the human sciences, it could be that more 'flexible' voluntaristic models are more appropriate.

At the present time, the vagaries of human behaviour – like the indeterminacies of human disease – are becoming increasingly dominated by the 'gene-for-everything' mentality which, in itself, is another form of determinism. We all have to accept that there are certain biological givens, things we cannot change, nevertheless even radical biologists concede that there has to be a social dimension to behaviour. Nature may supply the basic parameters, but only experience can supply the 'content' of behaviour. Just how much can be attributed to nature and how much to nurture is anybody's guess – even the experts are not agreed on this – but no one should be surprised at this, because the respective determinants are notoriously difficult to measure.

The problem of volition has long exercised the minds of psychologists. Much of their thinking has centred on the notion of *intentionality*. This is seen by some as the key to the will, and it is argued that one cannot have intentionality without values and purpose. And the capacity *to choose* this or that value, or reject this or that possible course of action are seen as genuine options. These are real existential acts. There are those, however, (for example, Erich Fromm) who would maintain that we cannot speak of freedom in general, only of the freedom of a particular person to act in a particular way in a particular set of circumstances. We are all, in our own ways, subject to irrational passions, therefore awareness is an all-important factor; knowing our weaknesses and proclivities, and recognizing the limits of our abilities. Long ago, Kant argued that regardless of our natural impulses, we should strive to act in accordance with what we know to be right. But this begs the inevitable question of what determines our conceptions of right and wrong. This still leaves out the matter of compulsion, so we are left with a basic problem for philosophers and psychologists alike, and that is that no matter how much they – and we – would like to believe in the freedom of the will, there is no ultimate argument against determinism. No matter how much our everyday experience may suggest the contrary, the sense of having potential behavioural alternatives may be a delusion.

Freedom and the exercise of the will are important presuppositions in the world of parapsychology. Studies of clairvoyance, telepathy and especially telekinesis presuppose certain capacities that may be innate

THE PARANORMAL AS A FORM OF SOCIAL COMPENSATION

and/or which are developed by training and experience. (There are interesting parallels here with the Human Growth Movement encouraged by some humanistic psychologists who insist that many of us have unrealized potential for development.) Telekinesis, in particular, is really all about acts of will. The term, for which the eminent researcher Professor J.B. Rhine substituted the word *psychokinesis*, suggests the possibility of affecting physical events or situations by mental influence alone. Psychokinesis (commonly abbreviated to PK) literally means mind-movement, and although some researchers encourage an attitude of 'passive volition' in their subjects, the evidence often suggests that positive volition is more often the case. Parapsychologists talk of micro-PK where the effects are slight and perhaps not even noticeable, and macro-PK where the effects are clearly observable, such as, say, moving an article on a table by thought only. Macro-PK is unsurprisingly much rarer than micro-PK, and those unusual subjects who seem to be able to produce such effects are highly prized within the 'trade'.

There are a number of different theories as to how PK works. The term, after all, is not an explanation, merely a description. It is considered doubtful whether any current researchers can cogently account for the contradictory data which have so far accumulated regarding this still puzzling phenomenon. It is also uncertain whether PK should be regarded as a mental force or a biological force, or perhaps some inexplicable combination of the two. (Here nothing approximating to a physical force is implied; it might therefore be preferable to use the term capacity.) Is it, as J.B. Rhine suggested, a capacity that is somehow generated by the human mind, or is it something – at present unrecognized – which is part of the human physiology, but which is activated by the mind?

The recently retired University of Edinburgh psychologist (and an official of the Society for Psychical Research) John Beloff, has argued that we should discount the idea of 'psychic energy' such as one finds mentioned, for instance, in connection with spiritual healing. He questions whether some form of 'psychic energy' can actually flow from the healer to the patient. For Beloff, this is not so. Presumably, therefore, any alleviation of the patients' condition is effected by the subject himself. Similarly with PK: it does not really require explanation of a paranormal kind – it is simply 'an ultimate fact about the world' (Beloff: 1976, pp. 173–97). One critic of Beloff, however, argues that his ideas do not accord with the facts. Why, for example, do some known PK 'agents' often exhibit what appear to be a paroxysm of effort in order to activate their PK abilities? Research in both the USA and the earlier Soviet Union indicate that PK effects are often brought about by violent contortions of the body (and a certain agony of mind?) which then seem to project a mysterious energy (Rogo: 1980, pp. 359–77). Beloff's theory implies that everyone has an innate capacity for PK, something not substantiated by the evidence. But even if they have, why is it that it only seems to be manifested by so few?

A related theory is that PK is a biological force or capacity which is part of the natural human physical make-up and regulates the body's homeostasis system, but which occasionally manifests itself in other ways. J.B. Rhine, as the result of his extensive card and dice-rolling tests with many PK subjects, put forward a modified version of this theory. He suggested that the PK is a mediary force which links the mind, brain and body (Rhine: 1947). These ideas have been substantially supported by John Eccles (1953) and by Helmut Schmidt who extended PK capacities to other life forms, notably animals. But it has to be admitted that there is no scientific evidence to indicate, either in humans or in animals, that there is any neurological disruption when PK is ostensibly being exercised (Schmidt and Terry: 1977), although, it may be that our electroencephalogram (EEG) technology is, as yet, not sophisticated enough to detect it. If PK does have the natural function of keeping the body in balance, as it were, it might go some way to explaining why its outward manifestations are rarely seen. It might also support the view that PK operates on a seemingly involuntary basis. (Interestingly J.B. Rhine found with his dice experiments that a subject might score well above average on the first run of tests, but that this ability increasingly deteriorated with subsequent runs.) This suggests that PK operates when subjects are in a relaxed state of mind, and that the more they try, the more they are likely to fail, as indicated by Stanford and Fox (1975). Yet, as we have seen, this runs counter to other evidence which suggests that it all takes a considerable effort of will.

Psychokinesis does not appear to be subject to whim. It is not the kind of energy that can be switched on and off for the pleasure of either subjects or observers. In this sense it is rather unlike some other forms of energy which are not subject to 'exponential decay'. Experiments have shown that PK is not predictable and is affected by both spatial and time limitations. But as Rogo (1980) has pointed out, PK is a phenomenon of vast contradictions. All we can say at present is that it appears to be a psycho-biological phenomenon by means of which 'gifted PK subjects are said even to produce materializations (mists, lights, phantom legs, arms and so forth) under quite rigorous experimental conditions' (ibid.). The great problem with this study of PK is that tests indicate its 'presence' and in what directions it appears to work, but we still know nothing about the phenomenon itself. Is it a human capability, or is it a superhuman energy – a kind of cosmic force – which can occasionally be used? This has been seriously suggested, but like the transient – and quite unsubstantiated – pyramid power, which was all the rage a few years ago, there is absolutely no evidence for it.

Modern research into the effects and nature of PK tends to disparage, if not actually dismiss the spontaneous and the anecdotal accounts that claim public attention. Indeed, the experimentalists are inclined to outlaw macro-PK almost entirely, regarding such cases as unreliable and unsubstantiated. Instead, current research has concentrated on laboratory-based experiments which rule out any indirect ways in which the subject might influence the proceedings other than by mental 'energy'. These tests are designed not only to ascertain whether or not any physical changes have been effected, but also to explore the influence of external physical conditions, if any, and to see if there are any correlations with other psychological variables relating to the subjects, the experimenter or even the relationship between them. Researchers have long been aware of the 'experimenter effect', and if this can be eliminated from the proceedings, so much the better. The need for the greatest care is well illustrated by the experiments carried out in the Soviet Union with the subject, Nina Kulagina, which, in addition to close visual observation, careful examination of the equipment used (for instance, to make sure there were no magnets or other aids) and the screening of the test objects, there was sometimes the introduction of new tests without notice to the subject. The test equipment consisted of a table-like smooth horizontal surface on which were placed small movable objects of various types, textures and weights. According to reports, objects were made to slide over the surface at will, and on occasions two objects were moved at the same time although in different directions. Nina Kulagina has also been known to affect the swings of a pendulum, even to stop and start it, and to rotate compass needles. While tests were in progress, her heart rate was checked, and afterwards her weight and so forth were also checked for any abnormal changes or fluctuations.

Macro-PK events of this kind are relatively rare and highly individual in nature. Where someone develops a reputation for 'psychic' abilities such as Uri Geller, it is not unusual to try to persuade them to put their 'gifts' to the test under experimental conditions. In Geller's case, he was quite willing to do so, particularly to demonstrate – among other things – that the reports of his metal-bending abilities were well founded, and certainly not fraudulent, although it has to be admitted that on occasions SPR representatives found him 'tantalisingly elusive'. However, in one well-documented test, Geller was first allowed to examine a steel key supplied by the researcher, it was then placed on a glass-topped table and held at one end flat against the glass by the researcher who was also able to observe the underside of the key by use of a mirror. Geller then stroked the key (as he similarly stroked spoons in his public demonstrations), and the key was seen to bend. Admittedly, this was not psychokinesis as it is usually understood, but it was a clear example of a paranormal effect (Cox: 1974, pp. 408–11). An interesting parallel to this can be found in the work of D. Scutt of the Mechanical Engineering Department of the Cranfield Institute of Technology. After some experiments with Ori Svoray using a special aluminium alloy (reported in *JSPR*, 51, (787), February 1981), he concluded that Svoray actually changed the atomic structure of the metal in a way that cannot be duplicated by normal heat treatment or by any other method that was known to him.

For researchers such effects are extremely encouraging. One can perhaps be forgiven for suspecting that the current penchant for micro-PK has resulted from a lack of obvious success with macro-PK. No wonder Geller created such a stir in the trade, and why so many wanted to believe that he was a mere showman (Rush: 1977). Rush writes that though 'some macro-PK is impressive, it inevitably lacks the evidential force of the more consistent and sustained statistical findings' (Rush: 1986a, p. 244). One senses that parapsychologists actually find it difficult to believe in the paranormal they are studying. It seems a little curious to the outside observer that the professionals are a little like clergymen who spend much of their time in prayer, but can hardly believe it when it appears to work.

Sceptics – especially among natural scientists – point not only to problems of validation of the 'presence' of PK, but also to the apparently trivial nature of some of the reported experiments to locate or even establish its authenticity. Some PK researchers have felt that the best experiments are those which encourage a good, perhaps lasting, relationship between the subject and the target. They feel that this is better than the classical and rather impersonal laboratory test whereby a subject tries to impose his/her will on a passive or reluctant target. A randomly moving machine known as a tychoscope has been devised which can run for hours on its small batteries, and is able to trace and record its own movements. It is suggested that this machine will facilitate the 'progressive building of a deep-rooted, personal, affectively toned link with the user' (Janin: 1986, p. 342). In other words, the user will hopefully be able to develop a 'dialogue relationship' with the tychoscope in such a way as to influence or 'tame' its movements. So how has this been used? It will come as no surprise to critics that one way in which the tychoscope has been utilized is in experiments with mice, long favoured, of course, by the arch-enemy, the Behaviourist community. An experiment involved putting mice and machine in an enclosed circular area for a series of 45-minute time trials. Each mouse was tested four times at five- to seven-day intervals. The results of the tests were then statistically analysed, and it was discovered that a few mice gave 'specially good results'. How? Apparently by influencing the machine in such a way that they 'caused' it to move away from them even though they would be expected, because of the noise, to move away from it. This was taken as evidence of mouse PK. In true researcher fashion the parapsychologists took two couples of the 'best' mice and mated them so as to ascertain whether their offspring may have inherited the same PK abilities, but with the 20 second-generation mice they had 'little success' (Chauvin: 1986, pp. 348–51).

I have to say that these experiments in France are reminiscent of that other notoriously uncertain series of tests with mice in order to ascertain how – if at all – they prioritized their wants and needs. Male mice were placed on one side of an electric grid, and on the other side were female mice and some food. It was hypothesized that the males would choose food first and sex afterwards (presumably on the assumption that sex just makes you hungry, anyway). And they were right. The mice did what was expected. But then everything went awry. Once the mice were sated, they just roamed back and forth across the grid regardless of the electric shock they would receive. The experiment had proved nothing of importance.

The *JSPR* is a very scholarly journal, emanating as it does from the highly respected Society for Psychical Research. It is aimed primarily at professionals, and its not particularly numerous membership is drawn from devotees abroad as well as from the UK. But even the *JSPR* is not above clutching at evidential straws in an effort to promote its interests. Take, for example, its relatively recent articles on PK and plant growth in India. Plants and plant seeds have been used in a series of tests to try to ascertain whether a person or persons could influence plant growth and plant health by exercising their PK abilities. The tests were carried out using shamen (holy men) mainly because it is part of the Hindu tradition that the goddess Durga can be invoked to prosper the barley harvest. Indeed, it is even reported that some Hindu mediums are able to make barley seed sprout in their hands within a few minutes at the appropriate season given that they have sufficient devotion to the goddess.

In the published tests, wheat seeds were tried, but without success. Then the traditional barley was used, and the experiments were conducted very meticulously employing the necessary controls. Basically it came down to a test of will; if sufficient will-power was exerted it was believed that success was assured. Complementarily, if the test was a failure then it could only be that PK ability was not strong enough, and/ or that some combination of faith/will-power/devotion was inadequate. The conclusion was that PK only 'worked' when there was sufficient religious devotion present and the test was tantamount to an act of worship. Overall, the results were rather uncertain. Replication was not always possible. And just how experimenters can judge success simply by the growth or healthy appearance of plants is surely a problem. Can *all* other environmental factors be eliminated? Even the experimenters had to admit that PK effects do not seem to influence seed germination, although one must also take into account the fact that subjects were only asked to focus on plant height (Saklani: 1992, pp. 258–65).

The whole question of claimed paranormal powers by Indian holy men and especially cult leaders is particularly interesting and has been the subject of a number of tests. Religious leader, Swami Premananda, is a case in point. He claimed to be able to materialize small statuettes in his bare hands. Tradition had it that he had produced many 'miracles' since childhood, and that on one occasion scores of his devotees witnessed a bright and decidedly unnatural light emanating from his body. In the test in question, all possible precautions against fraud were taken as there had recently been a woman Hindu swami who made extravagant claims to PK powers, but who had been discovered to be a fake. After repeated attempts, Premananda was able to produce 'materializations' under *informal* conditions, that is, when his hands were not covered in plastic bags, but he was not able to do so under *controlled* conditions when events were being videotaped. Similar problems have been encountered with other claimants to psychic powers such as the cult leader, S'athya Sai Baba. However, the investigators found no direct evidence of fraud, but conceded that in the circumstances this could not entirely be ruled out (Haraldsson and Wiseman: 1995a, pp. 193–213). Unsurprisingly, Premananda wanted the experiment to be conducted in private, ostensibly because he could only give matters his full attention in such conditions, but one is bound to suspect that his reputation would have been at stake had he failed in the presence of his many devotees.

It is all too common to find individuals, especially among Indian cults, who establish themselves by the display of some apparently paranormal abilities. This gives them the kind of charismatic quality that often attracts huge numbers of followers. The same researchers decided also to investigate two others who insisted that they too could materialize objects such as tiny statuettes, rings and vibuti (a powder-like substance) with their bare hands. One claimant, Mrs Minu Bhowmick, said that Sai Baba spoke to her during her trances (something that was incidentally rejected by Sai Baba's camp), and that materializations were no problem for her. But she refused to allow herself to be searched prior to her performance, or to permit the investigators to watch her at close hand. The whole display was regarded as suspect because she did nothing that a reasonably competent magician could not have done. The second case, that of a man somewhat cryptically known only as Dr A.B., was not that different. He was able to produce that all-time favourite, the fine-grained powder, which appeared (or was dutifully applied) on framed pictures of some Indian deities (Haraldsson and Wiseman: 1996, pp. 109–13).

From what we have said it is quite obvious that demonstrations of PK lend themselves to imposture and charlatanism, but this should not blind us to the fact that quite remarkable things do take place which are not susceptible of simple explanations. There are instances of 'directly observable PK' which investigators have found quite baffling. These are quite distinct from 'PK effects' which can only be inferred on the basis of statistical analysis and the evaluation of a number or series of events, such as the results derived from dice-throwing experiments. Directly observable PK refers to physical changes that are either related to the movement of objects, or changes that can be witnessed and verified such as, say, an unusual change in temperature. It should also be borne in mind that not all PK refers to the movement of objects such as a vase on a table, but also to the stopping of a clock. A distinction is also made between involuntary PK such as the 'production' of a poltergeist, and voluntary PK which implies some degree of conscious control by the subject.

As we have already seen, Nina Kulagina is a notable example of someone who comes into this rare category. She has been tested repeatedly under the most stringent conditions and there is a consensus among researchers that with a success rate of 80 per cent her PK abilities are genuine. According to observers, Kulagina, who discovered these abilities almost by accident, gave the appearance of being a physically normal woman, although when she was exercising her PK powers her pulse rose to abnormal levels, and the magnetic field around her body was reported as being about ten times that of the average person. Many of these tests have been filmed, and no signs of fraud have been detected. Admittedly, the objects in question have been relatively small (though a vase weighing nearly 400 grammes has been mentioned), and the degree of movement was usually measured in centimetres rather then metres, but the feats were nevertheless remarkable, and defy any conventional scientific explanation. She is also said to have been able to stop and start the heartbeats of certain small creatures (e.g. a frog) and – more contentiously – to have revived fish that were pronounced dead in an aquarium. Such things have not been accomplished without considerable mental and physical strain. After sessions which might last up to two hours, Kulagina has been reported as being dizzy and exhausted, often with pain in the back and in her legs and feet, and with considerable changes in her EEG readings (Keil et al.: 1976).

It is inevitable that the literature on PK should concentrate on those who purport to have such abilities, or whose reputations otherwise demand explanation. Consequently, there is an understandable tendency to review their accomplishments, presumably as proof that PK – though inexplicable and not analysable – really does exist (see Braude: 1986). The same names crop up time and time again, D.D. Home, Ted Serios, Rudi Schneider, Felicia Parise and the like, possibly in the hope that with continuous rehearsal will come conviction. Whatever the verdict, it has to be conceded that there have been exceptional people, and that the phenomena with which they are associated have been exceptional phenomena. The debate will go on. Tests will become more sophisticated. Research may indicate not only *how* but also why such phenomena occur. Of course there has been – and is – fraud in PK 'exhibitions', but the very term fraud implies that somewhere, somehow, the real thing actually exists. It may not be there for everyone, indeed, current evidence belies this. But it is still possible for everyone to take comfort and consolation from the PK demonstrations of others. After all, PK studies derived originally from the seance phenomenon, and this, in turn, from concerns about survival. And, in one form or another, this is the hope of all supernaturalist belief systems.

Excursus: The 'False History' Problem

It hardly needs to be laboured that there is a considerable difference between the nature of scientific and historical explanation. In science, explanation normally consists of three elements:

1. The thing to be explained or deduced (the explanandum).
2. Particular (supporting) facts (the explanans).
3. Uniformities expressed as general laws such as, say, the elasticity of bubbles, i.e. why bubbles expand and then recede or burst under pressure.

When speaking of the laws themselves, theorists sometimes refer to the Covering Law Model. This is because laws – such as we understand or conceive them – are empirical generalizations which may well be explained by further more inclusive laws or uniformities. So, for instance, when physicists talk of gravitational forces they are also talking about the phenomenon of *spin* which characterizes both subatomic particles and galactic clusters (Davies: 1995). Furthermore, the fundamental concepts of cause and effect presuppose like conditions and like circumstances, and then only in relation to particular facts, not to universal laws. This is something which cannot be taken for granted in historical explanation.

Science is able to advance certain probabalistic (often statistical) models which argue that given specific conditions/antecedent factors, a particular event will result as a statistical probability, for example, lung cancer as the result of smoking a given number of cigarettes over a given period of time. The uniformities observed in nature make it possible for scientists to deduce that these operate at such a high level of probability that they can be expressed as laws. So in general conversation and everyday practices these laws are presupposed in such a way that they are said to be 'eliptically formulated', that is, tacitly taken for granted (for example, 'the ice has melted on my windscreen'). By comparison, explanations in history and the social sciences are often partial and ambiguous. Indeed, in some cases there may be no *one* explanation that will cover every contingency unless it is couched at such a high level of generalization as to be virtually meaningless. And in so far as they may be regarded as *interpretative* in ways that are specifically human such as, say, pausing before crossing a road, they too can be regarded as unexceptional human behaviour.

Nomological explanations such as we find in history and the social sciences are deductive rather than *in*ductive and therefore presuppose certain underlying causes and regularities. Such presuppositions may be *pragmatic* in kind. So if, for example, one were presented with a historical statement such as 'The Egyptians prepared for their spring campaign against the Asiatics' it would be taken for granted that the inclement nature of winter inhibited military action at that time. Armies in ancient times often wintered, if possible, in friendly territory before launching their spring offensives. Sometimes, however, we find that the presuppositions are implicitly psychological in nature. If we take another statement, 'Kindon was tricked into leaving Sparta so that he could be arrested on instructions from the Ephors, and made to betray his fellow conspirators', we understand that he was more likely to crack under interrogation when isolated from his friends. At other times history presents us with highly generalized pseudo-genetic statements such as, 'Nazi aggression in Europe was typical of the German imperialist temperament', or *ideological* presuppositions such as 'It meant everything for a Muslim to die for his faith – it was his entrée to Paradise'. (Interestingly, crusaders were also granted indulgences if they too died in battle against the infidel.) The main snag with explanations of this type is that they tend to omit the element of rational calculation which undermines the covering law idea as related to social phenomena.

Can human behaviour therefore be reduced to reasonably well-defined laws or must we make do with mere probabilities? A probabilistic explanation could take the form of a syllogism:

> Ego was in situation type X.
> Ego was disposed to act rationally.
> Any person who is disposed to act rationally will – in X type situations – do Y (or, at least, there is a high probability that he will do so).

This kind of explanation in terms of the *dispositions of the actor* marks it off from those explanations in terms of some presupposed laws of human behaviour. But it all begs some uncomfortable questions. For instance, what is – or can be – meant by rational calculation? Is it possible that some rational action (for example, swerving to avoid an accident) is so instinctive that very little reflection is actually involved? And is it not possible to reassess retrospectively an action and *attribute* some rationality to that action? Furthermore, such attribution may be a *rationalization* rather than an explanation. The real reason for an action – even if they can be adduced – may be no more than the reasons a person is prepared to give in his own justification.

It is Karl Popper's view that although history and the social sciences involve complex judgements, they must nevertheless adopt where possible the modes of explanation appropriate to general science. But he insists that:

1. All covering law explanations must be strictly universal.
2. All laws must be empirically falsifiable.
3. Analytic (logically necessary) truths cannot be universal laws; specific conditions are only specific to an event.

It follows from what we have said so far that explanation in history and the social sciences has its problems:

1. Expectations must not be confused with explanations. If a person flips a coin and expects 'heads', this is not the same as winning the jackpot on a fruit machine. Yet the basis as to why the first is more reasonable than the second (which is obviously a matter of odds) does not actually explain why he succeeded in the first and not the second. Statistical probability cannot *explain* chance.
2. The one is not the many. A statistical probability that one in four unmarried men over 40 is a homosexual, does not tell us anything about the sexual proclivities of any *one* man that we are likely to meet at a conference, party or whatever. Similarly, the fact that there is a homicide in the USA every 24 minutes does not enable us to make predictions about any person in any one town.
3. Macro and micro events. In history especially it is often possible to see the micro in terms of the macro, i.e. some general uniformity, but it is rarely possible to see the macro in terms of the micro. To take a simple but unusual example, a person may fall 200 feet or more and not be killed, which seems to be a violation of a macro physical law. It can happen – but it is so rare as to be negligible. Truly universal laws are those which are amenable to verification by repetition and hold true for all or most individuals under all – or most – conditions.

Generally speaking, we cannot speak of laws in relation to history or society. We can only speak of logically necessary or contingent statements which cannot be universal laws. If, for instance, we consider the statement, 'Caesar fought a civil war in order to become leader in Rome', we know that leadership in Rome – or anywhere else – is not necessarily dependent on winning a war. War may be a necessary antecedent factor, but it is surely not a sufficient one. Similarly, the famous aphorism of Lord Acton that 'Power tends to corrupt, and absolute power corrupts absolutely' may sound psychologically plausible but although not actually false, it does remain uncorroborated, and is certainly not a universal law.

With these general reservations in mind about the nature of historical explanations, it could prove instructive to look briefly at the 'false history' problem which is part of the stock-in-trade of some of para-psychology's keenest critics. While not exactly at the heart of para-psychological studies the issue of *human genesis* is the preserve of certain cultists on the fringe of the discipline. This is described by critic Kenneth Feder as the 'twilight zone of psychic archaeology' which has given rise to bizarre interpretations and misrepresentations of accepted scholarly research (Feder: 1986, pp. 274–84). Feder cites the work of Jeffrey Goodman, a popular American writer (whose academic qualifications are apparently in dispute) whose book *American Genesis* (Goodman: 1981) is said to have 'stunned the Anthropological World'. Feder describes this as a 'disingenuous fantasy' that completely mis-represents the prehistory of the New and Old Worlds.

Goodman's thesis is that:

1. Our understanding of the American Indian has been hindered by racism and prejudice, and that American Indians have been ma-ligned and persecuted.
2. American Indians have been in the New World for at least 12 000 years and possibly a great deal longer.

With statements (1) and (2) few anthropologists and historians would probably disagree, but Goodman then advances hypotheses which are considerably more contentious:

3. There were people – presumably American Indian in type – who were in the New World as long as half a million years ago. These were of thoroughly 'modern appearance' thus *pre*dating similar types in the Old World.
4. These proto-Americans lived in California – a veritable 'Garden of Eden', and migrated throughout the world. In effect, a kind of 'out of America' argument. (In an interview in 1981, Goodman main-tained that the eminent archaeologist, Louis Leakey, said he thought that the earliest humans came from Southern California. Feder asks if Leakey did say it and did believe it, why wasn't he excavating in California and not in Olduvai Gorge in Africa?)
5. America was not only the home of the first truly human beings but it was also the cradle of civilization, and that all the most impor-tant inventions normally associated with prehistory, such as weaponry, ceramics and so forth, first saw the light of day in what most people erroneously term the New World. This apparently even extends to astronomy and the applied understanding of the physics behind electromagnetics and Einstein's gravity waves.

Needless to say, this is reverse diffusion. Goodman's thesis turns usually accepted pre-history on its head. Sensational as it is, and satisfying to the most culturally introverted Americans, there is barely a shred of empirical evidence to support it. Goodman puts forward the extremely tenuous argument that the antiquity of American Indian culture can be 'proved' from the nature of prevailing Indian myths. But it is the contention of many scholars that with a little ingenuity it is possible to prove almost anything you want from mythology – no matter whose corpus of myths you use.

When it comes to the origins of these precocious early Americans, Goodman hints darkly that their cultural development may have been inspired from some outside source. But as if in anticipation, he reveals more clearly what he has in mind in an earlier text (Goodman: 1977) where he suggests that they may have emanated from the now 'lost continents' of Atlantis (in the Atlantic) and Lemuria (in the Pacific) – a 'fact' revealed from a psychic source. Again, there is no valid evidence for the existence of these continents, and if there were we would then be involved in a seemingly infinite regression because we would have to ask just how the Atlanteans and the Lemurians came by such advanced knowledge. Before we knew it we would be back with some fanciful 'cosmic visitors' hypothesis which, although not entirely impossible, is certainly unprovable.

There is no doubt that pre-history, as far as we are able to reconstruct it, testifies to both cultural relativism and cultural diffusion. There has been both independent development and the obvious transmission of cultural elements. This goes for both artefacts and ideas. We can give some respect to a pre-scientific people struggling to understand the nature of the world and coming up with bizarre notions about the Earth resting on a Giant Turtle or whatever, but we do not have to endorse the 'reality' of their conclusions. So when cultists invoke science to validate their ideas about ancient astronauts and psychic archaeology, we should surely cock a sceptical snook and ask to see the evidence. The Native American supremicist theory is only one among many that deserve more than cursory investigation. Only a little less doubtful is the view that *all* cultural development in the pre-Columbian New World can be traced to the Old World and was diffused by ancient migrants, usually from the Mediterranean area well before 1492 (see Fell: 1977; Gordon: 1971). Similarly the even more ridiculous claim that the most important cultural artefacts and inventions emanated from Black Africa. This and related reductionist assertions can be found in the work of Martin Bernal (1991) among others – ideas that are proclaimed as 'fact' and which are put forward with plausible and Procrustean ingenuity.

There is a dearth of evidence to support any of these claims, and they are particularly suspect when advanced by sensationalists and psychic seers who only contribute to science's uncertainties about the paranormal.

CHAPTER THREE

The Paranormal as an Aetiological Device

Aetiology is concerned with forms of explanation. The classic example of the aetiological device is the myth. Not all myths, of course, have an aetiological function. Many stories, as with the elaborate corpus of Greek myths, may simply have been concocted and recited as a form of entertainment. But many others may have arisen as ways of explaining a society to itself by giving it a 'biography' – explaining how it came into being. Not infrequently, myths underpin and 'explain' current social institutions, such as the Sumerian myth that kingship (i.e. monarchy as an institution) was 'lowered from heaven'. For those in power such a myth conveniently justified the practice and reaffirmed the structural *status quo*. For people in traditional societies, in particular, myths 'explain' why things are done the way they are, and how certain norms have evolved. Thus the Jewish creation myth will help pre-scientific enquirers to know why it is that Jews keep the Sabbath. In short, as anthropologists are quick to stress, myths exist to justify current social practices. The paranormal too can be a form of explanation. This can be well illustrated from the occult practices of witchcraft.

For those who accept witch beliefs, these are the answer to those things which cannot otherwise be explained. In this sense, witchcraft – or the *belief* in witchcraft – constitutes a closed intellectual system. So in a case of misfortune, say illness, the question may well be asked, why this particular person at this particular time? Those who believe are possibly already aware of the natural order of things, but for believers the context becomes as important as the intrinsic nature of the event. To ascribe misfortune to 'bad luck', as we more sophisticated beings are likely to do, is really not an answer; and to speak of an unanticipated conjunction of events is certainly not an explanation. Indeed, it is hardly better than attributing it to witchcraft. To resort to either interpretation is a circular procedure, and to interpret misfortune in terms of misfortune really tells us nothing at all.

What is often called the 'witch experience' has a near universal distribution. This does not mean that it is found in every society but that it is found in just about every *type* of society from primitive pre-industrial societies to complex centralized societies including, of course, relatively modern Western society. As we have seen, the last witch to be burned in the UK was in Scotland in 1727, but the repeal of the Witchcraft Act which included not only the practice but also the pretence to practise witchcraft, did not take place until 1951. But so much depends here on how witchcraft is to be defined. The witch myth varies greatly from society to society, but conventionally it has had a number of features in common. It is usually associated with the 'black arts', and as such has strong moral connotations; the witch is traditionally seen as someone who is evil and malevolent, and who possesses uncanny powers. Witches may be thought to be capable of flying or have the ability to change their form (Mayer: 1970). They are almost invariably adults, and not infrequently women – a view commonly held in medieval and post-medieval Europe as well as in many tribal societies. Their bestial practices were guardedly acknowledged, especially in post-medieval Europe where they were held to keep unspeakable compacts with the Devil.

In Europe, it is estimated that the Inquisition burned some 30 000 of those it claimed to be witches, and it may be that between c. 1450 and c. 1750 as many as 200 000 suffered in one way or another (Robbins: 1964, pp. 6–8). It is notable that in England a statute by Elizabeth I in 1563 made witchcraft punishable by death only if it resulted in the death of the person who was bewitched. How a causal connection could possibly be ascertained given that a witchcraft case usually began with the *effect* is a source of bafflement to the modern reader. Guilt or otherwise could only be decided by a 'read-back' method which could only satisfy the accusers. The actual practice of witchcraft, *per se*, was a lesser offence. But this changed under James I (1604) who revised the statute so that the practice of witchcraft alone was made a capital offence regardless of its believed effects.

Actually the Elizabethan statute was little more than a confirmation of what had been done for the best part of a thousand years. The whole issue of trying to control or, at least, manipulate nature has existed from time immemorial. Sorcery and magic are, after all, world-wide. This involved the invocation of spirits – good and bad, as they were believed to be – and the accompanying use of amulets and charms, mostly in the interests of health and fertility. It was during the thirteenth century that ecclesiastical law became more clearly and comprehensively formulated concerning sorcery and magic. In 1310, the Council of Treves forbade divination, love potions and 'conjurations', and by 1330 Inquisitorial trials began in relation to witchcraft itself. The Church now faced a problem. It was not opposed to seeming contraventions of natural law; the Church had long promoted the possibility of miracles. But the question was, by whose agency had these come about? Were they divine acts, or had they occurred as the result of magic spells and incantations? If so, they could only be the work of evil spirits. The theologians went to work, and before long whole groups of daemonia had been identified together with the particular evils with which they were associated, and the saints who could give special help as occasion demanded. The head of this assembly of demons was, of course, the Devil himself, 'the Prince of darkness' whose intention was nothing less than the subversion of the faithful and the overthrow of the eternal order. Concourse with this daemonic hierarchy was therefore, *ipso facto*, heresy, and heresy could only merit the most fearful punishments.

Demons were believed to seek out those who would serve them, and it was these that were designated witches. By 1350, it is thought that as many as 600 people found guilty of such practices had been burned in southern France. Before long the contagion of persecution had spread from France to Italy and Switzerland where more trials and executions took place. At first the civil courts took no part in this. Matters of orthodoxy were left to the Inquisition. In formulating the appropriate – or necessary – criteria, the Inquisition generated the fear, and the fear produced the victims. In effect, the Inquisition fed upon itself. All sorts of heterodox, opinion was pronounced heresy, and persecutions were authorized by the Church, including the unwarranted Albigensian massacres in France (Carlton: 1996).

Even though the Protestant Reformation brought with it a great deal of new thinking, this did not extend to a reappraisal of witchcraft. Indeed, the sixteenth century brought extensive speculation and even more elaborate formulations of the phenomenon. In Lutheran Saxony it became a capital crime in 1572; likewise Calvinist Geneva ten years later. Witchcraft, which by definition now implied a pact with the Devil and a denial of the true faith, reached its full development by 1600 and continued in full spate for a hundred years. The persecutions not only brought increasing power to the prelates and to the civil powers who now assumed relevant responsibilities, they also proved to be a valuable source of income. Both the inquisitors and the civil authorities shared the proceeds of the confiscated properties of those who had been condemned. Gradually ecclesiastical law was codified as criminal law, and became a powerful agent of social control.

Witchcraft came to be looked upon as the gravest of crimes, but because it was difficult to prove, in 1468 it had been declared a *crimen excepta*, an exceptional crime, in which ordinary legal rules did not apply. Heresay evidence was allowed, and so torture was used in order to force confessions and to make the accused name (or invent) their accomplices, and then, of course, for the accomplices to name yet others, and so on. Torture could be frightful (indeed, without it confessions were regarded as unreliable); few could resist naming names and even concocting 'special evidence', that evidence derived from dreams, visions and so forth, as in the now well-known Salem witch trials in the seventeenth century.

How much *actual* witchcraft was practised is anybody's guess. Few, if any, were caught *in flagrante*. And it is difficult to know how many people really believed it had any effects, as Thomas Hobbes noted 'I think not that their witchcraft is any real power'. Yet, in England, after the severe persecutions during Elizabeth I's reign, the whole process received new impetus under the non-conformist Commonwealth which as a political experiment, some regard still as an enormous advance in social thinking.

It is perhaps significant that the demise of the 'witch scare' coincided with the rise of capitalism and commercialism in Europe. Whether this was induced, encouraged by the Protestant Ethic, as Max Weber once argued, or whether there were common factors underlying both capitalism and Protestantism such as the inspiration of post-Renaissance thinking, is a moot point. Perhaps the rationalism of capitalism and the essential irrationalism of the whole demonological structure of witchcraft just did not mix. But for many hundreds of years witchcraft had served as a convenient pragmatic fiction, an aetiological device which 'explained' that for which there were not other suitable answers.

Women were regarded as being more volatile and coitally unpredictable than men, as was evidenced by their sexual shenanigans with the demons. In some ways this harks back not only to Tantric cults in India, but also to the Dionysian orgies in ancient Greece where, if Euripides (the Bacchae) is to be taken seriously, frenzied women performed rites which involved the killing and eating of raw flesh. Similar bizarre practices were evident in the Middle Ages and particularly in the post-Reformation period. But how much of that which was reported *and confessed* actually took place and how much can be attributed to the fetid, sexual fantasies of bored, frustrated women is anyone's guess.

It is now reasonably well known that the only sure way to ascertain if a person was a witch was by a confession. These could be obtained by persuasion (compare the farcicality of the confessions at the infamous 1930s treason trials in Soviet Russia) or by torture – perhaps the most common method – and, if all else failed, they could be manufactured. If, as so often happened, a person was unable to prove they were not a witch (and how do you prove a negative?) it was known for a person to refuse to plead. This happened in the Salem witch trials in New England in 1692 when, among others, 80-year-old Giles Cory was found guilty by refusing to recognize the charge, and was actually pressed to death by the daily application of iron weights to his prone body. During this period, the accused had either to enter a plea or die.

In relatively recent times there has been something of a revival of witch beliefs both in modern transitional societies where such ideas have become syncretized with those of various religious cults, and in the West where they have commonly found expression as so-called 'white magic'. Here it can encompass all sorts of pursuits from the bizarre sexually oriented antics of self-styled witches cavorting in woodlands in those diaphanous shifts so beloved of the Sunday tabloids, to the practice of the healing arts as part of their 'earth magic'.

In *The Witch Cults in Modern Europe* (1921), Margaret Murray put forward the theory that witchcraft was – or is – a legacy of the early fertility religion in which the horned-god Pan became transmuted over time into the traditional Devil. The earth religion was attacked and gradually driven underground by the incursions of the new faith brought by monks from overseas. In this she may have been echoing the work of Charles Leland who, in 1899, published a book called *Aradia, or the Gospel of the Witches*, which had what can only be described as a disguised revolutionary message. In the book, the heroine teaches the people the secrets of magic so that they can strike back at the priests of the Church and at the established aristocracy. The Murray thesis is now widely discredited. We know something about Celtic religion and Druidic practices from the writings associated with the Roman invaders (such as Julius Caesar and Tacitus) – admittedly a biased source. It did, like so many early religions, have a definite fertility dimension, and we probably see vestiges of this 'old religion' in such activities as floral dances and harvest festivals, but it is hardly to be equated with what is commonly construed as witchcraft.

This notion of witchcraft as worship of the Earth Mother has been popularized by Gerald Gardner who was a Director of the Museum of Magic and Witchcraft on the Isle of Man, and the revival of witchcraft in its modern forms has been at least partly attributed to his book *Witchcraft Today* (Gardner: 1968). In this text, first published in 1954, Gardner sought to repudiate the work of Pennethorne Hughes who maintained that witchcraft is a cult of evil and perversion of the true faith. Instead, he reiterated some of Murray's ideas though in a much more elaborated form, and was keen to lay stress on the idea that witches were decent people who wished to remain unmolested by a prying public, and allowed to continue with their practices which were in no way socially harmful. However, he added that coven members have an esoteric knowledge which only they possess, and which cannot be divulged to the uninitiated and the curious.

In some ways, Gardner's views echo those of the Order of the Golden Dawn, a movement associated with the notorious Aleister Crowley, a magician-cum-writer whose self-promoted diabolism scandalized British society in the late nineteenth and early twentieth centuries. The Order of the Golden Dawn was dissolved in the mid-1930s, but enjoyed something of a revival of interest in the mid-1960s. Gardner's book is suffused with a kind of sexual hedonism. It may well be true that Gardner, who died in 1964, was a sado-masochist with a penchant both for flagellation and voyeurism (King: 1970). He was certainly a flamboyant character, an exhibitionist who 'developed a taste for voyeurism and being spanked during boyhood travels in the Middle East with a buxom Irish nurse' (Wilson: 1973, p. 597). As a result of his book, it is believed a number of covens sprang up in England whose express purpose was to practise 'white witchcraft' including curing the sick, increasing harvests and the like. But the ceremonies had a very strong sexual emphasis, and one suspects what was done was little more than an excuse for erotic high jinks. Such practices as ritual intercourse between the 'High Priest' and a 'Priestess', animal sacrifices, and almost mandatory nudity, meant that a good orgiastic time was apparently had by all.

This tradition has been carried on by a host of successors, including the self-proclaimed 'King of Witches', Alex Sanders, who has achieved considerable notoriety through newspapers and television. Sanders freely admitted that he has used 'black magic' to obtain money and sexual gratification with his female acolytes (Smyth: 1970), and one suspects that he is not entirely alone in this respect. From what can be discerned, however, many covens these days are very much under the authority of women. White witchcraft is no new phenomenon. There are references to it in European literature as far back as the ninth century. Curative sorcery was no new thing, and was liable even then to result in the death of the accused. Even in those days, it had anticipatory hints of a feminist flavour. But, contrary to some modern opinion, the white witch for all her herbal remedies and good intentions, was regarded as a 'more horrible and terrible monster' than her 'black' counterparts. Some theologians argued that this was merely evil masquerading as good, and therefore merited the most heinous punishment.

Leaving aside for the moment the matter of modern 'white witch-craft', the seemingly simple question that is often asked is whether witchcraft really took place. Did people *actually* practise the black arts, or is it all part of a witch myth? Given the fact that it obviously paid some people to *say* that it did, and for others to *believe* that it did, it must be open to question as to whether it actually did. Did people genuinely make pacts with the Devil, or what is perhaps more to the point, did they *think* they had come to such weird arrangements with the powers of evil? Montague Summers, an earlier authority on the subject argued that because so many descriptions of witches' sabbats are so similar even though the sites were geographically far apart, this constitutes proof that the Devil does exist and that the ceremonies occurred as the accused said they did. The Devil was almost always described as a large goat-like creature with an ice-cold – sometimes scaly – phallus that ejaculated very cold semen (Summers: 1965). On the other hand, Margaret Murray, possibly resorting to well-known hypotheses about primitive rituals in Neolothic times, opted for the reality of the sabbats but suggested that the 'Devil' was probably represented by a man with an animal mask and artificial phallus who squirted the women with cold milk!

Colin Wilson speculates that such fantasies arise from minds that cannot or do not otherwise give full vent to the creative imagination. 'Boredom or emptiness allows the mind to fill up with unused energy' and adds that more important than the question of ecclesiastical politics was the matter of sexual repression (Wilson: 1973, pp. 558–9). This rather Freudian interpretation sounds somewhat shallow, but perhaps he has something when he implies that the Inquisition influenced the accused with a prepackaged body of myths and symbols by which to interpret their experiences – whatever they happened to be. It may be that these gave a *meaning* to those experiences which they found stimulating and exciting. Certainly one can hardly account otherwise for the highly coloured confessions from people – commonly women – who were just about to be burned. In the circumstances, it would surely have paid them to dream up something rather less incriminating and prurient than they often did.

Despite the evidence that most of those who suffered in the persecutions were women (numbers vary with the sources), it is very doubtful whether we should 'explain' those persecutions as part of the 'war against women' (Briggs: 1996) or again, that blame should be laid at the door of Non-conformity which developed in the hey-day of the 'witch-craze' (Hill: 1966). Certainly in the much quoted case of Salem, the Puritan ethos had much to do with the eventual deaths which resulted from the trials. But there is evidence to suggest that, very broadly speaking, it was the tolerance of Non-conformity which inhibited the persecutions in the New World generally (Harrison: 1992).

Today the whole thing is taken far less seriously. Earlier cases may be compared to the near farcicality of a relatively modern trial where it is to be doubted whether the authorities really believed in the case. Helen Duncan was the last person to be prosecuted in England under the more or less defunct Witchcraft Act. She was tried at the Old Bailey in March 1944 for pretending to 'conjure spirits' and imprisoned for her trouble, but doubts remain as to whether she was really a charlatan (Cassirer: 1996).

One of the main lessons to be learned from any study of witchcraft is that the causes of the 'witch craze' in Europe were very complex, and the dynamics varied according to place and time. Why, regardless of the awesome reputation of the Inquisition were such a small proportion of those executed (perhaps 500 in all) to be found in the Mediterranean areas of such Catholic states as Portugal, Spain and Italy? Was the Catholic Church more intent on persecuting Protestants? Yet why were some 10 000 witches executed in Poland (also largely Catholic) in the eighteenth century when almost all other states were easing up on their persecutions (Levack: 1995)?

There is some truth in the idea that times of political and religious upheaval leave societies vulnerable to crazes of various kinds. In such circumstances it is not unknown for scapegoats to be identified and singled out for special treatment. As in Nazi Germany, a myth is fostered, in this case concerning the Jews, which then takes on the semblance of a universal 'truth'. In some ways the witch craze was like this except that in this case there may have been *some* substance to the myth. There were probably witch practices even if the witches in question were not doing what they thought they were doing. The acts were almost certainly objectively meaningless, but they were real enough to both accused and accusers to generate confessions which further substantiated the myth. And then, as Rebecca Cardozo puts it, 'a craze develops, a climate of fear and suspicion permeates ... society; and the consequences of the widespread fear and intolerance is the madness of "the hunt" [resulting in] false confessions, torture ... ruined reputations, and death' (Cardozo: 1970). It is the fear, once generated, that is then perpetuated. It suppresses dissent. Any kind of protest or resistance is likely to result in a suspicion of guilt by association. So the persecution continues.

It is all too easy to dismiss these phenomena as mass delusion. Yet it is still not simple to *explain* witch beliefs. One way in which we can begin to understand them is to see them as *a form of aetiology*. In this sense they are rather like religious beliefs which, as such, surely merit explanation, but which themselves provide a form of explanation about good and evil, our place in the cosmic order, and so forth. So it is with witch beliefs. In tribal societies they once explained everything that could not otherwise be explained, especially misfortune and disease, and there is some evidence to suggest that there has been something of a resurgence of these ideas, especially in some African societies (contra Postscript in Marwick: 1970) possibly in part because of the post-colonial trend to hark back to what are popularly referred to as 'roots', i.e. traditional native codes and practices.

In pre-scientific cultures it made a certain kind of sense to attribute abnormal behaviour to the activity of spirits. The world was a world of spirits: those that caused lightning, thunder, earthquakes, floods and so on. It was also reasonably certain that malevolent spirits were responsible for illness. Only a few more quizzical souls thought that other agencies might be at work or, in our terms, that other models or metaphors would be more appropriate. The idea of spirit possession seemed to fit what were perceived to be the facts. Thus trepanning, the opening of the skull with crude instruments, has been known from earliest times. This was regarded as essential to let the spirits free, and was quite consistent with the initial premises. Much later, towards the end of what we now regard as the medieval period (fourteenth century) the phenomenon of dance manias was also attributed to demon possession. Men and women seemed to have had little control over their actions. They danced in the streets and were found leaping about in their homes shouting out strange names of what were thought to be devils. And when they collapsed exhausted, they only appeared to come to their senses after exorcisms had been performed to banish the evil that was believed to possess them. In the following century, there was a similar outbreak, the Saint Vitus dance phenomenon, which was characterized by twitching and other convulsive movements in people that seemed to be in some kind of ecstatic state. Women seemed to be mostly affected, and the artist Peter Brueghel captured something of this in some of his paintings.

It could be argued that the 'witch scene' in the post-medieval period was a form of the same phenomenon. The symptoms were different but the attributes were the same. And there is a similar demonology abroad today, although it is usually seen as an alternative to the dominant scientific paradigms. Demon possession can hardly be tested experimentally, and as a theory it has little predictive capacity. But we should always remember that our current ideas, too, leave much to be desired. Terms such as hysteria, phobia, psychosis and the like are only descriptions not explanations.

Modern witchcraft in its 'white' resurrected guise is, if anything, inclined to be non-aetiological or, to be more specific, it does not purport to be an explanatory mechanism in the once accepted sense of the term. It does not pretend to give us a theory of evil, nor does it claim to solve the problem of theodicy as it did for those who lived in a pre-scientific world. If it did not actually solve the problem, at least it suggested *an* answer in terms of an ongoing conflict between the forces of good and evil which were vigorously competing for dominion of the human soul. Modern witchcraft with its strong ecological emphasis, is not out to answer perennial philosophical questions. Its affinities are with the environmentalists, naturalists and, particularly, with the Gaia movement which sees salvation in a return to nature and all its earth-borne benefits. There is a marked de-emphasis on the vagaries or the unpredictabilities of the natural world; all that is wrong is blanketly attributed to science and post-industrial hubris. In this sense and *only* in this sense, can modern witchcraft be seen as explanatory. Hence we have turned a full circle in the West in so far as elements of medieval daemonology are now being re-emphasized by certain charismatic religious groups. Exorcism is very much part of their rituals, and some of the behavioural phenomena (such as swooning and screaming) found in earlier times are being witnessed again today as 'evil spirits' are banished from believers (Howard: 1997).

In Britain, modern witchcraft's most notable figures after Gerald Gardner have been Monique Wilson, High Priestess of the Scottish covens, and effectively heir to Gardner's estate; Eleanor Bone, who came from nowhere to act as 'coven liaison officer' under the witch name of Artemis – a rather grand title for a Tooting housewife; and Patricia Crowther, the ex-dancer from Sheffield who had no inhibitions about posing topless for the tabloids. To the observer, they appear as an unlikely trio. Monique Wilson who liked to think that she had inherited Gardner's mantle; Mrs Bone (who found it frustratingly difficult to get her husband to join in the ceremonies) who specializes in curses but refutes the allegations that she uses them for evil purposes; and the 'tall and willowy' Patricia Crowther 'with a cascade of blonde hair and a totally engaging smile' (Haining: 1972, p. 32) who was the first to introduce green leather garters and blue silk into her rites.

Even a perfunctory glance at the literature shows much modern witch-craft to be little more than a syncretistic mish-mash of imagined ancient Greek religious revels with a dash of pseudo-Celtic ceremonial. There are hints of Sappho and her girls frolicking among the anemones and applauding the munificence of nature and the beauty of youth. There are elements of feminism in the worship of the Mother Goddess, and a nostalgia for a fairy-tale world that has never existed. Replicas of horned-gods, candles, altars, incense and robes together with ornamental swords, all serve to enhance the heightened theatricality of the rituals. Books of a suitably esoteric nature underpin the procedures. Such titles as the *Gospel of the Witches, The Book of Ceremonial Magic, The Book of Forbidden Knowledge, The Book of Shadows* and so on, provide a very profitable line for the movement. Merchandising of this kind brings in much needed funds from the curious as well as from the devotees.

Sex and sorcery tend to go together, although some adherents deny that it is in any way integral to the ceremonial. The truth is that while some deny it, or at least play down the sex angle, there are others, notably the self-styled 'King of Witches', Alex Sanders and his wife, Maxine, who provide plenty of talking points for the prurient. Sanders, who reputedly attended his first witchcraft ceremony at the age of nine, went on to develop his precocious talents staging magic rituals in which sex often played a major part. According to Sanders these were 'pretty lurid and orgiastic', and included such a variety of couplings that straight-forward heterosexual coitus could almost be considered a perversion. He later claims to have 'purified' such rituals and returned to the basic tenets of the Murray-Gardner teaching of Wicca ('wise one') and the 'old religion' which recognizes the Mother Goddess as the supreme deity.

Very similar movements can be seen elsewhere, particularly in the USA where, for some time, witchcraft was associated pre-eminently with Raymond Buckland and Sybil Leek who for several years appeared fairly regularly on radio and television talk shows. As in the UK, American witchcraft had its fair share of crooks and cranks which caused the covens to tighten their admission procedures. Buckland ran a museum on Long Island devoted to the study of witchcraft and pro-duced a monthly magazine called *Beyond*. Sybil Leek, on the other hand, was a far more flamboyant character, given to posing for the media in ritual cloaks and jewellery. Before long she had her own restaurant, a boutique and her own radio show, besides running a monthly magazine. She began her career in England, and was appar-ently in great demand when she went to the USA in 1964 where she had considerable success by ascending the feminist bandwagon and claiming that 'witchcraft is the only religion which enables a woman to take a major part in when initiated ... the orthodox religions do not seem to encourage women to lead ... In my religion, the High Priestess is re-spected as a woman and a spiritual leader ... ' (Haining: 1972, pp. 98–9). It was incorrect, but it got her a hearing.

With the revival of interest in the occult, certainly from the 1960s onwards, any number of groups have sprung up with their own distinc-tive emphases and practices. Sybil Leek was soon challenged for the

'Witch Queen of America' title by a much younger woman, Louise Huebner, who claimed descent from a witch dynasty in the Balkans (always good copy for anything from vamps to vampires). She too made her name on television by unashamedly plugging the sexual theme. Her record album, *Seduction through Witchcraft*, set the tone, and she claimed to be the possessor of arcane spells which could ensure sexual potency and fulfilment.

Although paying lip-service to the 'Old Region', to a large extent Louise Huebner and her ilk have departed from the ways of Wicca, and have promoted a more aggressive form of the occult. The close – almost guarded – esotericism of the earlier practitioners has given way to active proselytizing for a movement which has some resonance with American get-ahead social values. This new 'mood' was represented in New York by Leo Martello with the Witches Craft Association, the occasional 'Witch-In', and the Witches Encounter Bureau. Such occult groups come and go – almost like fashion. Among the more notable have been those operating in California. There was the Leda Amun Ra movement whose High Priestess ordered acolytes to sacrifice the swans in her 'temple'. Similarly, the Order of Circe dedicated to the service of a 'devil woman' who is thought to be a reincarnation of Circe the sorceress (from Homer's *Odyssey*). They are believed to indulge in animal sacrifices, and this is also said to be true of such groups as the Chingons and the Solar Lodge of the Ordo Temple Orientos which was once popular among certain university students. There was also the Process Church of the Final Judgement which insists that the most important commandment is 'Thou Shalt Kill'. Sex and drugs were part of its programme, and it is not surprising to learn that the notorious Charles Manson was once one of its members.

The *ne plus ultra* of quasi-occult hedonism, however, was reached with the establishment of the Church of Satan in San Francisco. Its founder, Anton le Vey, who referred to himself as a 'Doctor of Satanic Theology', complete with black garments and pentagram medallion, insisted that Satan was a 'symbolic personal saviour' who encouraged moral – meaning largely sexual – behaviour. Le Vey advocated that people should cast off their inhibitions and give vent to their 'true' feelings; one should not eschew the seven deadly sins for they are, in fact, virtues – expressions of our 'real' selves. Have no truck with false humility; conventional religion is a guilt-ridden philosophy. The Golden Rule should really be 'Do unto others as they (actually) do unto you'.

Le Vey insisted that modern Satanism has little time for 'white witchcraft' which is seen as something and nothing. He draws no clear distinction between 'white magic' and 'black magic' (sorcery). It is up to devotees to decide for themselves how they should act in any particular set of circumstances. Actually this is another variant of good old-fashioned relativism. There is no good or evil, merely what is expedient in given circumstances. The important thing is to avoid self-delusion and misconceived altruism. Le Vey would probably have argued that all so-called altruism is really hedonism, anyway. Ultimately, we all do what pleases us ('I love you' means 'I love *myself*', and I only love you as long as you please me – when you cease to please me, I will cease to love you'). True to his inclinations he believes in the efficacy of the curse, and once claimed to have brought about the death of the actress, Jayne Mansfield, a member of his 'Church', and her current lover who was antipathetic to the Satanist movement. Both were killed in a car accident. Obviously it can never be verified that magic was the agent of the tragedy.

There are a number of ways in which we can try to explain witchcraft – none of them wholly satisfactory. There are *psychological theories* which purport to explain witchcraft in terms of inner predispositions. These are closely related to *cathartic theories* which concentrate on the apparent compulsion for emotional release. On the other hand, we have the popular blame-deflection approach of *scapegoat theories* which are certainly relevant to many historical situations. Selectively focused animosities can often be explained in this way. Of course, witchcraft can be a very potent weapon for social control, something which has been very evident in tribal societies (Parrinder: 1970). And, as we have seen, there are *cognitive theories* which concentrate on trying to explain these things that are only partly understood (Carlton: 1994). The aetiological value of the modern movements we have been discussing is necessarily limited. They are not setting out to explain any of the great philosophical issues which have vexed thinkers of the past. The questions, Why are we here? Where are we going? have little meaning or purpose. The cardinal consideration seems to be 'we are here, let's make the best of what we've got – and if we can get a little more, so much the better'. It is no longer a matter of explaining the ways of the gods to men; it is more a question of explaining ourselves to ourselves. Aetiology is out – self justification is in.

Excursus: Astrology and the Determinants of Fortune

Astrology, the belief that individual fates are somehow linked to the movements of cosmic systems, was losing its appeal by the end of the nineteenth century but, as we all know, has returned with added entertainment value in the modern age. It seems preposterous that anyone can give credence to the notion that human destiny or human personality is influenced in this way, but the incomprehensible popularity of astrological predictions in the press and elsewhere obviously proves otherwise. Is this another symptom of human irrationality or is it – as some insist – just a form of amusement? One wonders if for those for whom 'reading their stars' is just a kind of novelty there is a vestigial suspicion that there might be something in it, after all.

It may be that ancient megalithic monuments, standing stones etc., were intended as ways of marking the positions of cosmic bodies, and thus astrological rather than astronomical. Certainly we can say that the principles of astrology have barely changed since the days of the proto-astronomer, Ptolemy. Those who still practise the ancient 'craft' do so in much the same way as it was done in the first century. Horoscopes still flourish despite the fact that we now live in a time of post-Newtonian physics. There are those, of course, who insist that astrology is not an occult practice at all, but a science, yet it does not observe the vigorous standards we usually associate with the scientific method. Cause and effect can only be adventitious; outcomes and predictions can be no more than fortuitous. Even those who have tried to bring astrology up to date such as Michel Gauquelin who has tried by statistical methods to establish correlations between cosmic configurations and personality characteristics have found that it is not generally recognized as having any real validity.

Astrological horoscopes have been traditionally cast according to the Sun or Zodiac sign of the month in which a person was born (Aquarius, Pisces etc., which may roughly coincide with our months), and the 'Rising sign', i.e. the constellation coming over the horizon at the moment of birth. On this basis some kind of character assessment is made and 'fortunes' are predicted. The idea is that the ecliptic is divided into 12 roughly equal parts or segments and that each is believed to exercise a different influence on the various areas of human life: the personal ego, possessions and finance, personal relationships and so forth. Much depends on one's 'birth chart', i.e. the conjunctions and oppositions of the planets at the moment of birth. This is done on the assumptions that the planets exert their own particular influences (needless to say, modern astrology has had to make modifications with the discovery of more planets).

How is this supposed to work? One theory is that if the planets, for instance, can gravitionally affect the thin crust of the Earth (thus making earthquakes astrologically predictable), then perhaps they can also affect the human nervous system via the Earth's magnetic field (Wilson and Grant: 1981). It all sounds like mumbo-jumbo although *aficionados* like to refer to it as an 'intuitive science'. It goes without saying that predictions are either highly generalized, making it possible to read almost anything into them, or – as in the case of 'special readings', i.e. personal horoscopes – highly inaccurate. It was obviously because astrology was held in such disrepute that more recent theorists have tried to give it a more rational basis. Therefore, at the turn of the century, traditional astrology metamorphosed as 'astro-biology'. Paul Choisnard, a French army officer, tried to 'prove' astrology using statistical methods, and his work was improved upon and popularized in 1939 by Karl Krafft (1900–1945), a Swiss mathematician. He had some success with his predictions, most notably in connection with the attempt on Hitler's life in November 1939, but after enjoying a brief period as a consultant astrologer to some of the more superstitious members of the party, he fell into disfavour – perhaps because of the want of more accurate and optimistic predictions – and died in a concentration camp.

The very notion that celestial objects can actually have any kind of determinative effect on terrestial life seems impressionistically to be quite ludicrous. (Why, for example, because Mars is 'red' does it have to be associated with blood, and thus with war and aggression?) But even the most ardent detractors of the 'arcane science' argue that it is no use just dismissing the whole idea as nonsense. Criticism of a pseudo-science must be refuted by true science. Work has been done to see if there is really any marked correlation between a person's Sun sign and their profession/occupation and therefore their life chances. In one particular study, John McGervey tested the statistical association between the astrological signs of 16 634 scientists and 6 475 politicians. The results were entirely negative, and McGervey asks why can it be that this revered and ancient 'science' has not measured up to its claims? How can the time of day when one is born (if it can even be ascertained) possibly have any influence when it varies with the seasons (McGervey: 1981)?

Another test of popular astrology, also done in the USA, established that astrology had more believers than most religious organizations, and that horoscopes were to be found in two out of every three American newspapers – and this despite the fact that the public is largely unaware of how astrological calculations are made. This study which investigated the relationships – if any – between star signs and personality characteristics, also found that the claims of popular astrology were untenable. The researcher, Ralph Bastedo, insists that his work was carried out in a broad-minded, unbiased, dispassionate kind of way and that his methods were logical and rational because he used his 'natural intelligence, genius, brilliance and inventiveness'. Above all else, he insists that he has remained 'sincere, honest, idealistic and serious in his never ending quest for truth'. He adds – with wry humour – 'it could not have been otherwise. Because I am Aquarian. And Aquarians are like that' (Bastedo: 1981).

There are echoes of the same sort of thing elsewhere. As I write I am looking at an advertisement in a British daily newspaper for a free offer of a talisman from Maria Duval who is said to be 'probably the greatest clairvoyant in the world'. Ms Duval, who is President of the French Parapsychological Institute, is also a lecturer at the 'Free Faculty of Astrology' and is said to be a consultant to bankers and industrialists who 'flock to her door' when they wish to recruit managers and the like. If this were not enough, she is purportedly regarded by the French press as 'the human radar', so it comes as something of a surprise that this high-powered psychic is prepared to send all and sundry a life enhancing bauble which might 'make ... wishes come true ... attract that new job offer ... and win ... a new admirer'. And all this together with a personal six-page glimpse into the future – at no extra cost.

Michel Gauquelin, as we have seen, created something of a stir in the world of astrology by his statistical work relating cosmic factors to the adoption of particular professions. In this he received some support from non-astrologers including the late, eminent behavioural psychologist, Hans Eysenck. To be fair, both Michel and Françoise Gauquelin and Eysenck remained sceptical about traditional astrology, but were intrigued by the statistical results obtained from the research. Among the variables, the Gauquelins looked at the 'Mars Effect' which was said to be influential as far as sportsmen in particular were concerned. However, the interpretation of the findings has come in for some criticism by other researchers. In a study of 564 champions in various sports in the USA, it was found that there was no evidence for the so-called 'Mars Effect' (Kurtz, Zelen and Abell: 1981).

We can say with reasonable certainty that scientific tests of astrology do not support its claims – and this despite the fact that believers insist on its veracity because it has withstood the test of time. We know that today it still has its devotees and the uncommitted who hover on the fringes of the movement. Among parapsychologists there is no consensus about astrology. At least one reputable professional has come in for serious criticism for his attempt to analyse the effect of 'Rising signs', and their relation to personality (Sargent: 1986).

One of the most notable pieces of research conducted by non-astrologers which gave aid and comfort to the cultists was that done by Mayo, White and Eysenck (1978). This again was an attempt to see if any correlations could be established between astrological factors and personality. The research was carried out using Eysenck's all-purpose Extroversion-Introversion model which it seems he has applied to just about everything from intelligence to sex. This study, too, has had its critics, most notably Kelly and Saklofske (1986) who contended that what at first appeared to support a paranormal hypothesis was unconvincing because it had not given due consideration to alternative hypotheses. A key factor – and also the principal weakness – of the study was that it relied too heavily on the ability or inability of respondents to 'know' the significance of their own star signs. So much, after all, depends upon prior knowledge and the question of self-attribution. This, of course, is the snag with so much empirical (i.e. survey-based) research. One is at the mercy of one's respondents.

CHAPTER FOUR

The Paranormal as Mental Aberration: Near Death and Out-of-Body Experiences

In recent years, psychologists and others have become particularly intrigued by what are commonly referred to as *altered states of consciousness*, more technically known as dissociative states. There is very little evidence one way or another for supposing that genetic or other biological or hereditary factors might predispose a person to dissociative reactions which may take many forms. Much of the technical literature concentrates on such things as amnesia (loss of memory and sometimes of personal history), fugue states (flights from reality) and more extreme conditions such as multiple-personality which are often confused with schizophrenia in popular texts. In the everyday world, however, dissociative disorders tend to be linked with meditation, hypnosis and especially drug-induced experiences, and are sometimes associated, either directly or indirectly, with the incidence of stress (a much abused and misunderstood term because stress can be constructive as well as destructive in its effects). The term consciousness, too, can be used in a number of different ways. It is particularly difficult to define, but usually it denotes total awareness – whatever that may mean – in a 'normal waking state'.

It would seem that from time immemorial people have experimented with ways of altering consciousness and of changing perception, especially by the ingestion of various toxic substances. This was clearly recognized by the early psychologist, William James, who wrote that the 'normal waking consciousness [or] rational consciousness ... is but one special type of consciousness, while ... parted from it by the filmiest of screens, there lie potential forms of consciousness [which are] entirely different' (James: 1958, p. 298). Obviously, consciousness can only be studied indirectly by self-reports, observed behaviour and to some extent by measuring physiological functions. All such methods have their own inherent weaknesses. Self-reports can be false, and observed behaviour can be misleading. Even physiological examinations may not produce the 'true' result, as in, for example, lie detector tests.

This all becomes much more difficult when trying to elicit information about an altered state experience. Not uncommonly a respondent's vocabulary does not extend to this, as for instance with people who are trying to describe an hallucinogenic experience. Drugs, of course, may produce such an experience but they cannot determine the *kind* of experience at any particular time for any particular individual. Fasting also (depriving the body of blood sugar) and meditation can also induce trance-like states. Such states are said to have an appeal because they deepen an awareness of the sensory and aesthetic aspects of life and because they produce feelings of unity and peace despite living in a troubled world (Ornstein: 1977, pp. 186–8). This sounds rather like a group indulging in drug-induced escapism, and tends to overlook the phenomenon of mysticism which, by its very nature, is intensely private and individual.

It may be that consciousness is influenced by parallel brain subsystems including those that underlie memories, emotions, dreams and that which comes close to the subject of our present discussion, fantasies. It is even speculated that these various subsystems actively register and process information independently, and are actually unaware of each other. Whether this is correct or not, it is undoubtedly true that waking consciousness is continually changing, and that sometimes our awareness is intuitive, say in our appreciation of art or music, while at other times it is more rational and analytic. The way we perceive the world is largely determined by mood, but just what determines our moods is yet to be discovered. Research has shown that the 'average person' experiences fairly regular cycles of mood (elation, depression, anxiety, etc.) which would seem to have a biological basis.

Hypnosis and its companion state, meditation, can possibly give us certain clues as to the nature of fantasy and dissociation. In the hypnotic state, the subject is 'detached' from ordinary preoccupations and self-control. By no means everyone is able to achieve this state. Research indicates that probably about the same number are not susceptible at all. If we ask how is it that we know that someone is really hypnotized, the answer – not always foolproof – is that we can tell by their behaviour. They lose a sense of spontaneity and do not initiate action or discussion. They also become selective in their mode of 'attention', that is to say, they focus on limited objects (for instance, the hypnotist's voice) and block out all other distractions. Not least, if they are particularly good subjects, they may be tested for their susceptibility to post-hypnotic suggestion, say, go out and buy a certain unfamiliar magazine, and not be able to explain their actions. Our understanding of exactly what hypnosis is, and how it works, is still deficient. According to some theorists hypnotism is made possible because the brain has dissociated subsystems. Other more sceptical experts insist that it is all a matter of heightened suggestibility and the willingness of the subjects to contribute to the experiment. So in stage-hypnotism subjects merely participate in their own embarrassment. Suggestion alone, it is argued, can even produce effects such as pain reduction, changes in heart rate and control of blister formation (Barber, Spanos and Chaves: 1974).

In many ways, meditation functions in a similar way to hypnosis. It normally consists of a set of diverse exercises which are intended to alter the state of consciousness either by quiet contemplation, as in the case of Buddhist monks, or by feverish activity such as dancing or chanting as in certain Hindu cults. In either case the aim is to drown out external distractions and open the mind to some special experience or truth. Research done with novices indicates – as with hypnosis – that some people respond very well while others are unable to achieve any real sense of detachment. Further experiments conducted with those seasoned in transcendental meditation (TM), which is supposed to en- gender a blissful 'oceanic state', were tested for all manner of physiological reactions. It was found that the heart rate slowed, the metabolic rate was unusually low, and that respiration and carbon dioxide elimination were both reduced. However, not all research has confirmed this (Wallace and Benson: 1972, pp. 84–90). The long-term effects of meditation are still not clear. For some it is obviously a joyful experience, but others testify to its adverse effects such as depression and confusion, and – interestingly – hallucinations (Davidoff: 1980). Research certainly does not unambiguously confirm that meditation always leads to creativity, happiness and increased efficiency, nor can it substantiate claims that it brings subjects into contact with some ill- defined life force.

The ingestion of intoxicants as a short cut to an altered state of consciousness has a very long history. Drugs such as marijuana and peyote have been used for hundreds of years to induce mental states ranging from ecstasy to oblivion. Herodotus, who travelled quite exten- sively in the Middle East in the fifth century BC wrote of the Scythians who threw hemp seeds on open fires and inhaled the vapours. The Egyptians, the Persians and the Greeks used forms of opium as an analgesic, but – interestingly – there is no known reference to its addic- tive properties in those societies. A wide variety of cultures is known to have used drugs to reduce pain, induce sleep or to give individuals sought after pleasurable experiences; as one Meso-American Indian answered when asked why he drank so much, 'a man must take a rest from his memory' (quoted in Taylor: 1963).

Drugs, and intoxicants generally, alter thinking processes and affect both mood and perception. They are now commonly regarded as relaxants or medical aids, but were used – and to some extent still are used – as ritual accessories to induce the appropriate state of euphoria. We all know, though, that there is a downside to drug-taking – impairment of judgement, lack of co-ordination, depression of the central nervous system (CNS), delirium and possible delusional reactions – besides being indirectly responsible for all manner of social ills such as broken homes, violence and sexual abuse, car and fire accidents, and the like. Much depends on the drug in question, and to some extent on the user. For amphetamine users the long-term result may be irrationality and instability; for those on LSD, panic and anxiety. However, as far as the present discussion is concerned, certain drugs can generate the kinds of dissociation in which we are interested. There is an increasing sense of 'distance' from the world. Troubles lose their impact and significance. Receptor sites in the brain have been affected and there is an – albeit temporary – reduction of stress in what has become a distorted reality.

Are there here any parallels with paranormal experiences? Are there certain stress-induced states which lead not to meditation or to drug-dependency, but to analogous altered states of consciousness? And are these to be considered 'true' experiences or merely a form of dissociative disorder? There are no unambiguous answers to such questions. What we can say is that there is no clear evidence that, in general, those who claim to have had paranormal experiences are any more neurotic, strange or odd than those who make no such claims. Furthermore, we are not sure how many of those that make such claims were *actively seeking* these experiences. Some obviously were – and are – such as those who organize and attend seances, and, arguably, those who carry out experimental tests to establish the existence of PSI or PK. But many insist that their experiences are spontaneous; quite unlike those who indulge in meditation or dabble with drugs. Nor can we argue with any degree of confidence that the stresses of their individual lives are such that they are looking to escape from reality. The paranormal is not a coping strategy, and – as far as we can make out – these people are not practising denial or adopting defence mechanisms. In fact, far from denying reality, they are hoping to discover some new dimensions of reality.

In this connection it might be instructive to look at some of the research that has been carried out into near death (NDE) and out-of-body experiences. There is a great deal of anecdotal evidence for remarkable near death experiences in which the subjects insist that they have 'seen' dead relatives and friends, or in some cases idyllic landscapes which indicate a future existence. And where the patient has made a sudden or unexpected recovery, it is not unusual to find that they no longer have any fear of death. But not enough work has been done by professionals in this area, possibly because, by its very nature, it is a very difficult subject to research. Among those who have carried out investigations, some of the best known are the eminent psychiatrists, Kenneth Ring and Elizabeth Kübler-Ross, who have accumulated records of many such cases, as has also Raymond Moody, a physician (Moody: 1975), and more recently another doctor, Michael Sabom (1982).

Further studies of deathbed observations by doctors and nurses conducted in the UK and the USA confirmed the general nature of such experiences with patients claiming to have had visions which portended a future blissful state (quoted in Rush: 1986c). Yet other research carried out in India found that although the apparitions experienced by patients had come to take them away to a future existence, it was something that many of them regarded with apprehension. In the Sabom study (reflected also in Moody's research), of the 116 cases investigated, many subjects claimed to have been travelling in a dark tunnel and then emerging into the light. Some 43 per cent of these also claimed to have had out-of-body experiences. Margot Grey, calling on the methodology of Kenneth Ring, identifies five stages of the NDE which confirm the same pattern:

1. Peace and a sense of well-being.
2. Separation from the body.
3. Entering the darkness.
4. Seeing the light.
5. Entering the light.

She also reports that those subjects who had accidents or were attempted suicides did not experience the last two stages, and that about 13 per cent of her respondents testified to a 'negative NDE', i.e. a feeling of anxiety and fear (also confirmed in a larger American Gallup survey). As in so many other surveys, she found that her respondents testified to a subsequent belief in survival after death, and some even claimed that they had now been blessed with certain spiritual gifts (charismata) such as telepathy, clairvoyance and healing (Grey: 1985). Her work has been criticized for a certain ingenuousness and its all too willing desire to discount possible naturalistic explanations, and to take her respondent's accounts at face value.

A quite different approach was taken in an earlier study by veteran OBE researcher, Susan Blackmore, who is obviously conversant with the literature and who propounded a very different thesis (Blackmore: 1981). She is patently not over-impressed with the large body of anecdotal OBE reports from a number of different cultures. In her own study she analysed case reports and, after looking at the physiological correlates of the experience, she advanced the thesis that OBEs are neither paranormal nor astral in any sense, but are simply psychological phenomena. Blackmore argues that the OBE is an altered state of consciousness characterized by vivid and detailed imagery. In other words, she is claiming that no one actually leaves their body, and that the whole thing is a kind of hallucination. By this, she is not saying that people do not have genuine experiences, but that they are mistaken in the *interpretation* of those experiences.

There is clearly a conflict between those who adopt what some modern researchers regard as a traditional spiritualist or paranormal interpretation of the OBE in which the spirit or 'astral body' actually leaves the physical body, and those who see it all as a product of vivid dreaming or an over-heated imagination. The problem in the 'trade' is just how to verify OBE reports. Experimental evidence is not conclusive, although some respondents are known to 'bring back' information (for example, about conditions in the hospital in which they were patients) which would have been difficult if not impossible to have obtained in any other way. An out-of-body experience is considered to be significant if it involves observing scenes from the vantage point of another (duplicate?) body. It may be regarded as paranormal not only if the events 'seen' by the experient could not have been known by other means, but also if some other person or persons at the scene somehow senses or perceives the experient at the scene. Needless to say, such reports are extremely uncommon.

An OBE does not have to be part of a near death experience, though in many such reports they are complementary phenomena. Some psychics claim that they are able to accomplish the feat of 'astral projection', that is, leaving the body at will and returning again. In the USA, the psychic, Ingo Swann, has confounded at least some of his critics by apparently identifying, in his astral mode, eight target objects which were set for him as a test. But his performances were not all as successful as this. Whether or not we can completely rule out fraud is a moot point, but Swann is not alone in these claims. There are a number of others who have survived similar tests (Mitchell: 1982). Another American study conducted on quite a large scale was done by Gabbard and Twemlow (1984), two psychoanalytically oriented psychiatrists, who solicited responses from readers of a national periodical. Surprisingly, of their 1 500 responses, nearly half (700) claimed to have had an OBE, and were consequently sent follow-up questionnaires. On the basis of these further responses, the researchers concluded that they were not dealing with psychotics but with normal 'healthy Americans'. They also found that adults' OBEs were very similar to those of children, but that in adults near death experiences were different from those with 'after death' (say from cardiac arrest) experiences. They also tend to agree with other studies which show that regardless of the 'healthy Americans' there is *some* correlation between the OBE and symptoms of schizophrenia – a pathological state.

The highly contentious issue as to whether or not people really can have spontaneous out-of-body experiences has generated a considerable volume of literature in recent years although the phenomenon has been reported from classical antiquity. And just as intriguing is this question of whether it is accompanied by this ESP capacity for seeing what could not otherwise be known or inferred from normal processes. Some reported small-scale research in *JSPR* found only a small proportion (5 per cent) of the sample satisfied the criteria for ESP during such an experience (Alvarado: 1986). A great deal, of course, depends upon the way the questions are framed, and the answers interpreted. Work with students concerning OBEs, lucid and 'flying' dreams (and the degree of recall) showed that there was a strong correlation between all three phenomena. Significantly, too, those who claimed to have had one or more OBEs said they did so in a waking but relaxed state often after taking drugs (LSD or marijuana). Most respondents could not say just how long their experience lasted, and only a tiny minority (three) displayed knowledge which was evidential of a capacity for ESP (Blackmore: 1982a).

Common sense suggests that the questions asked in OBE research must be reasonably similar, but the actual experiences themselves vary quite a lot in their length and complexity, for example (Ibid.):

1. A person who fell about 20 feet on a rock face and suddenly had an image of being apart from their body and watching it fall ... .
2. A clergyman delivering a sermon who became aware of a 'detachment' from his body and listened to his voice from another part of the building. (*Note*: It is not entirely unknown for teachers, preachers and the like to be, as it were, 'beside themselves' while speaking – in effect, watching themselves deliver material with which they are already over-accustomed).
3. 'While driving fast along a road the drone of the engine and vibration seemed to lull me into a stupor and I remember I seemed to

leave my motorbike like a zoom lens in reverse and was hovering over a hill watching myself and friend tearing along the road below and I seemed to think I shouldn't be here ... and the next instant I was in the saddle again ... .'

In a subsequent postal survey conducted in Bristol, Blackmore tried to cover a wider range of phenomena including not just OBEs and dreams, but also hallucinations, mystical and other psychic (i.e. telepathic) experiences together with questions concerning beliefs about the paranormal generally. In all, 593 people were selected randomly, but only 321 (55 per cent) usable questionnaires were returned. Just 12 per cent reported OBEs, most lasting no more than five minutes. There was a marked association between those who had 'lucid dreams' (47 per cent) and those who had 'flying dreams' (28 per cent). Given that, as far as we know, everybody dreams, these may represent only those who could recall their dreams with any clarity. A significant number (45 per cent) claimed to have had hallucinations of various kinds, and a modest 19 per cent said that they had had at least one 'mystical experience'. There was a relatively high belief level in ESP (36 per cent) and survival (42 per cent), and 25 per cent actually claimed to have experienced telepathy. In short, there was a strong correlation between the various psychic experiences and belief. The problem, of course, is to know which determines which.

Unlike some other surveys, only 10 per cent of those in Blackmore's (1984) study claimed any lasting benefit or effect from their OBEs in terms of changed attitudes or beliefs. Blackmore concluded from this study that people who have these experiences, especially OBEs, are those who have 'the ability to become convinced of the reality of an imagined world instead of the normally perceived world', thus supporting a psychological rather than a paranormal interpretation of such experiences. Somewhat different conclusions can be found in work by Harvey Irwin in Australia. In a study among university undergraduates, he assumed that out-of-body experiences required a high level of skill in the art of 'mental imagery' but it was discovered that this was not the case. In a sample of 177, Irwin found that 36 claimed some kind of OBE-type experience, but on Irwin's criteria this was whittled down to 21 (12 per cent). His research indicated that the OBE was not a hallucinatory experience, but was related to the subjects' capacity for 'absorption', i.e. the ability to shut out all extraneous distracting sounds and images, rather like those who are susceptible to deep hypnosis (Irwin: 1980). Elsewhere (Irwin: 1985) he makes clear that he rejects any PSI or supernatural interpretations of the OBE, and says that such ideas are too presumptuous to pursue any further. Yet his own 'synesthetic model' says nothing more than that a person – for reasons that are not clear – loses bodily sensations and thus 'feels disembodied'.

There is a long tradition in many cultures which indicates that psychic abilities and/or experiences are most commonly developed in children, i.e. in those whose cognitive faculties are not fully developed and who have not been 'contaminated' by worldly scepticism. But there is an alternative viewpoint. If the influential psychological approach is something like right, then it may only be when those faculties *are* developed that such 'skills' can be experienced. The problem is again one of testing. It is well known that young children endow toys (dolls, teddy bears, etc.) with human qualities, and have a predilection for 'constructing' imaginary figures with whom they confer on a more or less regular basis. One survey among children whose confidence was first cultivated over a period of several months revealed only one reported OBE in a sample of 52 children from a variety of ethnic backgrounds (Blackmore and Wooffitt: 1990). Knowing that children are not above concocting something quite fantastic in order to make an impression, this was a surprising result.

Experiments have actually been carried out with students (who else?) in which the experimenter, a psychology teacher, attempted to induce the out-of-body experience. This was done by trying to 'convince' the sample group that conscious experiences are not automatic records of outer reality but rather that we construct our conscious experiences. But if awareness is a construct, can our bodies be simply creations of our minds? If so, then perhaps the mind can 'move' wherever it wishes – hence the OBE?

The subjects of this experiment were given 'relaxation exercises' – often a very unconvincing procedure – and told to imagine that they were taking a 'trip through outer space' in which they left their bodies, went through the roof of the building and into the sky. From there they were to imagine entering the void at the heart of the galaxy. After taking the return trip by the opposite route, they were required to fill out questionnaires and write brief accounts of their experiences. Amazingly, 44 of the 45 students reported some kind of out-of-body sensation, 21 mildly, 18 'out into space', and five 'out into the white light'. All but three reaffirmed that their experiences were pleasurable, but there was no attempt to test the veridicality of the OBEs. Further tests, however, were unable to yield such impressive results, and one wonders if suggestibility and cultural setting did not play their part in the original experiment (Schmeidler: 1983).

The evidence for an *actual* OBE is still not forthcoming. Some researchers have even tried to establish the possible veridicality of the OBE by trying to measure the 'shock' to the body at the end of the out-of-body experience, that is, when the astral or alternative self is assumed to return to the body (Alvarado and Zingrone: 1997). But these 'shocks' may be nothing more than 'sleep starts' so nothing conclusive was established – certainly nothing that would convince the impartial enquirer, least of all the sceptical scientific mind.

There is a considerable body of literature which is extremely critical about parapsychology in general and the out-of-body experience in particular. Some writers have argued that 'hypnagogic sleep' accounts for the overwhelming majority of reported OBEs. John Palmer, himself a professor of parapsychology writes, 'the OBE is neither a potentially nor actually a psychic phenomenon. It is an experience or mental state, like a dream or any other altered state of consciousness' (Palmer: 1978, p. 21). This is really just another way of saying that the OBE is something that can be *thought to happen* during that uncategorizable time between sleep and wakefulness. This can involve dreamlike fantasy mixed with some elements of reality, though this can, of course, be true of the dream state itself when reality can unaccountably intrude, as when, say, an elderly person dreams he is running effortlessly, yet knows somehow even in his sleep that this is not possible. Palmer argued that if the dying patient, possibly preoccupied by thoughts of death, passes through a physiological state such as hypnagogic sleep, then an OBE cannot be regarded as in any way extraordinary (Alcock: 1981).

Similarly the OBE can – and has been – seen as a hallucination. Experiments conducted with subjects who have used marijuana reported images which might be interpreted in OBE terms, a bright light in their field of vision. Vivid imagery was even more evident with some of those who have taken LSD, again a characteristic of many OBEs where there is sometimes a 'meeting' with dead relatives and – most importantly – a feeling of dissociation from the body. Seigal (1977) argued that this emanates from a particular kind of excitation of the central nervous system, though exactly what triggers this excitation is not specified. The general theme of the sceptics is that just about everything that features in the out-of-body experience can be duplicated in some way (which means *explained* in some way) either by dreams or by drug-induced fantasies which are found in non-death circumstances. Having said this, however, it is important to note that some of the least critical commentators are not professional parapsychologists but researchers from other disciplines, especially medicine, such as Moody (1975) and

Sabom (1982). Even sceptics are often generous enough to concede that some people do have mystical experiences, and that we should not reject the experience even if we reject the explanation.

Inevitably, studies of OBE and NDE phenomena overlap considerably with those who try to test the survivalist hypothesis (Chapter 5). Raymond Moody, an American doctor, has listed what he feels to be the typical sequential features of the NDE, some of which would apply to the OBE and – some might presume – to the death experience itself (Moody: 1975):

1. A loud ringing or buzzing.
2. The sensation of moving rapidly through a long dark tunnel.
3. The feeling of being outside the body.
4. Seeing his own physical body from a distance.
5. As a spectator, watching attempts to resuscitate the body, he is in a state of emotional turmoil.
6. He notes that the 'body' he now possesses is quite different in nature and ability from his earlier physical body.
7. People – dead relatives and friends – come to meet him.
8. A kindly 'being of light' whom he does not recognize comes to greet him, and he is asked non-verbal (i.e. telepathic) questions.
9. He is asked to evaluate his life which he is shown as a kind of panoramic playback.
10. He then approaches a 'barrier' which represents the limit of his earthly life.
11. He is confronted by the choice of either going back or going on.
12. He has such a feeling of joy and peace that he does not want to return, but is, nevertheless, united with his physical body.
13. When he has recovered he tries to tell others of his experience but they tend not to take him seriously.
14. Regardless of others' opinions this experience profoundly affects his subsequent attitudes towards life and death.

Other writers have also given their views on the stages of the 'core NDE' (for example, Ring, 1992) but other than stressing an enhanced sense of awareness these are really only abbreviated restatements of Moody's schema. However, it should be emphasized that research has shown that not all near death experients testify to such sensations, though some had partial experiences. For example, Sabom who interviewed over a hundred (mostly cardiac arrest) patients, found that less than half (43 per cent) had had a near death experience (Sabom: 1982). A somewhat different approach was adopted by Noyes and Kletti (1977) who questioned 85 victims of falls, car accidents, near drownings and other near fatal events. Of these, 75 per cent experienced a slowing of (clock) time yet, simultaneously, a quickening of the mental processes. Almost as many had a feeling of detachment – a sense of unreality. About a half felt themselves to be out of their bodies, although visions (36 per cent) and far away voices (23 per cent) were only experienced by a minority. The researchers began with a theory of depersonalization to account for NDEs, but found elements of reported hyperalertness which the theory could not explain.

It is always as well to maintain a healthy scepticism regarding such *outré* experiences as OBEs and NDEs. After all, it can be cogently argued, certainly about NDEs, that no matter how close a person is to death, his experience is still that of a *living* person. Can it therefore be evidence of survival? But this is a point at which we may have to suspend critical judgements and allow that the exceptional may be possible. In the case of the various surveys we have discussed – and there are many more – there is every reason to think that the majority of respondents are reporting what for them was a true experience, however they are to be interpreted. Furthermore, we have to admit that there can be no conceivable philosophical or epistemological *a priori* argument against the *possibility* of such an experience (Hovelmann: 1985). What is disputed is the *nature* of the experience. While the 'typical' OBE/NDE is said to take the idyllic form we have described, some research points to a very different format. A recent British study of 230 accounts of near death experiences showed that approximately half were hardly blissful in nature. Respondents recounted 'negative' – sometimes frightening – experiences, such as being 'pulled down' into a void. However, not all these patients were near death subjects who had 'died' and then recovered, but persons who were gravely ill or under the influence of anaesthetics (*Sunday Times*, 5 October 1997).

So are OBEs and NDEs merely mental aberrations? Are they just subjective experiences? Writers at the popular end of the genre are often more generous in their assessments, but are their anecdotal accounts indistinguishable from fiction? Ian Wilson has given numerous examples of reported OBEs and NDEs not only from the past but also from the present day (Wilson: 1987). These range from Plato via the Venerable Bede to veterans of the war in Vietnam, to modern cardiac patients. On his own admission, Wilson, a convert to a liberal brand of Catholicism, entertains an unconcealed bias. As a professional writer, it is natural that he should choose to relate the most appealing accounts of such experiences. For instance, he relates the story (first reported by Kenneth Ring [1992]) of a would-be suicide who threw herself into a 'bone-chilling sea' and despite being dashed against the rocks, insisted that an incredible feeling of peace came over her: 'all of a sudden there was no pain ... [it was] perfectly beautiful' (Wilson: 1987, p. 117). But how far can such accounts be trusted? This is not to impugn the writer's honesty, but simply to ask if we can readily accept second- and third-hand reports that cannot be tested and for which there cannot, by definition, be any corroborative evidence.

As we have seen, some of the most interesting examples of the OBE/NDE phenomena have been recounted by the doctor, Michael Sabom, who admits that at first he was 'less than enthusiastic ... [and] just couldn't relate seriously to these far-out descriptions of afterlife spirits and such' (Sabom: 1982, p. 3). But after being persuaded that the subject was worth further research, he found that he became more and more impressed. His book was eventually based on carefully researched case studies only 12 of whom said they had ever heard of an out-of-body experience, and he was intrigued to find an amazing consistency in the various accounts. He was, if anything, even more surprised to find how many of his research patients reported facts about their physical surroundings that they could not otherwise have known. For instance, a woman heart patient who was *face-down* on the operating table yet was able to describe how the surgeons were operating on her back. Another patient who had suffered a cardiac arrest said to Sabom 'I could see anywhere I wanted to. I could see out in the parking lot, but I was still in the corridor ... ' (Sabom: 1982, p. 34). Another patient undergoing resuscitation was able to describe just who and how many relatives were waiting to see him in the hall of the hospital. Even more startling is the testimony of Dr Elizabeth Kübler-Ross who insists that she has known blind NDE patients who have been able to describe what was taking place in the operating theatre.

None of this constitutes concrete evidence for the out-of-body experience, and it certainly does not amount to irrefutable proof of the paranormal. But it is intriguing, and does indicate the need for more research. Many parapsychologists readily agree that the Occam's Razor approach to the paranormal should be tried first; conventional scientific analysis should always be applied where possible. As we have seen, many types of explanation can be advanced to account for OBEs/NDEs: pharmacological explanations which stress drug-induced sensations; physiological explanations which point to lack of oxygen and the reduction of blood sugar; and – not least of all – psychological explanations. The naturalistic possibilities have to be exhausted before other, more conjectural, theories can be entertained. But it is difficult to avoid the impression that some researchers wish to confirm the validity of the naturalistic approach, and that there is an actual *preference* for this kind of interpretation. The possibility – and certainly the probability – that we should consider or accommodate any kind of 'objective' para-normal explanation is often ruled out automatically, surely a denial of an open-minded, truly scientific espistemology.

Excursus: The Reincarnation Issue

It might be as well to look briefly at the question of reincarnation as not a great amount has been written about it in the West in recent years. As a subject, it has not exactly been taken up with alacrity by the academic community, but it does have its enthusiasts, especially those with Buddhist leanings. Professor Ian Stevenson, for example, who has almost made the parapsychological implications of reincarnation his own has produced several studies since the 1960s in which he has accumulated over 2 000 cases to date. These are necessarily 'spontaneous cases'; they could hardly be anything else, given that what is purported cannot ultimately be proved either way. Some of the cases in question relate to children, as are also the cases examined by Satwant Pasricha (1990) who found it difficult to reconcile children's claims/statements with any particular deceased personality. Other cases under consideration have related to hypnotically induced regression – a much debated procedure (see Wilson: 1981). Other lines of evidence, for instance those resulting from certain forms of past life therapy including drug-induced therapy (especially with LSD) have not been critically examined by many parapyschologists (for one exception, see Rogo: 1985).

By and large, reincarnation has not had a very good press in the West. Sometimes this has arisen where critics are anti-survivalist generally (for example, Edwards: 1996), but often the criticisms are directed towards the idea of reincarnation in particular. Impressionistically, the very notion of reincarnation strikes people as an absurdity. There are so many objections that can be raised. When and how do the changes occur? It was once said that a boy's best friend is his mother, and that a man's best friend is his horse. When does the transition take place? Furthermore, it is interesting to ask if demographic trends are genuine. Are world population figures increasing or are people mere replicas of former selves? There are, of course, different kinds of reincarnation. But can we, as in Hindu philosophy, accept the ideas of an endless wheel of life – and not necessarily human life, at that?

The problem of reincarnation, at least as far as its critics are concerned, may be broadly categorized under the heading of cryptomnesia. The well-attested assumption is that we all acquire knowledge unconsciously. This *is not* the kind of knowledge that is suddenly inaccessible because memory fails us, as we all know it does from time to time. This is especially true of names and dates; as we age this happens to most of us (at home, it has been commented that I can remember when Caesar crossed the Rubicon, but not what I had for dinner yesterday – and now even Caesar is getting a little hazy). No, it is more the kind of information that comes to us and is not consciously recorded, but which appears, perhaps in a new guise, later on. This is known in the trade as cryptomnesia or buried memory. Psychologists assure us that we have more ability to acquire, process and store information than we realize, even if we cannot always retrieve it on demand. But it can resurface, sometimes when we least expect it. So it may be that we have here one explanation for cases in which people appear to remember details of past lives.

As we know from various popular media reports, people do claim that they have 'lived before', but attempts to track down the persona described has proved rather fruitless. Hypnotism, the favourite tool of the 'past lives' enthusiasts has also been shown to be hopeless as a means of providing *evidential support* for the characters 'revealed' by regression techniques. Their identities seem to be more a production of the subconscious mind than an actual recollection of a previous existence.

Ian Stevenson has proposed three rules which should be followed for establishing cases of cryptomnesia, always given the possibility of unconscious borrowing (as opposed to conscious borrowing or plagiarism) from identifiable sources perhaps as the unusual phenomenon of xenoglossia, i.e. speaking in a foreign language that has never been consciously learned. First, there must be a close correspondence in detail between the information expressed by the subject and that normally available to him from another person or source. Second, given that we define cryptomnesia as remembering particular information while forgetting how or even if it was learned, it is important that there must be evidence that the subject did at one time learn the information, or at least, that it is more probable than not that he did so. In practice, it may be difficult to apply these two 'rules'; for example, not everyone would agree on what constituted a 'close correspondence'. Usually such cases can only be assessed on a balance of possibilities. Third, all elements of a case should be taken into consideration because selection of certain elements *only* (say, background information about a particular historical period) can lead to an erroneous assessment.

In any particular case, it is always wise to look for the most obvious or 'natural' explanation first before considering the ostensibly paranormal alternatives. We could take an instance of a claimed psychic communication which took place in March 1949 (Stevenson: 1983, pp. 1–30). The 'message' came to a Miss Geraldine Cummins, and the purported communicator was a certain Colonel Fawcett, a well-known English explorer who disappeared in a Brazilian jungle in 1925. Rumours reached England that he may have gone native, or that he may have been killed by tribespeople. Attempts were made to try to locate him, not least by his son, but all to no avail. The colonel was interested in psychical matters, and had written an article for *Occult Review* which was published in 1923, and in the communication Miss Cummins repeated – though not verbatim – some ideas and phrases from that article. The correspondence was not exact, but it was close. Stevenson states that the similarities could not be regarded as accidental. Miss Cummins, herself, suggested three explanations:

1. She had read the article probably some years earlier and it had become a 'buried memory'.
2. Colonel Fawcett was really in psychic communication with her, or
3. A certain Miss Gibbes who was her 'companion' and who had also probably read the Fawcett article was communicating with her telepathically.

To the observer (1) seems the most likely candidate, while (2) was to be a little suspect considering that Miss Cummins also claimed to have a 'word for word' outline of a new work on which the deceased poet, W.B. Yeats was currently working.

The ability of a subject to retain what must be considered the vaguest information was put to an unusual test by Bayer (1973, pp. 57–8) some years ago. The subject was shown 30 completely blank white cards about 8 cm square, and asked to 'see' on each card an object that the researcher suggested to her. The researcher made a list of the objects and wrote them on the back of the respective cards, which were numbered. The cards were then shuffled and then presented to the subject one at a time in such a way that neither could see the numbers or the names of the objects. Remarkably when the subject's answers were checked against the list she had made no mistakes. Yet more remarkably, when the test was repeated with the same cards two weeks later, she still got them all right. Neither test was conducted using hypnotism, and telepathy was ruled out by the design of the experiment. It is difficult to explain how anyone can do this. It was hardly cryptomnesia, after all, the knowledge was not known by anyone else, nor was it recorded anywhere. Very possibly it was hypermnesia – though even an exceptional memory would barely account for such a feat. It is certainly the sort of thing that makes the recollection of 'buried' facts that much more understandable. Even in cases of xenoglossia, it is rare to find anyone who can actually *converse* in the unknown tongue (usually they simply repeat a few phrases), and Stevenson states that he has never known of anyone who was capable of this who did not know that he had actually learned the language at some time in the past.

So do some people really recollect something of their purported 'past lives'? And is this proof of reincarnation? What is known is that memories can, under hypnosis, be planted artificially. The eminent psychologist, Ernest Hilgard, has recorded how he implanted a false memory of a bank robbery that had never occurred in the mind of a subject, and the person was actually able to 'identify' from a series of photographs the picture of an employee at the bank he had robbed. On another occasion, Hilgard deliberately assigned two concurrent – though spatially different – life experiences to the same person who was then regressed hypnotically at *separate* times to the *same* date. The subject then gave accurate accounts of both experiences. A believer in reincarnation would presumably have suspected that the man had really lived the two assigned lives.

We must distinguish between the retrieval of a lost memory, and a 'false memory' such as we find in certain purported child abuse cases where any explanation is better than no explanation, and the claim to 'past lives'. A reasonably typical example of a past life experience is that of Jenny Cockell, a Northamptonshire chiropodist now in her early forties who has recounted her youthful 'dream memories' of an Irishwoman named Mary who died in her mid-thirties. Jenny Cockell began to see herself as Mary who lived in a small cottage in a village (the main features of which she could draw on a map) just north of Dublin. Mary was desperately poor, burdened by children, and eventually died in the mid-1930s. When Jenny herself grew up, she married and had two children, and in 1987 she was introduced to a hypnotist who regressed her back to the early years of the century when she 'became' Mary once again. Under hypnosis she was able to reveal all sorts of finer details about Mary's life such as the names of neighbours and friends and so forth. In 1989, Jenny made a trip to Mary's village of Malahide and found that many of its features corresponded with those she had drawn in her regression sessions. Later still, she discovered that a person called Mary Sutton had lived there at the time recalled, and that she answered the description that Jenny had given. Jenny followed this up by ascertaining details about Mary Sutton's surviving children who had been sent to orphanages after her death, and actually met one of them in 1990.

So is this really evidence of a past life? Plausible as this all sounds, for believers there were some disquieting anomalies. For instance, the name given under hypnosis, for Mary's husband was Bryan O'Neal, hardly to be mistaken for Mary Sutton's husband the alcoholic John Sutton. Furthermore the names of the children were quite different from those elicited during regression. Jenny Cockell thinks she is another incarnation of Mary (Cockell: 1993), but is she? The evidence – though intriguing – is far from satisfactory, and leaves us with the suspicion that this could well be another case of cryptomnesia.

It is one thing to recapture, say, some youthful episode under hypnosis, and quite another to recall a past life. Recent research at the University of London involving 690 cases of patients with recovered memories who consulted qualified psychologists found that about 35 per cent remembered forgotten childhood events before therapy and a further 50 per cent after therapy. Researchers admitted that some memories are false, but the therapists reported that 41 per cent of these past events had been corroborated from non-patient sources (reported in *The Times*, 30 October 1997). By contrast, accounts of past lives by hypnotherapists such as Britain's Joe Keeton and the late Arnall Bloxham are quite a different matter, and have been ably criticized by a number of professionals. Ian Wilson (1981) is particularly sceptical about cases of so-called past life regression. Keeton, for instance, claimed in the early 1980s that he had investigated some 9 000 cases many with a wealth of circumstancial detail including attitudes and beliefs to go with the 're-lived' characters that have been seemingly dredged up from the past. But doubts arise when the historical details are inaccurate for many of these incarnations, and when specifics such as names and places cannot be checked. Are these accounts, therefore, conscious fabrications which, in general, seems a little unlikely, or – more probably – are they unconscious feats of creative imagination?

In another text, Wilson (1987) again has reincarnation 'proofs' as his target. In their fantasy lives he found that subjects were skipping from the Stone Age to ancient Egypt, Inca Peru and South Wales with equal facility, the 'rules' for reincarnation varying from one hypnotist to the next. He also castigates the 'muddled thinking' of other notable devotees of reincarnation such as the actress, Shirley MacLaine, and her friend 'David' whose ideas are at best unusual, and at worst frankly preposterous. They belong, among other things, to the 'aliens-are-among-us' brigade. Among other far-fetched claims, David has asserted that a girl named Mayan came from a planet among the constellation of stars we call the Pleiades.

If reincarnation does exist, its advocates seem to be most unclear on the details. Does the spirit immediately transfer to another body after death? Or is there some kind of intermediate stage which is not exactly earth-bound (as a ghost?) but not fully possessed of another incarnation? There could be a future eternal life, but there is precious little evidence for a succession of lives.

CHAPTER FIVE

The Paranormal as Ethereal Hope: The Question of Survival

The out-of-body issue is inextricably linked with that of survival, that is, the continuing existence of the self in some form after death. Indeed, for many the OBE/NDE is an indication – if not actually a proof – that somehow humans survive bodily death. The very idea that death is not the end, that we are not all destined to the extinction of our selfhood is extremely potent, and besides being the ultimate hope of so many religions was originally the *raison d'être* for much parapsychological research. Indeed, in the early days of the British Society for Psychical Research members who had been reared in a religious tradition but who were shaken by the implications of Darwinian theory 'saw in the claims of the spiritualists a possibility of salvaging something of the unique spiritual status accorded to human kind. Proof of personal survival of bodily death' (Rush: 1986c, p. 23). The main focus of much of this research was the spiritualist movement. Experiments by small groups of devotees had been taking place since at least the latter part of the eighteenth century, and by the middle years of the nineteenth century table-tipping, automatic writing, spirit voices and even 'apparitions', while not actually commonplace, were very much part of the repertoire of many self-respecting spiritualist – or, as some would prefer, *spiritist* – gatherings. Mediums were in great demand for seances, especially those who were apparently able to produce sensational results often before quite critical audiences. Some were only too ready to lease out their services for private sittings for the well-to-do, often for not inconsiderable sums. After the First World War in particular, it was understandable that those who had lost loved ones wanted the reassurance that they were in a 'better place' and that one day the bereaved and those who had 'passed over' would be happily reunited.

It was patently obvious to serious researchers that much of this activity was fraudulent. A variety of techniques were discovered for producing spiritist effects, and the unscrupulous were only too ready to exploit the unwary. The sad, the curious, and – not least – the gullible, were prime prey for fake mediums and opportunists. A particular problem, however, arises in relation to those mediums over whom there is still some debate. Some were never detected in overt fraud such as D.D.

Holme and Rudi Schneider, or were rarely detected such as the Fox sisters and Eusapia Palladino (whether this, therefore, undermines *all* their work is still a matter of opinion). What seems a little sad for the modern parapsychological point of view is that these now rather dated cases are still being rehashed and re-evaluated in the pages of the *JSPR* as though the whole enterprise stands or falls by the veridicality of these few – if important – cases.

As an example of this, let us consider for a moment one of the classic cases from the history of trance mediumship which was still being reviewed 50 years later. In August 1915 a 'message' was received via a very well-known medium, Mrs Leonore Piper, which to all intents and purposes was addressed to the scientist, Sir Oliver Lodge. It was couched in rather cryptic quasi-classical terms and appeared to allude to Lodge's son, Raymond, who was killed in action the following month. The message, known in SPR circles as the 'Famous Message', was eventually taken to mean that Sir Oliver and Lady Lodge should not despair because their boy was still living – albeit in another dimension. This seemed to be confirmed in a further sitting, this time with another well-respected medium, Mrs Leonard. The Lodges were obviously delighted, and Sir Oliver – a firm believer in the paranormal – eventually wrote a book, *Raymond, or Life and Death*, which became extremely popular, especially among those who had become similarly bereaved. Understandably, it made the mediums concerned national figures (although it was the last significant 'performance' by Mrs Piper).

The whole matter did not rest there. It was taken up many years later by, among other people, parapsychologist, Scott Rogo (1971) who suggested a more complex interpretation. Lodge had first introduced the American, Mrs Piper, to British sitters in 1889, and Rogo sees the 'Famous Message' as an indication that this was to be her swansong. The message had a double significance. It referred to Raymond Lodge's death, and also to the fact that the SPR was to lose its most famous 'sensitive', Mrs Piper. But this loss was to be lessened by the new discovery, Mrs Leonard. This interpretation seems rather strained, but the conjunction of events did give the SPR continuity of trance mediumship of a similar kind from the 1880s to the 1940s.

It is all too easy to mock early spiritualists (see Brandon: 1983, and the devastating critique of her book by Brian Inglis (1983)), but arguably the intentions were laudable and the results still open to discussion (see Gregory: 1977).

Although mediumship continues to flourish elsewhere, there does seem to be a dearth of professional mediums in our modern scientifically oriented society. It is argued (Braude: 1986) that this is not due to earlier gullibility or to increased technological sophistication but to the changing social and psychological attitudes which permitted spiritualism to develop so rapidly in the first place. However, as we know, there is still a fashionable occult culture in the West where fads come and go with the seasons. The earlier view of the adherents, and sometimes of the mediums themselves, was that they really were in touch – or could be in touch – with some non-human agency. Whereas today, in keeping with current trends, the tendency is to ascribe the phenomena, if not to some – as yet – undetected sleight of hand, then to possible PK. Anything that now savours of the supernatural (paranormal?) is often found to be faintly embarrassing.

The scepticism even of card-carrying researchers is an open secret. This is well illustrated by the work of the late, eminent philosopher, Professor C.D. Broad who assured his readers that 'most of the well attested mediumistic phenomena which are commonly cited as evidence for survival of a deceased human being's personality seem to me not to support so strong a conclusion'. He further argued that

> many mediumistic communications which take the dramatic form of messages from the surviving spirit of a deceased human being, imparted to and reported by the medium's 'control' (i.e. the sensitive's 'spirit guide') obviously require no more radical assumption than telepathic cognition on the medium's part, (and/or) facts known (consciously or unconsciously) to the sitter or to other living human beings connected with him.

However, Broad was prepared to admit that this kind of naturalistic explanation (if we can call telepathy naturalistic) seems rather contrived when related to certain kinds of mediumistic phenomena (Broad: 1958, pp. 28–30). Regarding survival, he was ready to accept reincarnation as a possible hypothesis, but compared with the 'vast coherent mass of ascertained (biological) facts' there was nothing to counter it but 'a few pinches of philosophical fluff' (Broad: 1953).

It is probably true to say that today there is nothing like as much discussion about survival in parapsychological literature as there was early in the twentieth century. There are a number of reasons for this. Perhaps the most important is that parapsychology is now intent upon being accepted as a 'legitimate' science, and has therefore expressed less concern about such amorphous – and perhaps ultimately unanswerable – issues as survival. We can probably say, too, that the notion of survival has almost always been linked with religion, and there is little doubt that religion – certainly in its institutionalized forms – has lost much of its cogency in modern day society. Yet it is interesting to find those with a strong disposition towards the paranormal but who have no conventional religious beliefs obviously intrigued by the possibility and even the hope of eventual survival in some form (Spedding: 1975, pp. 1–18).

There are, in fact, several non-religious ideas about the nature of survival and ostensible communication with discarnate entities which have been developed in the last hundred years or so. Ducasse (1951) tries to counter critics by questioning:

1. The dismissive notion that all so-called 'contacts' can be attributed to ESP, itself not that easily explained.
2. The spiritualist idea of 'passing over' to an 'astral' dimension in which astral bodies – the nature of which is not specified – inhabit a non-physical world.
3. The transition to a permanent dream-like state.
4. Reincarnation, though not necessarily (contra Hinduism) in anything other than self-conscious 'human' forms.

This kind of classificatory scheme by no means exhausts the possibilities. Very similar types of categorization have been put forward, for example, by Thouless (1979). He suggests seven possible kinds of survival theory ranging from non-survival (if that can be considered a survival theory) to timeless survival. By survival Thouless is referring to what he terms the 'stream of consciousness', something that can only be known to the individual himself.

1. Non-survival: the view that the individual – rather like Monty Python's parrot – is indubitably and irreversibly dead. This cannot be proved any more than any other theory of survival can be proved, but on a priori grounds it is a theory that has much going for it.
2. Continued survival: the evidence for this – if such it can be called – is culled from mediumistic seances and the reported existence of apparitions which are assumed to be the spirits of the dead. The belief is that the individual no longer inhabits a physical body but is a spirit that under special circumstances may manifest itself in an identifiable form. The interesting variant of this, found pre-eminently among Buddhists, is that although there is continued survival there is no continuation of the individual self. Every individual is absorbed with the great Cosmic All.
3. Bodily survival: this theory holds that individuals retain a kind of body sometimes referred to as the 'astral body' whose structure and composition are left unspecified. As we have seen, this is the kind of body most commonly associated with out-of-body experiences.

4. Reincarnation: this is found mainly in the Hindu and Buddhist traditions, is another obvious candidate whose appeal rests largely on the notion of virtuoso-like self-improvement. Thouless classifies this as a theory of 'intermittent revival' because the individual becomes successively re-embodied, perhaps in human or animal forms, until final absorption takes place.

5. Terminal revival: this is found in ongoing Western religious traditions and involves the idea of a resurrection of the dead at some future date. Whether it is to be assumed that this stream of consciousness ceases temporarily or whether some awareness of selfhood continues is not made clear. But in its most refined Pauline form, this theory posits not the revivification of the physical body – which prayers for the dead might imply – but the endowment of a 'more glorious' spiritual (astral?) body.

6. Timeless survival: would seem to be another version of 'continued survival' except that greater emphasis is placed upon the un-imaginability of life in endless time.

7. Extradimensional survival: this is really yet another variant but with the interesting additional idea that after death the individual enters into a different time dimension which has no direct correspondence with his former earthly time-bound existence. If true, this would certainly cast doubt on the validity of mediumistic communications. A further implication of such a theory is that perhaps there is continued survival but the conditions of survival are such that no communication between the living and the departed is possible – a view held by many religious people.

It is notable that despite their suspicions to the contrary, a number of parapsychologists are reluctant to abandon the well-rooted notion that survival can be proved by the mediumistic experience. A number of professionals prefer to plump for 'super-ESP' to account for validatory survivalist phenomena, a hypothesis which postulates a power of telepathy for which, as yet, there is not sufficient experimental evidence. Others try to reconcile the ESP hypothesis with that of the 'overshadowing' of the medium by discarnate spirits (Gauld: 1982). What this really means in practice, and how it actually operates, is left to the imagination of the reader. But some kind of survival still seems to be the most persuasive hypothesis if we wish to reconcile under one explanatory umbrella all the phenomena concerned. After all, is it so impossible that the supervenient principles which constrain the neural activities of the brain cannot be reinstated in some other setting (Gauld: 1982, p. 214)?

It is important that we should bear in mind the fact that if the survival of the consciousness should prove to be true, it would not actually affect scientific theory given that scientific theory has not – and probably never will – prove otherwise. The mechanistic presuppositions of much of physics is already being questioned, and as for biology, it would probably carry on much as before (Braude: 1986). Indeed, some survivalists have gleaned new hope for their position in the light of some of the implications of the new (quantum) physics (Rees: 1997).

It is largely because of the – as yet – seemingly insurmountable logical and methodological difficulties involved, that survival issues are no longer a number one priority even among the professionals. The very ambiguity of the evidence has been the problem. To be verifiable, a material record of some kind must be accessible, and there is still no certainty that it is or ever has been. In our present state of knowledge we have to admit that a direct demonstration of survival may be impossible, although some might consider that if telepathy exists (i.e. mind-to-mind activity) then the mind could be a separate entity that survives bodily death. Critics, however, argue that a 'disembodied person' is a contradiction in terms. Can a disembodied person, the kind of spirit-being implied by the very notion of survival, be located in time and space, and possess the kinds of senses we associate with human beings? Furthermore, does a disembodied person possess agency, i.e. the ability to act, to change or influence our physical environment? Even the idea of an 'astral body' does not really overcome these difficulties. C.D. Broad alludes to the possibility – not too far removed from the philosophy of certain forms of Hinduism – that some vestigial element or 'dispositional consciousness' may survive like radio waves continue after the station has gone off the air (Edge: 1986). This idea must give little emotional satisfaction to those who harbour an 'eternal hope'. It is true, as Broad reminds us, that 'dead men tell no tales' (or as my old grandmother used to say, 'There's Aunt Flo and Aunt Em gone, and not a word from either one of them') but then would they – or could they – if they only possess the low-level consciousness of an oyster?

An even more amorphous state awaits us if we are to experience the conditions of survival posited by what parapsychologists term 'field theory'. William Roll (1974), for instance, suggests that after death consciousness may become involved in a 'field relationship' with a certain space or object, and it is this relationship which survives the bodily system. Again, it is a hypothesis fraught with difficulties, not least the problem of how such a relationship is created in the first place. Field theory really suggests that there may be a dissolution of the ego, in other words there will be continuity of the personality or self only in so far as it is specifically located within a subsystem of consciousness.

Presumably this means that the individual consciousness will eventually be absorbed into a kind of all-embracing cosmic consciousness. Such theories militate against our feelings/wish that what we sense is ours – our subjective awareness or selfhood – is really ours. Does this mean that what has been developed will be eventually lost to us?

Again we are forced back to the conclusion that there are a number of theories, but no actual proof either way. Yet there is quite a lot of intriguing evidence that indicates at least the possibility of survival. Mediumistic communications, admittedly, have to be treated with considerable scepticism, but it is virtually impossible not to be beguiled by some stories of 'cross-correspondence', i.e. when several mediums who have no known connection with each other, impart fragments of information to a particular subject which not only correspond with the facts but also with one another (see, for example, 'The Missing Fingers Case: Corroborated Evidence of Survival', *JSPR*, 1993). Absolute sceptics would undoubtedly put forward some kind of counter-explanation for such experiences, while more moderate sceptics might just accept the paranormality of these phenomena but would disavow that they could bear any sort of survivalist interpretation.

The question has also been raised especially in connection with the survivalist implications of out-of-body and near death experiences whether such phenomena can be associated – even correlated – with a certain type of personality. In a fairly recent study by McCreery and Claridge (1995) involving 450 people who claimed to have had at least one OBE, plus a group of 214 controls, they unsurprisingly concluded that both sets of subjects differed very little in terms of neuroticism. The researchers used the model of the 'schizoptype' (*not* schizophrenic), a functionally, well-adjusted individual due, in part at least, to his/her anomalous experiences. The schizotype, they concede, is a 'relatively new, emerging concept' which can be likened, by analogy, with blood pressure, a continuous condition, whereas schizophrenia can be likened, say, to breakdown processes such as a stroke or series of strokes. Several measures were used, and the whole carefully analysed in statistical terms, but the results were not so much unconvincing as inconsequential. The researchers concluded that their work provided 'a considerable degree of support for the hypothesis that schizotypy, considered as a long-term trait or set of traits, is a contributory factor in the aetiology of the OBEs' (ibid.). In other words, people who have or claim to have OBEs have certain personality traits which are not disturbed by their experiences – hence the 'happy schizotype'. Surely, a modicum of common sense would have told us as much. Like so much experimentation in the field of parapsychology, a great deal of effort produces precious few significant results.

We still have very little understanding of the brain and its processes. Its capacities and incapacities are still a puzzle to us, and its behavioural expressions never cease to amaze us. It is both predictable and unpredictable by turns (see, for example, the popular works of Dr Oliver Sacks). If the workings of the brain are largely beyond us, are we therefore in a position to pontificate about what we refer to as consciousness which is normally thought of as a function of the mind? So what is mind? What is its relationship to the brain? Is it a case of the car and the driver; the computer and the operator? Basically, we are left with two main theories, the monist and the dualist. Either we adopt a mechanistic or monist position which regards the body/brain as a kind of fallible and impermanent biochemical machine. This is more or less the generally accepted scientific position which sees mind as matter conscious of itself. A position which seems to be firmly supported by everyday experience. To say that the evidence for survival is *incompatible* with a hypothesis is not proof. Therefore it is argued that compatibility is not enough (Moore: 1981). But if we think that the evidence is still persuasive, we could adopt the more tenuous position of the dualist who sees the mind and the body/brain as separate interacting elements. It could follow from this that when the body/brain dies the mind/consciousness lives on.

Critics of the dualist position – perhaps rightly – call for more evidence. But exactly what is expected here? A new kind of evidence, whatever that might be, or more research of the now familiar kind? If so, the issue can become quite arbitrary. Do they wish to specify the number of 'positive' results that would settle the matter? Would they agree to five or 500 and, if 500, why not 499 (Lorimer: 1984, p. 183)? A variant of an old idea to establish evidence was suggested by Robert Thouless some years ago. He devised a test with enciphered passages for which he alone knew the key words. Another researcher, J. Pratt, devised a similar test using a lock combination of random numbers and remembered as an mnemonic which only he knew. Since that time, both Thouless and Pratt have died (1984 and 1979 respectively), and although numerous trials have been carried out by aspiring mediums and sensitives in relation to both the key words and the lock combination, only one has been broken, in this case by a computer expert. In the Thouless case, it is worth recording that one medium 'revealed' that the now departed Thouless was becoming so distanced from his earthly life that it was unlikely that he would be able to remember his own key words!

Even closer to the fringe, as it were, are the isolated attempts that have been made to verify the survival hypothesis by what is known as the Electronic Voice phenomenon. A notable experimentalist in the field, Samuel Alsop, or 'Alsoppa' to his voices, insists that communication with the 'spirit world' is possible by electronic means, including video (Alsop: 1989). Like so many of his ilk, Alsop is almost totally dismissive of science, although obviously happy to utilize scientific equipment in order to contact his voices. He readily admits that it often takes months to track down communicating entities and that, when he does, the messages are often either mundane or unintelligible. Where he can make sense of them, he tries to follow up the leads that seem to be indicated, but investigators are increasingly convinced that these have no objective validity. Again it raises the perennial debate about whether so much that is construed as paranormal is not, in fact, a projection of the human consciousness. Of course, if it is, it is still an interesting phenomenon which is also in need of explanation.

Really, we are back with the old question of whether consciousness depends upon a living brain, and whether consciousness is to be equated with *self*-consciousness. If consciousness is wholly dependent on the brain then, of course, there is no survival. If on the other hand, consciousness is somehow independent of the brain, perhaps survival *is* possible. But – and this is a point being taken up by some of those who write on the paranormal (e.g. Darling: 1995) – if we wish to distinguish consciousness from self-consciousness, the implication is that perhaps we may survive not as selves or personalities but (as in some Eastern philosophies) as constituents of some amorphous cosmic entity. This unsatisfactory compromise seems to be the last, vestigial hope of the parapsychologists.

We know from experience the human ability to fantasize given the appropriate stimuli. There are all sorts of circumstances and conditions in which humans can be induced to exchange their everyday view of reality for something more exotic. And it could be argued that nothing is more enticing than the prospect of life after death. So why is the 'dying brain' hypothesis so appealing – or so we are told – to most scientists (Blackmore: 1993)? Is it a question of the experimental proof versus the spontaneous experience all over again? Believers counter with the argument that the evidence *for* survival is so overwhelming and obvious that it is a wonder that people cannot see it. The arguments are not as irrefutable as Williams suggests (Williams: 1989), but there are transcendental pointers there for all to see, and the anecdotal evidence of spontaneous cases is so compelling that the issue demands reconsideration. There is certainly more to the OBE and the NDE than can be accounted for by reductionist arguments in terms of body chemistry, physiological states or psychological predispositions. Perhaps as

William James once suggested, survival is one those things which were intended to remain baffling so as to prompt our curiosity, hopes and suspicions, all in equal measures. Something that can never be explained away, but also something that is never susceptible of complete corroboration.

Excursus: Ambiguity and the Psychic

We have already touched on the fact of fraud and charlatanism, and the ways in which they have brought the whole idea of the paranormal into disrepute. We have noted too the tendency of reputable writers on the paranormal constantly to refer back to earlier demonstrations of apparently paranormal powers, especially those of certain physical mediums. It would, therefore, be interesting to look briefly at some of the research that has been done concerning a well-known modern psychic, which will point up also the ongoing conflict between those who tend to favour spontaneous cases and those who advocate experimental procedures.

The psychic, Matthew Manning, has travelled world-wide displaying what appear to be unusual gifts, and has been tested by many professional researchers ever since his youth. He was born in Cambridgeshire, the eldest of three children, and in 1967 at the age of 11, he seems to have been the centre of some poltergeist activity which involved the displacement of certain household articles, taps and rappings, and creaks which seemed somewhat unusual in a modern detached house. A doctor was called in who verified these odd occurrences. The following year, the boy took Common Entrance Examinations and went to public school where there was a temporary craze for seances, but the boys became scared and soon gave it up. In the same year, the family moved to a sixteenth-century house where, at first, there were no abnormal happenings. However, in 1970 the disturbances began again. There was the usual repertoire of noises, doors opening and closing for no apparent reason, and – most alarming of all – boots and shoes were thrown about in a quite inexplicable manner. A year later, the disturbances seemed to 'follow' the boy to school where the phenomena were even more bizarre and it was naturally assumed that he was the catalyst for all the paranormal activity. The doctor was again asked for advice, and everyone had their work cut out trying to persuade the headmaster to keep the boy at school.

Manning seems to have been rather a dreamy boy who liked gentle pursuits and hated games, and it was during this period, the summer of 1971, that he had what is reported as being his first 'spirit voice', that of 'Henrietta Webbe', and only a month afterwards he had his first experience of writing 'automatically' in a script quite unlike his own while he was doing a pre-'O' level essay. After this there was more automatic writing which had a 'paranormal content' in that the messages purported to come from deceased persons, although to be fair to Manning, no specific claims of this kind were actually made. He demonstrated this ability in front of friends, and found that if he sensed any poltergeist activity, automatic writing was the best way of preventing what he regarded as unsought psychic manifestations. He claimed to have a message from a 'Thomas Penn' who could diagnose illnesses, and another from the seventeenth-century diarist, Samuel Pepys, but afterwards declared that he hardly thought that Pepys would write something so naïve. More strangely, he is also said to have received messages in various languages (Stemman: 1979), but to what extent this has ever been corroborated is not certain.

As the automatic writing phenomenon developed, so the poltergeist activity gradually ceased. It is claimed that at this time he received more communications including some from a 'Robert Webbe', and that soon there were names and dates written all over the walls and ceiling of his bedroom. His parents obviously indulged his 'gifts', and late that same year (1971), his mother suggested that he try his hand at automatic drawing by calling on the spirits of certain dead artists. Although the boy was said to have no special artistic ability, he did begin to produce drawings in the style of such people as Dürer, Goya, Klee and others, and some of them were said to be very accomplished even though done at speed, and certainly beyond the capacities of the 'natural' Matthew Manning.

In 1971 also, he is said to have had his first visual encounter with 'Robert Webbe', and here it may be significant that in 1969–70 he had been engaged in a history project on the Webbe family from contemporary sources held in the Cambridgeshire Public Records Office. This was chosen because it was known that the Webbe family had once occupied their house, and the name of 'John Webbe, 1731' was scratched on a brick in the house. Manning carried on with his automatic writing, and later wrote some books about his experiences: *The Link* (1974); *In the Minds of Millions* (1977); *The Strangers* (1978). From 1973 he was giving public demonstrations of his 'power' and, following the example of Uri Geller, he tried his hand at metal-bending with considerable success, but soon gave it up – perhaps because it was becoming every would-be psychic's party piece.

Nevertheless, the public performances continued. By now he was in some demand, and he visited several countries displaying his gifts. In an interview given in 1978, he related that he had had 'waking dreams' of a psychic nature since he was 10 or 11, and came to think of himself as not being quite like other children. He made no pretensions to be religious, and considered the formality of being confirmed as 'a waste of time'. However, in 1977 while looking at a sunrise in the Himalayas he said he suddenly realized how completely unimportant he was physically, and how transient human life is. Yet he claims to have also felt a tremendous sense of 'harmony and unity' – presumably with nature – and became convinced that a power was telling him how he should and should not conduct his life (Gregory: 1982b).

Until his Himalayan experience, Manning seems to have taken a rather ambivalent attitude to the phenomena he appears to have generated. He suggested that the incidents may well have arisen from his own subconscious rather than from some spiritual source. For instance, he regarded the 'Thomas Penn' communications as having 'nothing to do with spirits'. He even speculated that Penn did not actually exist until during one of his public demonstrations the Penn messages reached such a high degree of accuracy that he was convinced that there might be an external, spiritual explanation for what was taking place.

By the time he was 24, Manning's success was such that he was sporting many of the embellishments of a pop star; long hair, flared trousers and a bright orange Lotus car. His popularity was such that he now felt confident enough to allow himself to be tested by professional parapsychologists. And it is here that the image becomes a little uncertain; acclaim becomes somewhat diminished and ambiguity takes over. In fact, after some experiments, some of which were never completed, Manning began to express his distrust of researchers generally. 'I've been abused by so many researchers ... They do experiments, they waste my time. I never charge for such research – and then they don't even bother to write up their work ... The amount of material they are wasting is criminal' (Stemman: 1979, p. 11). Actually, quite a lot of very meticulous research has been done on Manning, and has been written up in authoritative journals. As is perhaps to be expected, the results of some of the tests are impressive, some not so impressive, and much that is unsurprisingly inconclusive. It will suffice for our purposes to report briefly on three sets of tests for which he volunteered, two in the USA, and one in the UK.

After the automatic writing/drawing phase, Manning's interest turned towards healing, and it is with this that the first set of tests is indirectly concerned. As part of a larger experimental programme organized by Dr William Brand of the Mind Science Foundation in San Antonio, Texas, Dr John Kmetz designed some tests to see if Manning could manage to affect a culture of cancer cells under laboratory conditions. If successful such a PK experiment would have very significant implications. Manning in an interview for the – admittedly popular – magazine, *Alpha*, reported that the results had been impressive. Kmetz initially believed that these effects were paranormal, but further tests with the equipment showed that similar results could be achieved by non-psychic means. Manning was understandably deflated by Kmetz's volte-face, because he was convinced that this test would provide further evidence of his healing potential. Was there something to it, after all? And was Manning sincere yet mistaken when he insisted that when he 'gives healing', be believed that the power of love was being channelled through him, and that this was being directed by spirit entities?

Interestingly, this interview made no mention of the tests that Manning had undergone with Charles Tart and John Palmer at the University of California in May 1977. This research consisted of a series of different tests each comprising a number of trials which were run and rerun and analysed meticulously. In most it was reported that the results did not differ significantly from randomness and, in some, Manning was so discouraged that he did not wish to continue. However, the experimenters did admit that the results were such that the phenomena in question merited further research.

Later in 1977 and during the first weeks of 1978, Manning submitted to further experiments also conducted at the Mind of Science Foundation (which some might argue prejudiced the experiments anyway). Unlike the Tart and Palmer (1979) PSI research, these tests were mainly concerned with possible PK influences on biological systems, and were conducted by William Braude, Gary Davis and Robert Wood. Perhaps Manning wanted to confirm his own purported gifts experimentally in order to give them a recognized scientific respectability. There were five tests in all, each carefully set up and analysed, though an insider might be forgiven for thinking that some, at least, were somewhat trivial. They ranged from the subject's attempts to affect the revolutions of an activity wheel on which was riding a Mongolian gerbil, to trying to affect the electric signals given off by an Amazonian knife fish. There was yet another test on cancer cells the result of which was described as 'dramatic' compared with the appropriate controls. These effects were achieved by both the 'laying on of hands' (i.e. on the flask containing the cells) for about half an hour, and at a distance in an electrically shielded room.

The general conclusion of the researchers was that overall Manning was able to exert a significant psychokinetic influence on a variety of biological systems. On some tests his performance was not that different from the controls, but on those in which he was intensely interested, most notably the cancer cell test, his rating was considered to be 'most impressive'. Manning was least effective in tests where he expressed doubt about success. Test data sheets which record comments such as 'this experiment won't work' and 'this is a silly experiment', suggest that there was a definite anticipation of failure. On tests of clairvoyance his performance was erratic; there was sporadic success only, and this was ascribed by the researchers to Manning's 'lightning flashes' (Braude, Davis and Wood: 1979).

Anxious to improve his performance, and concerned to show that a prophet can indeed be accepted in his own native land, Manning offered to undergo tests organized by the SPR in London in the summer of 1978. The experiments were carried out at City University and at Birkbeck College (University of London), and involved a number of different experimenters besides a few other interested parties. They tried as best they could to fit in with Manning's other arrangements – it is reported that he is the kind of person who expects this of others while being quite impatient with timetables which impose restraints upon himself (a trait, incidentally, which he personally repudiates). It may be facile to suggest that this could be a reaction against his father who led a very structured existence (in Manning's view the reason for the earlier disruption by the poltergeist) or it may simply be an indication of an over-indulged childhood.

This series of tests were somewhat different from those in the USA. They consisted of an attempt to affect the growth rate of some Mung beans without any perceptible result; an attempt to influence the movement of a pendulum, again with no positive result; and an ostensible effort at clairvoyance using a Random Event Generator, yet again with no satisfactory result. In addition, there was what, in effect, was a form of remote-viewing test in which Manning was to sketch pictures corresponding with 20 separate brief extracts from poems. In this 'blind-match' experiment, the results again were negligible. A further test similar to that which had been used many years ago with the physical medium, Rudi Schneider, was tried with Manning, largely – one suspects – at the instigation of one of the researchers, the late Anita Gregory, who had a special interest in the Schneider case. The object was to influence the occultation of an infrared beam. Several trials were done on different days. At one point Manning refused to work with a session organized by a notable parapsychologist because he thought that the man who was miles away might be exerting a malign counter-influence on the proceedings. The equipment was complex (although on at least one researcher's estimate not sophisticated enough) and the scores conscientiously calibrated, but the results – though a little unusual – were far from conclusive. The final experiment was an attempt to influence the growth rate of a particular mould, but Manning could produce no consistent effect (Gregory: 1982b).

After the tests Manning made it clear that he was only really interested in experiments that had useful applications and would benefit humanity in some way. This appears to have been a genuine sentiment and not just a *post facto* rationalization for his relative lack of success in the SPR experiments. Again he criticized researchers who simply regarded him as a novelty and took his work so lightly that it was never actually written up and published. He is obviously a great believer in the 'experimenter effect' and believes that the best results are achieved when there is near perfect rapport between experimenter and subject (*Alpha*, issue 5, November/December 1979). Indeed, he owns that the test can become a kind of competitive game. He denies that there was any actual friction between himself and the researchers in the SPR tests, but does own to an element of boredom with tests he regarded as severely limited in their usefulness. For a test to 'work', he argued, for him there are necessary preconditions – he must *want* and *expect* a successful outcome, only then can he psych himself up to a state whereby it actually does work. This may involve stress and irritation expressed as arm waving or 'stalking' the equipment. At other times, effects may be achieved by distraction and reverie – the positive images of a kind of waking trance. This is the technique he advocates and markets in his self-healing books, tapes and lectures. Even a psychic is not above a little commercial enterprise to help his mission along.

CHAPTER SIX

The Paranormal and Mass Hysteria

The term hysteria is used mainly by contemporary psychiatrists to denote a loss of perceptual functioning for which there is no apparent physiological or neurological basis. It can be used also to indicate not so much a loss as an *inexplicable change* in perceptual functioning which seems not to accord with normal standards. Sometimes it is associated with persistent delusions, hallucinations and other perceptual distortions. There are well-documented studies (e.g. Farina: 1976) which indicate that a number of these disorders are specific to particular societies. The condition known as amok (from which we derive our expression 'to run amok') in Malaysia was characterized by extreme aggression where victims destroyed both property and people, and sometimes themselves. Something similar has also been reported in Siberia (Arctic hysteria) and among certain Canadian Indian tribes with cannibalistic tendencies as one of its features. This can possibly be related to other forms of bizarre tribal behaviour. Among the American Mandan Indians there was a collective ritual in which young tribesmen would skewer their chests and amputate fingers in what appeared to be a state of religious ecstasy.

In the West there were a number of outbreaks of hysteria in the eighteenth century which sometimes resulted in deafness, blindness and other forms of physical incapacity. Why was this? What are the causes of hysteria? It has been argued – perhaps rather simplistically – that mass hysteria can be accounted for by the existence of a 'group mind' whereby people are overtaken by an emotional contagion in which their individual identities tend to become fused or submerged into the mass. As in cases of stage hypnotism, there may be an element of imitation, even a desire not to be left out of a shared experience. In earlier times, as we have seen with the medieval 'Dancing Mania', there were strange 'epidemics' of hysteria in schools, cotton mills, in religious communities and in evangelistic meetings. Sometimes the symptoms mimicked epilepsy, or hysteria might give rise to false pregnancies, and at other times people seemed to enter trance-like states. By the seventeenth century, it came to be thought of as a form of auto-hallucination, and although men were by no means immune, it was noted that women were particularly prone to its influences; but by no means all women – not those who were gainfully employed, but 'noble virgins, nice gentlewomen, such as are solitary and idle' (Robert

Burton quoted in Inglis: 1989, p. 43). Later, in the nineteenth century, Sir James Paget (soon to become surgeon to Queen Victoria) denied that it was most common among 'silly, selfish girls', on the contrary, he said, it was more likely to be found among the 'very good, the very wise and the most accomplished' (Inglis: 1989, p. 71). In fact, hysteria could produce a wide variety of symptoms convulsions, dizziness, loss of consciousness, all in all what some described as 'fits' or 'tantrums'. Yet some symptoms were often rather significantly related to the beliefs and expectations of the culture in question.

Increasing interest by the medical fraternity resulted in specialists beginning to think the unthinkable. In anticipation of Freud, it was hypothesized that hysteria might be due to some form of repressed sexuality – again, especially in women. It was even thought that when in a hysterical state, even well brought up young women might go further than just a 'touch of the vapours' and make immoderate advances to all and sundry. Some suggested that this might be connected with a disorder of the uterus, and recommended hysterectomy as a rather radical cure. While other Victorian doctors thought that the cauterizing of the clitoris (roughly the Western counterpart of female circumcision) would do the trick. Later in the century, the French specialist, Jean Martin Charcot, advanced the view that hysteria was a neurological disorder, although this was modified by further research which indicated that hysteria was not organic and was susceptible to treatment by suggestion and hypnosis. What was also discovered was that it was not only hysterics that could be treated by hypnosis, but that many other subjects clearly demonstrated the potency of this novel form of therapy.

Freud, who worked for Charcot as a young student, generally endorsed the views of his mentor whom he felt had rescued hysteria from its ill-conceived reputation. But eventually his ideas turned full circle when he propounded his pan-sexual theories towards the very end of the century. These rooted hysteria back again in the domain of repressed sexuality. Hysteria became psychoneurosis, possibly brought about by the trauma of sexual abuse in childhood – a safely unchallengeable assumption. Ironically, a more positivist approach by the medical profession early in this century proved equally illusory. Hysteria was again regarded as an organic disorder arising from 'focal sepsis', a toxic condition which could be treated surgically. Mercifully, this organicist 'diagnosis', which resulted in many unnecessary operations, enjoyed a very limited life.

More valuable research was done during the First World War on 'shell shock' victims and young pilots in training who 'froze on the joystick' – an involuntary pause that could easily result in their death. This increasing conviction that hysteria was a psychosomatic condition resulted in it being seen as both a blessing in that it could have a therapeutic function, and a curse because it might lead to neurophysical paralysis or worse. It remains for us to apply some of these ideas to the phenomenon of mass hysteria.

There are those who argue that some experiences of the paranormal fall into a similar category and constitute a kind of mass hysteria, for example, claims about alien abductions. How, then, are we to account for such phenomena? *Medical models* would suggest that the whole thing can be ultimately explained in physical terms – or, at least, *will be* explained when we have sufficient knowledge. It is all a matter of correctly identifying the disease or deficiency, or whatever, and the condition will no longer be a problem. *Behavioural models*, on the other hand, indicate that we are really dealing with abnormalities which are learned like anything else is learned, and can consequently be *un*-learned in the same way. This argument, for all its weaknesses, is certainly more convincing than the *psychodynamic model* which resorts to the interplay of barely understood unconscious psychic forces. As we have already indicated, it is *cognitive models* that seem to be most relevant to our discussion of the paranormal because these emphasize distortions of reality which may be what paranormal experiences are all about.

The phenomenon of hysteria, and its various manifestations, raises the whole question of suggestibility. A number of studies have been done showing that people have different degrees of suggestibility. Many of these have been carried out in relation to hypnosis and the extent to which particular individuals are susceptible to suggestion in this form. Indeed, the hypnotic state may be little more than a condition of height-ened suggestibility in which the people concerned contribute to their own trance-like state. Experiments among students – a favourite captive sample group of researchees who are surely atypical of the population as a whole – have shown that their susceptibility to religious conversion can be positively correlated with their susceptibility to hypnotic sugges-tion. Intellectual and social factors also play a part in predisposing individuals to such influences. A similar sort of relationship can be seen in the case of 'spiritual healing' but, oddly enough, the evidence here is not at all clear. There are just too many instances of people experien-cing 'cures' or, at least, therapeutic benefits even where there appear to be no predisposing factors. Indeed, the 'healed' often claim to be ex-treme sceptics who have been persuaded to try this kind of treatment by the entreaties of others (Weatherhead: 1951).

It is not unknown for those who witness the phenomena of hysteria to be similarly affected. In some cases, this could be merely copying for effect, but in others there is little doubt that the symptoms are genuine. We are perhaps dealing here with a little understood form of collective neurosis. Barclay Martin (1981) gives a graphic example of a schoolgirl who suddenly exhibited strange 'attacks' of twitching and crying. Soon other girls were similarly affected, and worried parents withdrew them from school. In some cases, the pupils took some weeks to recover. This bizarre behaviour may well have been reinforced by concern and attention, and it has been argued that similar conditions are present not only, as here, with convulsive seizures, but also, as we shall see, with such apparently paranormal phenomena as faith-healing and speaking in tongues.

Prayers for the restoration of health are among the most common forms of petitioning prayers. Indeed, prayer is probably the most commonly employed ritual in faith-healing. Yet it is by no means generally accepted, even among the 'faithful'. One informal study made among students at a denominational college found that only 5 per cent entertained such beliefs. None the less, it can still be said that faith-healing (given an appropriate definition) is 'as well established as any phenomenon of science' (Meadow and Kahoe: 1984).

In general, it can be said that faith-healing implies:

1. Appeals to agencies, powers or supernatural beings who are believed to exist independently of the person invoking them.
2. These powers are fully capable of producing the effects asked for or expected.
3. Specific rituals are required to activate these powers to consider the appeals in question.
4. If the request appears to be denied because no beneficial result is forthcoming, it is assumed that (a) the powers are unwilling to grant such a request, (b) that the rituals are in some way insufficient or that the exercise of faith is inadequate, or (c) that petitionary prayers have been too self-centred and therefore non-efficacious (see Krippner: 1980).

Needless to say, faith-healing takes a number of forms and occurs in innumerable contexts. Whether it 'works' in some paranormal way (as in what is sometimes termed divine healing) or whether it is the body healing itself, is much in dispute. It is even argued (Mes: 1975) that if the infirmity is such that the body cannot cure itself, then neither can faith, short of a miracle, and this would be a transgression of divine law

– a statement that seems to set arbitrary limits to both divinity and divine law.

We find in practice that healing most commonly takes place in one-to-one situations of healer and patient, or in group situations where, say, friends intercede for a sick person, or in congregations which may be convened especially for healing purposes. It is the congregational type of situation that most concerns us here, especially those congregations which are part of the charismatic culture. It is these which exhibit most clearly the phenomenon of mass obsessional behaviour, though it should be stressed that a variant of these, certain popular religious television shows which feature intercessory prayer, often claim similar results. Congregations of a Pentecostalist or Charismatic kind are typically suffused with emotion, and it is felt that miracles can happen. Those who come or are brought forward for healing are caught up in this maelstrom of emotion which may be enhanced by uninhibited clapping, shouting, singing, dancing and, not uncommonly, crying and fainting. Studies of faith-healing as a ritual have shown that respondents' perceptions of having been healed were related as much to their participation in a healing ritual as to the observation of changes in their physical symptoms. One study (Pattison, Lapins and Doerr: 1973, quoted in Meadow and Kahoe: 1984) neither supported nor disclaimed the physical reality of the healing experiences. The respondents did, however, insist that the experiences had increased their religious faith, and the researchers concluded – somewhat inconsequentially for such an extensive study – that the experiences had helped their respondents to deal more adequately with their psychological stresses.

It can always be argued that healing effects are really brought about by the power of suggestion. Here the evidence – such as it is – is not entirely clear. One particular study (Beutler: 1988) of hypertensive patients who were unaware that they were the subjects of 'distance healing' failed to demonstrate any paranormal effect. But in another experiment (Byrd: 1988), patients in a coronory care unit who had also not been told that they were *randomly selected* as subjects for intercessory prayers from a distance, fared significantly better on a number of measures than others in the unit who were also suffering from myocardial infarction.

In a much larger study by a psychiatrist (Benor: 1990) of 140 controlled trials of PSI healing published in English (12 of which were postgraduate dissertations) it is asserted that 61 demonstrated effects which could have occurred only once in a hundred trials or more. He argues cogently – if rather repetitively – that these are significant results which still continue to be ignored by the great majority of the medical fraternity. He insists that this is because PSI healing conflicts with the prevalent paradigms of medical science. Modern culture shrinks from non-rational intervention. It is resistant to change. In fact, Western culture's materialistic beliefs tend to exclude even the possibility of PSI healing; such 'healing realities' conflict with sensory reality and create a sense of cognitive dissonance. There is a tension between competing perspectives, and the result is that people tend to choose the easier option and deny that such things are achievable.

In conclusion, Benor hedges his bets. He admits that 'instantaneous, total cures are very, very rare. Healing boosts defenses and enhances recuperation' (Benor: 1990). This tends to nullify much of his thesis, and puts PSI/faith-healing on a par with a bottle of Lucozade. He also quotes with approval a person with cancer (and echoed by others) who said that he is glad of his condition because it forced him to face his problems and reassess his relationships with others: 'My quality of life is incomparably improved since I started working out *my unconscious reasons for letting this disease develop*' (Benor: 1990; my italics). This is really a thoughtless, dangerous endorsement from someone who should know better – but, regrettably, it is not that uncommon. In effect, the patient has become responsible for his own disease, and therefore, by implication, is also responsible for not getting better. This, sadly, is the logic of the we-have-the-power-to-heal-ourselves-if-we-really-want-to philosophy. It is not the position of one who believes in the paranormal at all, but who takes the view that the paranormal is really normal – albeit, as yet, not fully understood.

If we turn now to glossolalia (speaking in tongues) we find that here is another phenomenon which is categorized as paranormal which also has many of the hallmarks of social hysteria. The emotional fervour of old-time revivalism is now manifested in what is broadly termed the charismatic movement, ranging from relatively mainstream groups of Pentecostalists who emphasize such differentiae as speaking in tongues, faith-healing and prophecy, to more extreme religious groups whose activities may include taking psychedelic drugs, poisons and snake hand-ling – anything to make their rituals more exciting and to act as tests of faith.

Speaking in tongues has attracted quite a lot of attention from social scientists who differentiate between glossolalia, speaking syllables of a completely unknown 'language' (to charismatics, 'a heavenly tongue'), and xenolalia, speaking a known language which is allegedly completely unknown to the speaker. Speaking either spontaneously and without prior instruction is thus construed by the faithful as a kind of miracle. It is not always appreciated in the West that this phenomenon is known in a number of cultures, and not always as a divine gift. It is sometimes seen as a form of possession, even evil possession, and can be a characteristic of certain psychotics. Researchers (e.g. Samarin: 1972) have made linguistic analyses of glossolalia speech in order to understand its grammatical make-up, but they have been quite unable to discern any kind of rational structure. Yet it can occur in original and what appear to be stereotyped forms (in some contexts, seasoned practitioners are apparently able to switch to their 'heavenly tongue' at will). To the uninitiated, the words seem to be no more than meaningless sounds, yet it is an experience which is earnestly sought by those who have never had it. For them it is a sign of divine favour and acceptance. Needless to say, for those who aspire, the expected becomes the experienced. To what extent this can become a habit encouraged in the suggestible by charismatic leaders is still uncertain (Kildahl: 1972). The whole process would be more impressive if the 'translations' which should follow, were more convincing. If glossolalia *is* a 'heavenly tongue', one would expect the 'message' to be in some way revelatory, but it never is. Indeed, it is usually quite unexceptionally general in its applications.

Earlier work has suggested that more 'cultured people' find liturgical worship more psychologically satisfying (Clark: 1958). More formal church architecture and structured devotions being their own aesthetic pleasure. Yet many have rebelled against liturgical formalism with its stereotyped service orders and set prayers, and have reverted to more 'primitive' unthinking forms of religious expression. People feel that they have no need of priestly mediation; they want a direct experience of the divine. Hence the enlivening of worship with such non-rational features as glossolalia.

Whether this can be classified as a kind of religious infantilism is a moot point. Certainly to the observer it appears as a way of avoiding the cognitive processes and relying almost entirely on the experiential 'high' that such behaviour may bring. To this extent it may resemble the mass responses found at raves and pop concerts where devotees do not have to understand the music – if, in fact, there is anything to understand. It just has to be 'felt'. The general ambience, the lights, the percussive beat and the rhythmic writhing of fellow cultists are contagious. This shared experience constitutes a kind of hysteria. One is left wondering if the gathering of several thousand people for a candlelight ritual at Graceland to celebrate the anniversary of Elvis Presley's death (and resurrection?), and the massive outpouring of 'grief' over the untimely death of Princess Diana are not latter-day forms of collective neurosis. (As an appropriate postscript, it is perhaps worth noting the Greek aphorism that 'whom the gods love die young'. The adulation –

one might almost say, the canonization – of Diana would hardly have occurred if she had been a decrepit has-been of 86. She will now never have cancer, lose a breast, have a hysterectomy, heart disease or dementia. She will never have failing eyesight or poor teeth and be raddled by wrinkles. She will remain attractive, tender-hearted with foibles forgotten. A beautiful icon in the public memory.)

Perhaps the original Pentecostal experience of 'speaking in tongues' was actually xenolalia as the account suggests (Acts 2: 1–11). It could have been, as some argue, that the speakers had unconsciously absorbed certain linguistic cultural elements that they were able to utilize at the time, after all, it was a multilingual environment. Or – more problematically – perhaps there was some kind of telepathic rapport between the apostles and their hearers which was able to surmount language barriers. Among modern critics, the idea that it could have been paranormal in the simple sense in which it is recounted is seriously questioned; and the very notion that it could have been miraculous is regarded with grave suspicion. But that something very unusual happened, and that it inaugurated a universal movement, is hardly in doubt (Carlton: 1987).

To summarize, then, we can say that the mass acts in a way that any individual who might be part of that mass would almost certainly not act. So, for example, the behaviour of a lynch mob is likely to be much more extreme than that of any individual that comprises it. One might almost say that the mass seems to generate a character, a life, of its own. Numbers give it a feeling of power, and the individual's emotions become fused with that of the mass, and he or she is able to shed any sense of personal responsibility. One has only to witness some of the unruly behaviour of football crowds, the bizarre antics of rave enthusiasts and the tragic irrationality of mass suicides to exemplify this point. Are these different from the kinds of contagious hysteria we have been considering?

In the past group symptoms have been attributed to organic, perhaps viral, causes, yet with closer investigation nothing definite has been identified. Inglis (1989, p. 212 ff) gives the example of an 'epidemic' at London's Royal Free Hospital when some 300 fell ill with symptoms of dizziness, spasms, weeping and nausea. Every possible source of the 'infection' was tracked down, but nothing was found. Only 12 of the victims were hospital patients, the rest were staff, most of them women. When the evidence was reviewed in the *British Medical Journal* in 1970, the researchers concluded that it was a form of epidemic hysteria. This verdict did not please the hospital, and when a symposium was held in 1978 in which the matter was discussed again, the consensus was that it was a kind of neuromyasthenia, as innocuous title – really little more than a label – which indicated muscle fatigue. But no one seemed to know what was supposed to have caused the muscle fatigue, any more than anyone knows what causes mass or epidemic hysteria. Like so many high-sounding medical/psychiatric terms, these are just words, descriptions, nothing more.

Excursus: The 'Vailala' Madness in Papua

Utopian manias have afflicted both simple and complex societies through the ages. Ideas such as those of the Marxist 'classless society' and the Nazi 'thousand year Reich' which hold that current evils will be banished and a new order of society established, have been with us – in one form or another – for a very long time. No cultures are entirely immune. Teachings vary but the basic ideas are much the same. The inauguration of the new order may be seen as distant or imminent. It may be achieved violently or pacifically, and it may be part of the doctrine of a small sect or cult and thus the privilege of a favoured few, or it may be thought of as being society-wide in extent. Most important for our present purposes is that it may be conceived as being ushered in by human means or by supernatural forces. It is well known, for instance, that in the nineteenth century various groups of Bantu destroyed both crops and cattle in the anticipation of imminent 'deliverance'. Early in the twentieth century some Eskimo groups stopped hunting and consumed their meagre stores of food, all in the hope that they too were going to witness a miraculous change in their fortunes. In other cultures, massacre and suicide have even been thought to be necessary precursors to a people's or group's 'salvation'.

Is this a religious phenomenon or a political phenomenon? Or could it be a combination of both (Carlton: 1996)? These beliefs which are classed as millenarian have always had a considerable appeal to the oppressed and the unenfranchised just because they promise salvation or future compensation for known or assumed injustices and grievances. Social anthropologists have long been intrigued by such movements, and some of the best documented are those known popularly as the 'cargo cults' of Melanesia (Worsley: 1968). Such cults have appeared and disappeared on and off in Melanesia since the late nineteenth century. Usually they are syncretistic and often bizarre amalgums of the Western religious ideas to which the indigenes have been introduced, and native religious traditions. Typically a native prophet arises and announces that given certain conditions are fulfilled, the millennium (strictly speaking, a thousand years of peace and prosperity) will come in the very near future. The expectations are that ships and/or planes will arrive with the people's ancestors on board, and they will bring with them a cargo of the kind of material goods which their white overlords already have and which the people greatly desire.

The myths that lie behind such movements often maintain that the goods have been sent by the ancestors but have been criminally misappropriated by the whites – a fact that the whites have carefully tried to hide from them – but the belief is that when the ancestors return, the present order of society will be inverted, and the native culture will revert to its original state. In some forms of the myth it is believed that the whites will be driven out and the native chiefs will reclaim the authority which has been usurped by the white intruders. In another form, the skin of the whites will turn black, and that of the natives will turn white, and then the new 'whites' will rule the now humbled Europeans.

Before any of this can happen, certain conditions have to be fulfilled. Some prophets maintain that the whites must be banished first, otherwise the ancestors will not return; some maintain that there must be a complete break with the past and that all the old taboos must go. Others insist that it displays a disbelief in the coming millennium to carry on as before. So the people are enjoined to cease cultivation and to consume their existing stocks of food. On occasions this has resulted in the rapid squandering of money and the deliberate destruction of goods in order to demonstrate faith in the promised 'time of plenty'. Many of the prophets have provoked states of extreme religious ecstasy which has been typically accompanied by dancing, twitching and writhing – the features one might expect in conditions of revivalist hysteria.

It virtually goes without saying that the authorities were not particularly sympathetic to these goings on. Frankly, they were often baffled by such movements, and what they did not understand they sometimes persecuted. For them, such demonstrations must have seemed like forms of insipient revolution – which, in a sense, they were. One movement known as the cult of John Frum broke out on the island of Tanna in the war years 1940–41. It began – so it is said – when a local god appeared to some natives calling himself John Frum. He encouraged people to celebrate his appearance, and promised that he was going to bring the people of the island the material benefits which the whites had denied them. He prophesied that the whites would leave and that he would take charge of everything. He told them to destroy their money or give it back to the whites otherwise he would be unable to carry out his plans. Instead he was going to introduce John Frum money, and there would be no need for anyone to work anymore. Among the credulous the message spread rapidly. The missions and churches were soon depleted of villagers who danced and feasted in ways disapproved of by the Western missions. But soon the authorities clamped down on the unrest and exposed 'John Frum' as a native who had fooled the people by some astute stage management. Peremptory justice was administered and the fraudster and his supporters were shipped off into exile. This effectively ended the first incarnation of John Frum.

Not long afterwards a letter arrived from the place of exile. It was in pidgin English and interpretations vary as to exactly what was what, but the general message seemed either to be that John Frum was in America and would seek an audience with the 'king', and/or that he would send his sons to Tanna to prepare for his return. Coincidentally, American troops arrived and it would seem that these were identified as John Frum's sons. Thus began the second John Frum movement. Another native proclaimed himself John Frum, 'king of America and of Tanna', and organized the building of an airfield, ostensibly for the arrival of more Americans. A government agent was threatened with violence, so the authorities acted quickly to suppress the movement. There were a few sporadic minor outbreaks after this, but gradually the movement fizzled out.

Another later movement was associated with the Garia people of New Guinea. It seems to have begun with a native ex-soldier named Yali who, during the Second World War, had served for some time in Australia. He was regarded by the authorities as a person with a basic education and therefore someone with whom they could discuss native affairs. Then several men calling themselves his 'lieutenants' began to spread the story that Yali had in fact been killed by the Japanese but that it was his spirit that had returned, and that he had divine instructions to run the country for the people. He had also been told that a cargo was due to arrive with goods including weapons with which to drive out the whites. Yali's own position in all this seems to have been somewhat ambivalent, but – as was to be expected – the whole movement was soon suppressed by the authorities.

The movement – or phenomenon – known as the 'Vailala Madness' was first noted as early as 1919. Reports spread among the indigenes of Papua that their ancestors were about to return in the guise of white men. They would arrive by steamer or aeroplane and would bring a large cargo of goods of every kind. These goods – so they were told – were really theirs by right but until now they had been withheld from them by the Europeans. The leaders of the movement ordered the people to cease work and prepare feasts of welcome for the ancestors, and promised that the white authorities would be driven out of the country. Before this happened, however, the people were to abandon all their traditional ceremonies and destroy their ritual objects. In fact, it was a particular feature of this movement that unlike so many native uprisings in colonial territories, there was quite a violent reaction against *traditional* religious practices. Another features, and the one that caused the movement to be described as a type of madness, was the fact that the people were affected by a kind of giddiness. They lost or abandoned control of their limbs and staggered about the villages uttering wholly unintelligible grunts and cries. So much so that at times whole areas seemed to fall victim to what appeared to observers as a kind of disease.

The 'prophets' who generated these and other such cults were usually people of little education who had no particular standing among the natives until they made their appealing if outrageous claims. It was often the case that both they and their devotees were wildly misinformed about the outside world. The teachings of the cults with their marked millennial emphasis were invariably syncretistic in that native beliefs were grafted on to particular aspects of missionary teaching. It is possible that the natives may have assumed the disproportionate importance of religion to the whites. Only a small proportion of their contact time with whites involved missionaries. They almost certainly noted the disparity between missionary teaching and colonial practices.

To the observer a tragi-comic aspect of such movements was the indigenes' attempts to ape white practices in order to secure the 'cargo'. They had obviously witnessed these especially in connection with the military, and interpreted them as 'rituals' which ensured the arrival of the cargo. So they made crude dummy radios and mock telephones, and fashioned wooden rifles with which they paraded on the beach in the hope that the 'ancestors' would respond. They even improvised landing strips for planes and jetties for ships, and – in some ways most pathetic of all – spread table cloths and put flowers in bottles in a parody of European manners in order to welcome the ancestors back again.

It is understandable that there was disgruntlement at the marked disparity between native living standards and the relative affluence of the white traders and administrators. No wonder the indigenes resorted to magio-religious explanations and practices in order to remedy the situation. But whether these cults can be construed as pre-political movements is very much open to question. The neo-Marxist argument that native disquiet found its outlet in magio-religious gestures because there was little or no opportunity for overt political expression leaves a number of questions unanswered, most notably why the 'mania' took the form that it did. No-nonsense economic arguments cannot account for the collective hysteria and the bizarre behavioural manifestations which certainly require a socio-psychological explanation. And one also has to ask why it is that similar kinds of millenarianism can be found in Western society among relatively prosperous people. Certain adventist groups come into this category as do those who look for salvation – as we shall see – from anticipated alien sources (Chapter 7).

CHAPTER SEVEN

The Paranormal as Esoteric Cult and Media Craze: The UFO Phenomenon

In very general terms, a cult is regarded by academics either as a form of sect that is a breakaway group from a larger parent body, or as a separate type, *sui generis*. As a kind of sect it would probably have formed by some process of fission, perhaps because of disputes or possibly because of some heterodox views held by a minority group which is at variance with the larger community. Theorists who take the view that cults are a singular type of movement, sometimes contend that they are organizations which by their very nature are alien to the primary culture (see, for example, Nelson, 1968). In the senses in which they have been defined, cults are the special concern of sociologists of religion although they can obviously take non-religious forms.

The general characteristics of the religious cult only barely apply to UFO cult groups who are not usually in the thrall of some charismatic leader (though ufology does have its gurus), neither are they intensely exclusivist as far as membership is concerned. Furthermore, they do not normally have initiation rites of graded categories of membership (though note the quasi-religious nature of the 'Heaven's Gate' cult and its tragic aftermath). But there is one feature which they do tend to share with religious cults in a qualified sense, and that is that members of some groups may see themselves as recipients or beneficiaries of a special 'gnosis' or knowledge which is given or revealed to them. This is especially true of those who claim some ultimate experience of the phenomenon, a sighting, a contact, or whatever. This experience may be treated with scepticism or ridicule by those outside the movement, but it is all too real for those who have the predisposition to believe.

In this discussion, we are going to think of the UFO phenomenon in three senses:

1. In terms of the serious investigatory groups such as the British UFO Research Association (BUFORA) who publish regular critical reports.
2. In terms of fringe groups often of a quasi-religious kind which

conform much more closely to the conventional cult type (see Excursus in this chapter). Such cults usually posit some kind of end-state: in this sense they are rather like millenarian ideologies. Their eschatologies foresee or anticipate the arrival of alien beings with immeasurably advanced technologies who will put our world to rights. Such ideas are a far cry from the political aspirations of those who have seen salvation in this-worldly terms. Cultists have no truck with thousand-year Reichs or future classless societies, but pin their hopes on the advent of beneficent beings who will either usher in a time of peace and plenty in this world, or whisk the chosen off to better things in a life beyond the stars.

3.   The cult in the broad, imprecise sense of the term, as when writers refer to the media craze for science fiction films, the occult and so forth. Some writers, though, are openly hostile and allege that society is slipping into a miasma of mysticism characterized by 'glitzy TV series', television programmes extolling the paranormal – all of which are 'unashamedly irrational'.

Are we really experiencing a flood of ersatz science which is threatening to engulf our culture? There are a number of possible reasons for the appeal of these other-worldly cults, not least the despair that so many feel when confronted with the world's seemingly insurmountable problems. People are concerned about the breakdown of the current social order, and the traumas brought about by the rapid – and perhaps ungovernable – rate of social change. Cult ideologies may provide an outlet for extreme anxiety and disillusionment. Collective paranoia and irrational fears – according to some psychologists – can give rise to fantastic expectations. Consequently, UFO 'experiences' may not only have their own intrinsic interests, they may actually become a form of social protest or even a religious surrogate.

What we might term *contact myths* have been with us for a very long time. People have reported 'sightings' of one kind of another throughout recorded history. So much so, in fact, that some modern writers – a few of whom are serious researchers – have reinterpreted certain ancient phenomena in UFO terms. For instance, one hoary but nevertheless intriguing example is that of the Hebrew prophet Ezekial's description of a 'great cloud, with brightness round about it, and fire flashing forth continually, and in the midst of the fire, as it were, gleaming bronze'. According to ex-National Aeronautics and Space Administration (NASA) official, Josef Blumrich, this sounds remarkably like a spacecraft.

If we ask what has generated the modern attraction for contact myths, we could cite at least three main factors:

1. A basic dissatisfaction with conventional evolutionary hypotheses which are felt by some to be more like descriptions of possible processes rather than explanations of how such apparently bizarre developments and mutations came about (are birds and dinosaurs really related?). Those who reject conventional evolutionary theories have sometimes advanced ideas which seem positively eccentric. One is that at some time in the remote past, extraterrestrials interbred with Earth people (note the famous reference in Genesis to the 'sons of the gods' mating with the 'daughters of men'). A related idea is the hybrid hypothesis whereby extraterrestrials have genetically manipulated primitive (ape-like) people so as to produce more advanced mutations – an idea which has certain doubtful ethnic implications. A variant of this is that extraterrestrials have been transplanted to Earth thus ensuring that there is no direct genetic link between apes and humans – an idea which has a particular appeal for those who want to believe in a Special Creation. Then there is the much more plausible Panspermia hypothesis. This is roughly the position taken up by one of our most notable – if mildly heretical – astronomers, Sir Fred Hoyle (1983) and has also been hinted at by Nobel prize-winners, Crick (1973, pp. 232–3) and Watson (1976). Hoyle in particular maintains that preconditions on our planet were unsuitable for the spontaneous generation of life, and that spores, perhaps carried on meteorites from outer space provided the seminal possibilities for life on Earth. Was this done deliberately? Or did they simply self-seed in a conducive environment?

2. Furthermore, some writers point to the fundamental incomprehensibility of the 'breakthrough' i.e. the apparently sudden development of artefacts (especially monumental architecture), the inventions of written language, and the formulation of complex religious ideologies. There are 'natural' explanations for all this, but again, some scholars still find the whole process rather perplexing (see, for example, Covensky: 1966).

3. The abiding fascination with UFO stories generally which, as we have seen, have lent some credence to earlier myths concerning the contacts between mortals and the gods. For instance, the Greek myth of Chronos (Time) and the war in heaven with Father Zeus who eventually establishes his authority over the Earth can be seen as a feature of an ancient Star Wars scenario. Could this be, as some claim, a faint echo of a pre-human other-worldly conflict? Similar stories are found in Indian, Aztec and Islamic traditions.

The view that there have been interventions of an extraterrestrial kind have given rise to a wide variety of contact myths which are found in several historical traditions. There are reports of 'ships', 'globes' and 'shields' in the sky from at least Roman times. At Spoletum, north of Rome, in 90 BC, it is recorded that a 'globe of fire' fell to earth gyrating, and then rose again into the sky where it 'obscured the disc of the Sun with its brilliance'. Even the Egyptians over a thousand years earlier had written of 'circles of fire' in the sky. And it may be not entirely irrelevant that they believed that at death the souls of the departed returned to the sky.

There are, too, a number of literary traditions which tell similar stories. The Hindu Vedas, a collection of ancient hymns probably collated as early as 1000 BC also recount strange tales of celestial phenomena. The Vedas are generally regarded as a poetic record of the incursions of the Aryan peoples, possibly from the Caucasus area c. 1500 BC, who brought with them beliefs in aggressive sky gods. The traditions – undoubtedly distorted – speak of cloud-gods who were half-human and half-divine who had rapid cloud vehicles (vimanas) which changed colour with speed, and which seemed to be engaged in some sort of celestial conflict. In Chaldean (Babylonian) myth there is a tradition which even the late Carl Sagan (1974) – a severe critic of uncorroborated UFO phenomena – says deserves our attention. This is the story of Oannes, a half-human half-amphibian creature who was regarded as a kind of culture-hero who brought knowledge of the arts and sciences to ancient Babylonia (modern Iraq). The earliest known culture in this region was that of the Sumerians, and they were saying, in effect, that their civilization was founded by non-human creatures who when their mission was ended returned to the sea. This could, of course, be a charter story, an aetiological myth to justify or explain the Sumerian's singularity as a people, but it is interesting, nevertheless.

Received wisdom has it that modern ufology began in 1947 when Kenneth Arnold, piloting his own plane in Washington State saw nine shining discs flying near Mount Ranier. He reported that they were moving very quickly and performing twists and swerves over the mountain range. After the incident was made public, there was a rash of sightings in the USA, but within a matter of days an Air Force 'investigation' concluded that Arnold had been imagining things. How such an investigation could have been carried out in the circumstances is something of a problem – it is notoriously difficult to check on what appeared to be a spontaneous phenomenon. On the other hand, the fact that hosts of other people suddenly began to 'see' flying saucers as they came to be called, does suggest some kind of collective hallucination. Even so this does not have to invalidate the *original* experience.

These incidents prompted a further long-term investigation of the phenomena generally. This was an official US Air Force operation which began in 1952 and was published as *Project Blue Book* in 1969 (Steiger: 1976). It concluded that there was no real case to be answered, possibly to soothe public anxieties. The head of the project, Edward Ruppelt did admit that some of the sightings could not be explained by any known cause, but added that he felt that this still could not justify further investigation. A fellow sceptic, Dr Edward Condon, also thought that the study of UFO reports was not likely to be a fruitful direction of scientific advance. But afterwards *Project Blue Book* was dubbed a 'cover-up' by Allen Hynek (1974), a participant physicist, who came to believe that a small residue of the sightings might be genuine. Since this time there have been some slack periods as far as observations go, but still many hundreds of incidents are reported every year, and at present it is interesting to note that in the USA, Fox Television's *Sightings* documentary is one of the most popular programmes in the country. If anything, UFOs and the paranormal generally have a growing constituency.

There are – with some minor variations – four main schools of thought in relation to UFOs:

1. Those who are less than enchanted with the whole idea. At very best, people in this group wish to remain completely agnostic on the question, at worst there are those who dismiss the entire issue as nonsense or possibly as fraud, of which there are some classic cases in ufological lore (note, for instance, the case of George Adamski in the 1950s who claimed to have met people from Saturn and – better still – the highly inhospitable Venus, including an alluring spacewoman). Further research, therefore, is regarded as a complete waste of time.
2. Those at the other end of the spectrum who entertain the popular notion that UFOs are vehicles from outer space. They are alien craft from one or more advanced civilizations who may or may not be beneficently inclined towards people of the Earth.
3. Those who occupy one of the two intermediate positions and hold that UFOs do exist but are not extraterrestrial in origin. Rather they are secret, very high-technology craft of an experimental kind, possibly emanating from the USA.
4. Those who argue that if people believe something to be true then *it is true for them*, regardless of its possible non-objective validity.

This is a particularly common view among parapsychologists. The idea is that UFO phenomena are a projection of the human mind; they are either 'generated by the mind or symbiotically linked to it' (Rogo: 1984, p. 322). As such, these phenomena are regarded as the legitimate province of parapsychology, although – curiously – the British SPR is not altogether convinced of this, and except for book reviews devotes very little space in its journal to such matters.

The first position of the four is really untenable. After all, nobody can actually know for certain what lies out there. It is really quite unwarranted scientifically to assert that *every* sighting can be explained naturalistically. Logic demands that we abjure this kind of reductionism. It only require a single positive to refute a universal negative. Nobody is expected to prove every case. Only *one* sighting has to be genuine, and the case is proved. As far as the other three positions are concerned, there is no reason why they cannot *all* be 'true'. Providing one does not wish to adhere exclusively to one theory, the sightings in question – and they now run to many thousands – could be conveniently subsumed within all three categories. Some could be of advanced machines of human construction, others might actually be alien craft. Perhaps there is a psychic dimension; the main problem with this view is that in a number of well-known cases, the 'thing' has been witnessed by several – sometimes many more – people at the same time. As we have previously discussed, there is such a thing as mass hysteria, but unless we believe in collective hallucinations, this matter of multiple witnesses certainly presents the mentalists with a puzzle. There do seem to be selective perceptions. For example, how can a UFO land in a busy street – according to some accounts – and *not* be seen by other passers-by? But to suggest, as Rogo does, that the witnesses are 'enveloped in a distortion of reality' is simply to use words. What kind of a distortion? How is this precipitated? Why does it take this form? How easy is it for the mind to conspire with natural phenomena to produce a false image which for the witness(es) is indelibly real? It is interesting that subsequently Rogo admitted that the mentalist/psychic position was being overtaken by the wealth of empirical evidence that was accumulating about UFOs. This he felt points to the possibility of actual sightings of real objects (Rogo: 1989, p. 432).

Another form of this theory is that put forward by Hilary Evans, another long-term student of the genre. He suggests that 'within our minds there exists a creative, intelligent, sympathetic and understanding capability whose function is to fabricate non-real scenes and scenarios for purposes only some of which can be guessed at. This capability ...

may plausibly be conceived as a parallel personality to our conscious personality' (Evans: 1984, p. 308). This tends to make humans look like day-dreaming multiple personalities who resort to the comforting images of an unreal world because they are sadly disillusioned with this one. An entity-sighting (or what has been termed an 'apparitional drama') is therefore made to measure as one of several possible options whereby our subconscious can influence or speak to our conscious minds. For whatever reason 'our conscious selves are presented with the illusion of an entity experience' (ibid.).

There is, however, a variant of the psychic theory which attempts to marry it with the possibility that somehow the UFO mystery itself is being deliberately planted into the human consciousness, and that this may derive from a terrestrial or an extraterrestrial source. The former hints at some kind of darkly suspicious mind control, and the latter implies an alien source that is trying to communicate with us not by language but by a series of mental pictures (Randles: 1983). Just how and why this is being done is not made clear.

Ufology is virtually tailor-made for mockery and ridicule. A number of enthusiasts have formed UFO clubs, and it is all too easy to visualize ex-trainspotters in their anoraks keeping vigil on the hills in the hope of glimpsing strange lights in the sky. These days, debunking has become something of an art form. But given that there have been some wild and outlandish claims, there still remains a huge corpus of evidence for sightings, very many by people with unimpeachable credentials such as pilots, military personnel, etc., who are trained observers. Whether many of those involved have been effectively silenced by various governments' agencies, as some claim (for example, Good: 1987), is still a matter of some debate. When Admiral of the Fleet, Lord Hill-Norton, who was one-time Chief of the Defence Staff weighs in on the side of the 'believers', especially on the question of there being an official conspiracy of secrecy, it is perhaps time to give the matter some serious consideration.

Perhaps the main reasons why the UFO phenomenon has occasioned such hilarity in the press and elsewhere are the apparently bizarre claims to have had actual contact with alien creatures. Articles such as 'Happy birthday, aliens ... come down to the party' is typical (*Sunday Times*, 23 April 1997). It probably did little to help the cause when, to celebrate the famous Arnold sighting claim 50 years earlier, conventions took place, commemorative books were issued and the usual accusations were heard that the Pentagon was involved in a gigantic cover-up. When enthusiasts are pushed back into a polemical corner, their claims can take on a more sensational, and even sinister, form. These may be enhanced by the insatiable maw of the media. Neither sightings nor contacts are any longer enough. Abductions are now the thing. The American writer, Budd Hopkins, claims to have records of some 600 abductions often with titillating sexual overtones (Hopkins: 1987). The whole enterprise seems now to be more driven by commercial considerations than by curiosity. Serious researchers insist that ufology is being undermined by money and hijacked by mercenary sensationalists. For instance, on television *X Files* draws 7 million viewers in the UK, and on film the doomsday scenario *Independence Day* – apart from the effects, a truly mawkish offering – apparently grossed £500 million world-wide.

The 'missing time' syndrome, so closely associated with alien abduction claims, in which the percipient is unable to account for 'lost time', can be found elsewhere, especially in folklore (Spencer: 1989). But the forms that 'missing time' takes varies in different cases. Many 'victims' now insist that they have actually lost track of time. Abduction experience accounts can often be so meticulous in their detail that one wonders if this is quite the same thing as we find in folklore. On the other hand, some abductees maintain that they just do not remember what has happened at all. Thus the stories of abductees are frequently obtained by means of hypnotic regression, a dubious procedure in any circumstances but none so momentous in their implications as abduction experiences.

What is so astounding about all this is the scale of the phenomenon. A fairly recent analysis of data collected by the Roper Organization in the USA ('Unusual Personal Experiences: An Analysis of the Data from Three National Surveys') 'suggests that hundreds of thousands, if not millions, of American men, women and children may have experienced UFO abductions, or abduction-related phenomena' presumably for the purpose of medical examinations (Evans: 1994).

The whole idea seems so preposterous that it is more like a sales ploy dreamed up by *Sunday Sport* than an authentic study. But this is not the case. Noted American academics were involved, led by a distinguished Harvard Professor and included psychiatrists and other serious researchers who were admittedly predisposed to 'believe', and it was funded by prosperous individuals with a marked proclivity for the paranormal. All these high-profile people came to the conclusion that real physical abductions were – and probably still are – taking place, and that this is being done by alien intelligences. The study sample comprised 5 947 adults from representative occupational/class groups. The criteria employed were:

1. Have you ever awakened with a sense of paralysis and the suspicion that there was a strange presence in the room?
2. Have you ever found inexplicable scars on your body?
3. Have you ever seen unusual lights in a room?
4. Have you ever experienced the sensation of flying through the air without knowing how or why?
5. Have you ever had experiences of 'missing time'?

These were the indicators, and if respondents answered positively to any *four* of these key questions, it was taken that they had had – whether they realized it or not – a genuine paranormal experience. The survey findings were that perhaps as many as '2 percent of adults in the American population have had a constellation of experiences consistent with an abduction history' (Evans: 1994).

It is truly amazing to think that one in every 50 Americans has been whisked away and inspected in an alien craft – and not even know it. Evans is surely right when he says that we must distinguish between the *findings* and the *conclusions*. The former are probably beyond dispute, unless the public is having a huge laugh at the researchers' expense, but given the arbitrary nature of the criteria, the conclusions have to be open to more than one interpretation. Few would seriously doubt the integrity of the study team, but given the nature of the criteria employed, the final conclusions do not have to follow from the initial premises. Few in the SPR community would question the intellectual acuity of the reviewer/critic, but his alternative 'abduction-as-fantasy' explanation is also unverifiably weak.

The fact that the claims to UFO abduction experiences are so persistent, and because our intellectual natures abhor a cognitive vacuum, the phenomenon has been open to all manner of bizarre speculations. One thesis which has been seriously advanced is that abduction experiences are hallucinations caused by hypersensitivity to all kinds of polluting influences from power lines to childhood abuse (Budden: 1994). The 'trade' finds it difficult to take this at all seriously. As a mixture of dogma and distortion tricked out with a little pseudo-scientific terminology, it will do little to convince those seeking plausible explanations. Of much more interest is the amusing but well-crafted study by Jim Schnabel (1994). It consists largely of interviews with those such as the noted artist and abduction researcher, Budd Hopkins, whom we have already encountered, and relates a number of the case histories they have culled from 'abductees', some by regression therapy. Schnabel himself, a perceptive observer, is agnostic about the whole thing; he says he has 'a wary bewilderment' about it all. He agrees that regarding

UFOs 'there is something real and strange out there', but he recognizes that as far as abductions are concerned, we may not be giving due weight to the psycho-social or parapsychological aspects of the phenomena. There are undoubtedly parallels with other hallucination experiences and even similarities to other mass crazes which we have already discussed. So can these outlandish experiences be traced to common neurological reflexes which are then clothed in 'whatever idiosyncratic or cultural or archetypal material [that] is appropriate' (Schnabel: 1994, p. 283)? Are they forms of dissociative experience – a kind of cryptomnesia?

The main problem with the Schnabel text is its – perhaps inevitable – inadequacy at the explanatory level. Once it departs from the anecdotal to the analytical it tends to wriggle in all sorts of directions, trying psychology, then witchcraft and generous helpings of spirit-possession (Salem and the Devils of Loudun are invoked). Left brain–right brain hypotheses are included. Feminism and Freud are not left out. Suppression, repression and unacknowledged sexuality, are all there – indeed just about every possibility from Multiple Personality Disorder to Munchausen's Syndrome is considered grist for the explanatory mill.

Despite – or even because of – the scepticism, the UFO industry continues to flourish. Not only was 1997 the anniversary of the Arnold sighting, it was also the fiftieth anniversary of what has become known as the Roswell incident. The story/belief that an extraterrestrial craft crashed in the desert in New Mexico in July 1947 has now passed into UFO folklore. As also has the widely held view that one or more diminutive aliens survived but that the whole episode has since been shrouded in official secrecy. It is reported that there has been a four-year multimillion dollar investigation into the incident, and the Pentagon has declared that the whole thing can be explained naturalistically. Balloon-trailing disc-shaped reflectors as part of the Air Force Operation Mogul was the answer. It has recently been asserted that early accounts of UFOs were the US Air Force's way of diverting public attention from their own top secret spy planes such as U2 ('US Spy Jets behind UFO Hysteria', *Independent*, 4 August 1997). This is possible, but really rather implausible seeing that it was likely to generate a much greater scare among the population than any privileged knowledge of new high-technology reconnaissance aircraft.

Needless to say, 'believers' are unconvinced. A recent poll showed that 65 per cent of Americans believe that it was a UFO that came down at Roswell. So some thousands turned up at Roswell for the 1997 celebrations. The golden jubilee merited well-stocked gift shops selling UFO paraphernalia including T-shirts and 'alien glow-pop' sweets.

There were videos purchasable at the local UFO museum, and copies of sworn statements made by those who claim to have witnessed the phenomenon. It is estimated that Roswell profits to the tune of $5 million a year from the UFO industry (*The Times*, 25 June 1997). Roswell has its ripples as far away as central Nevada where at Rachel the Little A Le Inn does a brisk trade accommodating hard-core cultists who believe that the aliens who had the misfortune to crash at Roswell are being kept at a top-secret Air Force base nearby. Such is the American way; UFOs have a well-tried commercial dimension – but this might just disguise an actual incident.

At the extreme outer limits of the craze are those who patronize such organizations as the 'Heaven's Gate' cult (see Excursus in this chapter) and the high-sounding Urarius Academy of Science. The leader, Charles Spiegal, insists that spacecraft will land on Earth in 2001 to resolve the world's problems, and he has bought 67 acres of land near San Diego, California, to await their descent. Each craft – so we are told – will carry 1 000 advanced beings ('space brothers') with the knowledge we need to remedy society's ills. Through their ministrations, humans will be enabled to evolve to a 'higher plane'. Many of the public have already been apprised of these eagerly anticipated and momentous events through the writings of Spiegal and his group. These have been communicated to them by the 'brothers' in space. The 'messages' have also included information about the past lives of cult members, indeed, Spiegal himself claims to have been many notable people in his time, including Napoleon and an Egyptian Pharaoh (*Sunday Times*, 13 April 1997).

The other end of the UFO spectrum is peopled by those with a genuine academic interest in the subject, who obviously think that it merits serious attention. The autobiography of the former wartime pilot and later deputy Head of Strike Command, Air Marshal Sir Peter Horsley, recounts his own experience of aliens. This encounter is supposed to have taken place in his flat at Westminster in 1954. It will surprise no one to learn, however, that this is regarded by critics (*The Times*, 14 August 1997) as an hallucinatory experience. The problem here is, what was a man in charge of the nuclear force doing having hallucinations – hypnagogic or otherwise?

In the younger bracket of enquirers are those engaged in research theses regarding the UFO phenomenon. Particularly popular are those meta-treatments which concentrate on the philosophy of the subject, and examine how different methods of looking at alien life have been shaped by cultural attitudes. More empirical is the work going on at observatories as well as universities. At Arecibo in Puerto Rico, for example, the site of the world's largest radio telescope a new initiative has begun to try to detect extraterrestrial signals, with equipment which is 40 times more powerful than anything that has been done before. It (Serendip IV) can scan 168 million frequency channels every 1.7 seconds analysing them for intensities and background levels. Meanwhile there are moves afoot in the USA to convene a congressional hearing on UFOs. This initiative comes from The Centre for the Study of Extraterrestrial Intelligence (CSETI) which claims to have 50 witnesses with high-level security clearance, and also has the backing of former astronaut, Edgar Mitchell. Although most of us tend to think the 'aliens' are very coy, cultists in general and this organization in particular insist that the photographic, video and documentary evidence is so overwhelming that Congress must be apprised of the facts.

A commendably balanced view of the whole issue is that of Carl Sagan (1974) who adopts a position of the informed but open-minded sceptic. He suggests a number of criteria for judging the validity or otherwise of contact/witness claims:

1. They should not be invested with a supernatural content; it adds credibility to the accounts if they do not come into any of the traditional frameworks (it is worth noting here the view of one of the foremost authorities on myths, Professor G. Kirk (1974), that it is the peculiar character of myths – as opposed to other 'fabulous' stories – that they *have* a supernatural content).
2. There should be a clear description of the morphology of the non-human creatures including a convincing account of the astronomical realities that humans could not have acquired for themselves.
3. There should be a transparent presentation of the purpose of the contacts.
4. There should be information in the accounts (or past myths and legends) which civilization as we know it could not have generated for itself. (Certain ancient stories strongly hint at the possibility of extraterrestrial contact, but these are not evidence, let alone proof, that such things have actually taken place.)
5. Ideally there should be artefacts from a non-human source, i.e. something beyond the technological capabilities of human civilization which would help to establish a prima facie case for the authenticity of the contacts or whatever. (Good (1987: p. 102) cites an amusing exchange during a House of Lords debate in 1982 when the House was reminded that between 1978 and 1981 there had been no less than 2 500 sightings: Viscount Saint Davids – 'My Lords, has anyone found a beer-can marked 'Made in Centaurus'?'

Viscount Long – 'If it's a matter of beer-cans, I'm not a Minister for Conservation'.)

Excursus: The 'Solar Temple Cult'

The 'Sovereign Order of the Solar Temple' (sometimes associated in the popular mind with a similar but much smaller movement in San Diego known as the 'Heaven's Gate' cult) was one of the great unnecessary tragedies of our times. In some ways it is reminiscent of the People's Temple Sect led by the self-appointed Reverend Jim Jones which ended its days in the mass suicide of its 900 members at a commune in Georgetown, Guyana, in 1978. But whereas very many of the People's Temple Sect were simple, gullible people, the cult members were largely drawn from the well-educated, middle-class stratum of society. Indeed, as we shall see, even royalty may have been included, if recent reports are to be believed ('Fall from Grace', *Sunday Times*, News Review, 21 December 1997). But even sophisticated and successful people have no necessary monopoly of common sense.

The Order of the Solar Temple whose rituals were a mixture of Catholicism and the occult, probably comprised as many as 600 members found mainly in Switzerland, France and Canada (one set of computer records lists 576 paid-up members in ten countries). It seems to have been founded in the 1970s by a close friend of Prince Rainier of Monaco, Jean Louis Marsan, who was also involved with Monaco's flourishing casino industry. He ran the order from his villa, and at this time it appears to have been a relatively harmless enterprise associated – at least in spirit – with other Templar orders in Italy and France. As numbers grew, Marsan – a genuine occult enthusiast – bought a priory, and collaborated with a self-styled master of the esoteric, Joseph di Mambro, to absorb similar Templar organizations. He seems not to have appreciated that di Mambro who eventually took over the movement was a convicted confidence trickster who sometimes masqueraded as a qualified psychologist. The plans did not materialize as anticipated. Instead di Mambro gradually usurped Marsan's position, and by 1982 had taken over the entire Solar Temple set-up. Not only had he annexed Marsan's priory at Villie-Morgan, he also took charge of other chapels in Southern France.

Once in charge, di Mambro ensured that the movement was going to be profitable. Almost incomprehensibly, he recruited a wide spectrum of devotees who were mostly – though not exclusively – people with healthy bank balances. Members included the millionaire director of Piaget watches, a nuclear physicist and people from the entertainment world. These lent or gave some thousands of pounds to the movement in gratitude for the hologram spiritual experiences they enjoyed. Initiation into the movement was conducted as a solemn ritual involving a certain amount of arcane regalia and technical flummery which obviously impressed the candidates. The sprinkling of 'heavenly gold dust', the reiteration of obscure Latin phrases and the mounting crescendo of Wagnerian music all added to the illusion. The initiates were told that di Mambro was in contact with 33 'spiritual masters' who lived in the Himalayas (vague echoes of Shangri-La) and who were 'watching over the world'. Members of the order were thus a spiritual élite who were privileged to receive the wisdom of the masters. The general burden of the teaching – like that of so many eschatological cults – was that the world was 'hurtling towards oblivion', and that only the chosen would be saved.

The *éminence grise* of the movement was the young – some say charismatic – second-in-command, Dr Luc Jouret. As deputy he did a great deal to help with recruitment and to persuade members to part with their money (members paid a minimum annual subscription of £100 plus additional goodwill payments and had to stand the exhorbitant costs of their regalia, cloaks, swords, etc.). Jouret had studied medicine at the Free University in Brussels, and later took up complementary medicine, establishing a homoeopathy practice in the Ardennes. When his first marriage broke up, he seems to have sampled a whole range of ancient wisdom cults before finally teaming up with di Mambro in 1980 in what can only be described as mining a very lucrative pseudo-religious seam. Jouret also set himself up as principal of the Academy for Research and Knowledge of Advanced Science. This high-sounding establishment held seminars and conferences, and as an offshoot of the Solar Temple was able to create interest in the parent company. As part of his outreach programme, Jouret published a book *Medicine and Conscience* and marketed a series of consciousness-raising cassette tapes of his lectures at £10 each. These encompassed a wide range of his interests from healthy lifestyles to apocalyptic predictions.

As far as can be ascertained, di Mambro and Jouret used much of the money they fleeced from their prosperous cultist friends to buy property in Switzerland, France, and also abroad in Australia and Canada. But for a while nothing was seriously questioned. Whatever the 'high priests' taught was believed, and whatever they said was done. This included not only responses to appeals for ever more money, but apparently also requests for sexual favours. Di Mambro wanted these not just for himself; he also instructed one married lady to initiate his teenage son into the necessary mysteries. Jouret and di Mambro's control of the highest echelon of their devotees, the 'chevaliers' (resplendent in black capes with scarlet lining and gold trim) was virtually total. And di Mambro had no compunction in interfering in the personal lives of these members, even to breaking up marriages which were said to be 'cosmically incompatible'. Any opposition was dismissed as being the work of 'negative forces'.

A more sinister light was cast on the Solar Temple movement when in the winter of 1992–93, the Canadian police began hunting for a mysterious subversive organization known simply as Q-37, i.e. Quebec plus 37 founder members. The signs were that these were right-wing terrorists who threatened action against the government because of its relaxed racial policies. Undercover work revealed that there were some tenuous connections with the Solar Temple cult. However, despite phone-taps on some members of the cult and on Jouret himself, no concrete evidence was discovered. The publicity re the cult that followed from these investigations caused a number of people to resign their membership in 1993. In the light of subsequent events, it was the opinion of the Sûreté du Quebec that perhaps as many as 40 of the 80 that left the movement may have saved their lives by doing so. Sadly, though, others decamped to Switzerland, never to return. Just as unfortunate were the Dutoit family who were apparently murdered on di Mambro's instructions in 1994. He dispatched two absolutely trusted members of the cult from Switzerland, a man and a woman, who carried out the brutal, ritual killings of father, wife and child exactly to order – ostensibly because the child was designated as a satanic influence. Two other members cleaned up the blood – there were 64 stab wounds in all. At least some cultists were going to earn their journey to Sirius to join the 'Lords of the Universe'.

As early as 1989 some members were already becoming disillusioned. One woman, Rose-Marie Opplinger, sued for the recovery of £300 000 which she claimed her husband had been persuaded to donate to the cult after selling his property. But without doubt, the most famous person to be associated with the cult was ex-film actress, Grace Kelly, or Princess Grace of Monaco as she came to be known. In her premarriage days, Kelly had picked up a reputation as a promiscuous 'home-breaker' because of her many affairs with older married men, most notably her co-stars. But she had also had a strong Catholic upbringing which remained with her all her life. She was religious, curious and uncertain, and this eventually led (possibly via her husband's friend Marsan) to the Solar Temple set-up. Such evidence as there is, points to the 'fact' that some time in 1982 she was initiated into the cult as a 'priestess' (Channel 4, 29 December 1997). According to witnesses, this was done with considerable ceremony in great secrecy. One of the acolytes, a practised acupuncturist, said that the princess, as part of her preparation, had needles inserted in such a way as to excite her 'sexual meridians' which resulted in a double orgasm. Then robed, she underwent the initiation proper conducted by Jouret with all the customary theatrical trimmings.

As usual, there was a price. Di Mambro asked for £10 million as the royal family's contribution to the cult, but the princess told him she could only manage £6 million and hand over an apartment as security for the rest. The story goes that di Mambro was dissatisfied and became increasingly importunate in his demands for money, whereupon the princess grew impatient and disillusioned, broke off contact with the cult, and threatened to expose its activities. The strange – and tragic – sequel to all this was that only a few months afterwards, the princess and her daughter were involved in a car crash in which the princess was killed. It is an accident which has never been satisfactorily explained.

The end – or what is believed to be the end – of the Solar Temple movement came about equally inexplicably. In October 1994, five bodies were found in Canada and 48 in Switzerland in chalets belonging to the order. In December 1995, 16 more members were found in the Vercors area of France who are believed to have been murdered (two were police who had infiltrated the organization). In the spring of 1997 five more members died in Canada. It is not exactly certain just how many of these people were victims of mass murder, and how many were cases of suicide. Some died by shooting; others by intravenous injection, and a number were found badly charred by burning – probably as the result of pre-set incendiary devices. The dead included children as well as adults, and the adults included Joel Eggers and Dominique Bellaton, alleged killers of the Dutoit family, Luc Jouret, and di Mambro and his wife and two children. There is so much uncertainty about these deaths and whether other Solar cells still exist that the respective police forces are still continuing with their investigations.

Curiously, before the final denouement of the movement *as it was known to exist*, there was apparently some break between di Mambro and Jouret. The master blamed his deputy for botching the 'transition to the future'. In a letter to a Swiss newspaper which reads like a last testament, di Mambro wrote:

> to everyone who can still hear the voice of wisdom ... we today complete the requirements of a plan worked out in other times. We leave this earth to rediscover, in total lucidity and freedom, a Plane of Absolute Truth, far from the hypocrisy and oppression of this world, to sow the seeds of our future generation. (Millar: 1995)

It seems barely credible that otherwise intelligent people could be duped by this pseudo-religious *mélange* of mummery and mystical symbols. One is tempted to wonder if the message becomes more extreme when simple reiteration is not enough. This is often the way with cultists. It is as though they abandon common sense in the pursuit of some esoteric goal. In some ways the Solar Temple movement was not unlike similar cults elsewhere. Certainly there are certain parallels with the Hale-Bopp phenomenon at Rancho Santa Fe, near San Diego. The movement known – somewhat presumptuously – as 'Heaven's Gate' also taught that members' destiny was with the stars. There is, of course, a sense in which we are all 'starstuff', but this was something different. Members of the esoteric élite believed that they were due to be translated to outer space at the appointed time, and they – or their charismatic leaders – interpreted the appearance of the Hale-Bopp comet as a sign that their time had come. In September 1996, they attempted to recruit more members through the Internet, but surfers of the Web can be very unforgiving when what is being presented seems to be patently ridiculous. The devotees went ahead regardless. From their luxurious mansion, rented by the cult for $10 000 a month, they made their plans for even more intimate communion with the cosmos. For the leader, Marshall Applewhite, it was to be the culmination of a 20-year odyssey. The last message left on the Internet was that Hale-Bopp's arrival was the moment they had waited for, and that now they were due to 'graduate' to a new evolutionary level. Cult members helped each other to take a lethal cocktail of apple sauce, phenobarbitone and vodka, and then put plastic bags over their heads. The last two tidied up before dying. When found there were bodies of 21 women and 18 men, some of whom had been castrated. Only two were black, and only five were under 40. They were all neatly dressed as for a spaceship journey, and their suitcases lay tidily packed by their sides. As they put it, Hale-Bopp was going to bring a closure to Heaven's Gate – and who can argue with a comet?

More recently still we have the case of the Solar Temple satellite in Tenerife. Police believe that their raid on five homes in Santa Cruz following an anonymous telephone call prevented the mass suicide of 32 people including five children. It is thought that the members of the cult were going to kill themselves with poison on the summit of Mount Teide (*Sunday Telegraph*, 9 January 1998). All the followers of the cult were German, and were led by a German psychologist, Heide Fittkau-Garthe, who was arrested on the charge of trying to persuade people to kill themselves so that their spirits could be transported by spacecraft to another planet in order to avoid the imminent end of the world. Members of the cult which appears to have developed from an Isis holistic centre in Santa Cruz, had been under surveillance for some months, possibly because links were suspected with the lethal Solar Temple organization in Switzerland and Canada.

It would seem that such delusional thinking is in some ways related to 'pre-millennial tension'. The year 2000 was thought by some to portend cataclysmic changes – perhaps even the end of this world order. The future is therefore seen in terms of cosmic salvation, a rescue operation which takes the form of a spacecraft scenario. Naturally, this is only for the few. The plan is for the chosen, the élite, the cosmic cognoscenti – hence the esoteric and selective nature of the organizations in question.

CHAPTER EIGHT

The Paranormal as a Religious Surrogate

In a modern text on psychical research (Cerullo: 1982), it is argued that Western culture, particularly in its Protestant forms, is gradually undermining the traditional religious concept of the soul. It is said that the growth of scientism is slowly eroding the old familiar notions of a spiritual-psychic dimension, and supplanting them with a rationalized yet basically unsatisfactory brand of humanism. In some ways, this thesis is reminiscent of Peter Berger's charge that Christianity – again, especially in its Protestant guise – is 'its own gravedigger' (Berger: 1969). What he especially has in mind is that Christianity has become a rationalized form of Judaism, and that Protestant Christianity, in turn, has developed as a rationalized form of Catholicism. Each has helped to divest conventional religion of its miraculous content; by their questioning and scepticism, each has made a significant contribution to the evolution of the secularized consciousness. But what is more to the point is the additional contention that psychical research, especially in the view of its founders, was 'a gallant, nearly successful, bid to present an acceptable western vision of the secularised soul' (Gregory: 1983a). In other words, in their own ways, the early devotees of parapsychology – perhaps unwittingly – made their own peculiar contribution to the process of secularized thought.

Is this really the case? Has parapsychology really drawn needy souls away from the path of 'true religion' or is it that its somewhat negative findings have insidiously detracted from the certitudes of traditional religious systems? After all, unproven – and perhaps unprovable – survivalist hypotheses do little to buttress the wavering faith of the would-be believer. Even the trusting have doubts, and it is therefore only too understandable that they should look to a study of the paranormal for evidential support. The seance, the reported out-of-body experience, the odd materialization are all grist for the phenomenological mill. It is little wonder, then, that some will feel a little let down when the experts seem unable to produce the goods, at least, not with any satisfactory conviction.

Impressionistically persuasive as this may appear to be, perhaps the truth is both more subtle and more complex. Rather than directly

undermining traditional religion, it could be argued that parapsychology, for some, is really a kind of functional alternative to religion. In
effect, it is a surrogate religion.

The idea of religious surrogates is most commonly associated with
the sociologist (Weber: 1965), who maintained that in given circumstances, there are certain ideologies which act as the functional equivalents
of religion. This, of course, begs the question of how religion is to be
defined. The notion of functional equivalents implies an inclusive definition of religion which allows for a range of possible alternatives such
as communism, national socialism, or even, say, psychotherapy (Falding:
1972). Inclusivist definitions involve nominalist interpretations of religion which, in effect, hold that religion is what we *say* it is. Religious
institutions, like any other social institutions, are humanly constructed.
People decide what is religion *for them*. Whatever they 'name' as religion becomes religion for all practical social purposes.

This kind of definition is usually contrasted with the exclusivist approach which has strong essentialist overtones and emphasizes what is
believed to be the 'real' or essential nature of religion. On this kind of
interpretation it is held that at the 'heart' of religion there is a quality –
indeed, a mystery – which eludes our capacity for intellectual
conceptualization. Exclusivists maintain that all religion is ideology but
not all ideology is religion, and that for the term 'religion' to have any
academic credibility it must be distinguished from functional equivalents and alternative ideologies. This can only be done if it is definitionally
linked with the supernatural.

Many would hold that religion is characterized by a distinction between a real, tangible world, which can be ascertained through the
senses, and a postulated invisible world, which is equally real but which
is not discerned in the same way. Both are part of the same cosmos, and
each is indispensable to the other (Hill: 1973). This fairly traditional
view has marked exclusivist orientations, and the main difficulty with it
is that it tends to rule out many influential thought-systems which could
certainly be regarded as being, at least, marginally religious. If, on the
other hand, a more inclusivist approach is adopted which stresses the
social utility of religion, much will turn on the question of how religion
functions for the individual and for the community.

In discussing the functions of religion, we must be careful to distinguish between what people intend to achieve as members of any particular
group or organization, and the unintended effects of this behaviour
upon their lives. The objects of religious belief and observance obviously differ for different adherents. Some may have quite specific
objectives such as the realization of a blissful afterlife, or – more

amorphously – their union with the eternal principle of the cosmos, or they may be content simply with the occasional attainment of particular states of consciousness. These various objectives will obviously condition the attitudes and expectations of the here-and-now lives of believers, often in unintended ways. It is these unintended consequences of behaviour which are often of greater importance than those produced by conscious aims (Nottingham: 1964, p. 122 ff.). This well-rehearsed distinction between manifest and latent functions can be seen most clearly in relating religious ritual to patterns of behaviour. It is here that a complementary point must be borne in mind. It is important to distinguish between the purposes religion serves for the individual and how it functions for society at large. In pursuing his own religious aims, the individual may not only be reflecting the norms of society, but may also be contributing to some larger interest such as the greater union of society – or contrarily – the reform of its policies and practices. It follows that religion is no one kind of a thing, and that its functionality is largely conditioned by the field in which it operates.

One of the primary functions of religion is to give comprehensibility to individual and social existence. In short, religion is bound up with the problem of *meaning*. People have a desire to know, to understand (Spiro: 1966), to make sense of their everyday lives. Indeed, it could be argued that all religious practices are really institutionalized 'answers' to the perennial problem of theodicy, how to explain the ways of the gods to men, and how to reconcile the antinomic experiences of both good and evil. The biblical character of Job epitomizes the human dilemma: why is there a seemingly inequitable distribution of rewards and punishments, and why do the ungodly continue to prosper 'like the green bay tree'? In the 'high' religious tradition where God is regarded as merciful and just, this kind of question poses an intractable problem. How are we to square the omnipotence of God with the unabated suffering of His creatures? Theologians have a number of solutions to this problem, all of them partial and none of them wholly satisfactory. Many de-emphasize the singularity of our present human existence, and hint at some form of post-moral compensation. In centring on the possibility of survival after death they echo a perennial theme in parapsychological literature.

For a number of parapsychologists, the study of the paranormal has assumed a cognitive significance akin to that of religion. It is probably not too far-fetched to say that parapsychology has become a substitute for religion. For instance, it is doubtful whether Arthur Koestler's interest in the subject was wholly 'scientific'. The study of what he often called 'parascience' was obviously something more than a mere academic hobby. In his earlier writing about free will and determinism in *Reflections on Hanging*, he speaks of the possibility of making choices which are not completely determined by heredity or environment, but which are 'subjective reflections of an objective process, negating time and injecting moral responsibility into the amoral edifice of nature' (Koestler: 1956, p. 102). In other words, he is arguing that there may be no inherent meaning in the universe, but that we can nevertheless *invest* it with meaning and significance, and therefore change the nature of experience. Later, his neo-existentialism gives way to the suspicion that there may be rather more to it than this. *Roots of Coincidence*, though ostensibly a treatise on the relationship between the findings of physics and ESP research, has certain metaphysical overtones (Koestler: 1972). This is even more clearly brought out in *The Challenge of Chance*, significantly based on experiments conducted under the auspices of the Religious Experience Unit (later the Alister Hardy Foundation) at Oxford, in which he discounts the indeterminacy thesis of physics and comes down in favour of a 'hidden variables' approach. He has, by this time, dismissed the notion of a deterministic, mechanistic universe, and is searching for meanings in the study of the paranormal (Koestler: 1973). These ideas are further elaborated in *Bricks to Babel* in which he expounds on the ways in which his thinking has developed over the years particularly in relation to 'the implications of the integrative forces in the universe' (Koestler: 1980).

Closely allied to questions of meaning and explanation are those relating to 'proof' and validity. The concern with the possibilities of some supra-empirical dimension inevitably raises the issue of verification. Does such a dimension exist? If it does exist, what are the implications for the mundane world? Such metaphysical questions have strong religious overtones. Indeed, the 'quest' can constitute a kind of surrogate religious activity.

Concern with these matters informs a great deal of parapsychological research and writings, and is typically evidenced by a paper presented at the second International SPR Conference in 1978 (Thouless: 1978; 1984) on the subject of survival. Here an attempt is made to classify existing theories and clarify their interrelationships. As we have seen, a spectrum of theories is suggested ranging from non-survival to continued survival, and includes refinements such as the conjectured continuation of consciousness in a different dimension of time. The author makes it clear that his intention is not to rehearse yet again the evidence for and against human survival of bodily death, but his very preoccupation with the subject, and his assertion that the problem of survival may actually demand a way of thinking about it that has not yet been developed, suggests that it is more than a matter of mere disinterested academic concern.

Again, as we have seen, American parapsychologist Scott Rogo has re-examined the evidence for reincarnation (Rogo: 1985) which – it is claimed – has increased faster than evidence relating to any other topic in parapsychology (Matlock: 1986). Much of the case material in Rogo's book is culled from the work of eminent (e.g. Ian Stevenson) and no so eminent researchers in the field of reincarnation studies. This is a popular presentation of a much discussed theme, and therefore open to predictable criticisms, but both the book and its critics are, in their own ways, expressing concern about the whole question of proof and validity.

The question of survival is related to a further function of religion, namely that of consolation. Marx's aphorism that 'religion is the opiate of the people' or Freud's insistence that religion is a 'necessary illusion' both reflect the common view that religion exists primarily as a form of emotional comfort and support. And what brings more consolation than the possibility of survival?

It has been argued that the problem of survival is the main *raison d'être* of psychical research. Martin Johnson, for example, maintains that 'the question of man's survival of bodily death can be said to be the perennial question of "psychical research" and probably also ideologically the most loaded one within the entire realm of parapsychology' (Johnson: 1984). Perhaps therefore *all* survival research – no matter how broadly conceived – from the investigations of mediums and seance phenomena (Gauld: 1982; Lorimer: 1984) to analyses of out-of-body experiences (note especially the work of Blackmore: 1982b), tend to support the contention that parapsychology functions either as an adjunct to religion, where psychic phenomena may be seen as a kind of bridge between the sacred and the secular, or as a substitute for religion.

Sociologists in particular are often keen to stress the integrative functions of religion. The pioneer, Emile Durkheim, pre-eminently emphasized that religion was a source of social solidarity. He maintained that its rituals were forms of group reinforcement, and that its beliefs were collective affirmations of commonly held sentiments and values (Durkheim: 1968). It is further argued that this also holds true for the individual. Religion is psychologically as well as socially reinforcing. Symbols and beliefs enable people to cope with the unpredictability and insecurity of everyday existence (see especially El-Guindi: 1977, pp. 19–20). This argument has a certain cogency. In qualified ways religion integrates both in the social sense and in the conceptual sense by bringing customs and beliefs together in a unique and significant way (Keesing and Keesing: 1971).

Interestingly, the social and conceptual cohesion argument can also be applied to parapsychology. Students of the paranormal – despite their continuing differences – not only share a similar conceptual universe, but also enjoy a certain perverse yet proud insularity which serves to bind them together in the common cause. They have their factions and occasional bouts of academic in-fighting like any 'religious' movement, but in general such unseemly wrangling does not detract from the pursuit of their discipline. There is an almost Calvinistic certainty about the overall rightness of the cause, and an uncomprehending hostility to the dismissive attitudes of 'unbelievers'. In the face of continuing opposition from the majority of the scientific establishment, parapsychology has tended to become – paradoxically – both more intellectually adventurous and more defensively introverted in its orientations. (There are numerous texts concerned with the heart-searching of parapsychology about its 'role' as a science. See particularly, McClenon: 1984.)

Religion has the additional function of instilling or furthering a sense of purpose in its adherents. Throughout the ages people have asked about the meaning of existence. What is it all about? Why are we here? These common queries about the purpose of life are all part of the general problem of teleology. In one way or another they have generated the present variety of religious philosophies which claim to answer these perennial questions. Clifford Geertz, in a famous essay, has described religion as 'a system of symbols which acts to establish powerful, pervasive, and long-lasting moods and motivations in men by formulating conceptions of the general order of existence and clothing these conceptions with such an aura of factuality that the moods and motivations seem uniquely realistic' (Geertz: 1966). People want to see a shape to their lives, they want to detect a coherence in the ongoing flux of experience, and they sometimes perceive this in what Peter Berger has suggestively called 'signals of transcendence' (Berger: 1972), those intriguing experiential hints and cosmic clues which indicate that there might indeed be something beyond the mundane world.

Needless to say, such concerns are also to be found among parapsychologists. These concerns are both implicit in the general 'exercise' of the discipline, and explicit in some of the literature. Some observers feel that for many practitioners the study of parapsychology is, in effect, a substitute for religion, and that it is not exactly coincidental that psychical research took off in the UK at just about the same time that the verities of traditional religion were being questioned.

> The development of (psychical research) has in many respects a good deal in common with the history of religion. Indeed the very origins of psychical research as a branch of scholarly enquiry are

directly and quite explicitly related to the yawning inner spiritual vacuum experienced by the academic Cambridge founders of the SPR in response to the demise of religion as Victorians saw it. Was there, perhaps, in these phenomena with their potential promise of self-transcendence, a new way into the realm of the religious? If Darwin had killed the argument for the existence of God from design by exorcising teleology and hence any purpose from nature, was there not here a new way of pursuing natural theology? (Gregory: 1981).

At one level, then, religion exists to satisfy the need for both integration and a sense of purpose. These, in turn, are very much bound up with a desire for identity and esteem. Religion fulfils this function in a number of ways, not least of all by the transvaluation of the experience of the individual (see particularly the work of Wilson: 1961). In social terms the believer may be a nonentity, a person of no particular account. In the eyes of the world the believer feels he or she is no one, but he or she is also conscious of an alternative 'true' status as a child of God. The believer may then come to disregard and even despise worldly estimates of his or her social worth. It is faith that matters. This is his or her armour and shield which protect him or her against the taunts and indifferences of the world. The believer is not primarily interested in social esteem, and has a near imperviousness to public opinion. It is spiritual prestige that is important. Parapsychologists too are all too conscious of their minority standing, and they too are beset by indifference and even intolerance, but it does not nullify their convictions or belittle their endeavours. It clearly indicates that for them it has become more than a simple academic pursuit. For the earnest student of ESP it is not ultimately the endorsements of academe or the imprimatur of the scientific community, nor even the regard of the public that really counts. In the final analysis, his commitment is to a particular kind of truth. He has an alternative way of looking at the world, and is concerned with another dimension of reality. This quest can virtually become a way of life. Rejection only tends to encourage a closed society mentality in which all that really matters is peer group approval.

There is one further parallel between religion and parapsychology that should be mentioned. In both disciplines there is a spiritual–secular divide. The main cleavage is between those who are inclined to naturalistic explanations of paranormal phenomena and those who are not; between those who are prepared to adopt a parsimonious Occam's Razor approach, and those who see this as a virtual denial of 'true' realities. This dichotomy of outlook in the parapsychology community is reflected quite clearly in some of the current literature.

What appears to be gaining ground is the suspicion – and, in some cases, the conviction – that studies of the paranormal are not really dealing with the paranormal at all but simply with the 'normal' at a level which is still not clearly understood. For example, in a most interesting discussion of 'speaking in tongues', David Christie-Murray argues that the happenings at the feast of Pentecost (Acts 2: 1–11) can be interpreted not as glossolalia, i.e. speaking syllables of a completely unknown 'language', but as we have already seen, as xenolalia, speaking in a known language which is allegedly completely unknown to the speaker. This seems to accord with events as described in the New Testament. But Christie-Murray goes on to insist that this should not be seen as an inherently paranormal exercise, but in terms of the unconscious absorption of linguistic cultural elements deriving from a multilingual environment (Christie-Murray: 1978). On the other hand, other writers have interpreted the phenomenon as a form of glossolalia that was effective because of a 'telepathic rapport' between the apostles and their hearers which was understood despite the barriers of language (Perry: 1979). The view that it could have been paranormal is 'seriously questioned', and the very idea that it could be 'miraculous' is obviously regarded with grave suspicion. Whichever of these interpretations is accepted they appear to depart from the received text which insists that something very unusual definitely occurred, and that this inaugurated what is now a universal movement.

To take another example, the phenomenon of spirit possession – according to some observers – can now be seen simply as an altered state of consciousness possibly generated by opiate receptors in the brain. It is confidently predicted that the developing science of psychophysiology will help to 'demystify those strange phenomena reported by the study of religion' (Holm: 1982, p. 67). In other words, soon the paranormal will be paranormal no longer.

Religion and parapsychology have much in common. They both share an anamolous social position *vis-à-vis* the orthodox scientific community. Both give the impression of being beleaguered bastions of heterodoxy in the face of academic hostility and general indifference. Yet they tend only to co-operate at the margins, despite the fact that so many of their concerns coincide. Both are interested in what are essentially paranormal phenomena, but each invests these phenomena with a different importance and significance. For the parapsychologist they may be merely super-empirical, while for the religionist they are supernatural, with all that this term connotes. Yet if both approaches are seen in terms of their psycho-social functionality, there is considerable similarity. To speak of the social functions of religion is not to invalidate its claims to objective truth, however open to interpretation these may be. Similarly, to speak of substitution or surrogacy or exchanges of function is not necessarily detrimental to a discipline or an ideology, least of all parapsychology.

Religion and parapsychology – in their own ways – provide their adherents with a sense of purpose; a philosophy of life. Both have explanatory capacities inasmuch as they formulate different kinds of questions and suggest 'meanings' as to why things are as they are. Human nature abhors a cognitive vacuum, and both supply 'proofs' of the possibility of dimensions of reality as yet largely unexplored. What is particularly fascinating is to what extent continuing experimentation will give more verisimilitude to speculation.

Excursus: Credibility or Credulity: A Comparative Study of Beliefs about the Paranormal among Students in Higher Education

This discussion has centred on the possible relationship between paranormal beliefs/experiences and religious orientations. Such a relationship would seem to have a 'common-sense' plausibility. After all, religious studies and parapsychology share certain aspirations, and have a similar psychological functionality. In their own ways, they both have a teleological dimension, and are thus able to provide a sense of consolation and meaning for would-be believers (Carlton: 1973). Indeed, the apparent evidence for 'psychic forces' seems irresistible to many religionists. Extrasensory perception and the like appear to lend support to religion; they reinforce belief in the non-material world, and may even assume the role of science itself as an evidential adjunct for the 'truth' of religious ideas (Meadow and Kahoe: 1984, p. 139). There is little doubt therefore that some religionists look to parapsychology as a somewhat uncertain ally in their attempts to establish theistic truths. However, it might also be argued that some kind of inverse relationship exists between the two, and that actually parapsychology is, as we have seen, really a type of religious surrogate. Parapsychologists, unable to accept what they often consider to be the unsupportable claims of religion, resort to studies of the paranormal as a substitute for the religious quest. There is clearly some evidence that among active parapsychologists, their discipline can constitute a functional alternative to religion (e.g. Koestler: 1980). Although they are divided among themselves as to whether there is any actual correspondence between paranormal experience and the objective 'truth' that the experiences may represent, many are not immune to the lure of the metaphysical.

But what about the 'non-professional'? How do those with few disciplinary axioms to grind respond to such issues? Do they make any clear distinction between paranormal and religious experiences?

In order to test some reactions, a small-scale comparative study was undertaken among that ever-changing reservoir for all would-be researchers, the Higher Education student population. In this case, first-year students on Arts and Education courses in a university-linked college with a religious foundation specializing in Teacher Education were compared with first-year Humanities students at an ostensibly secular (= 'neutral'?) former polytechnic (now a university). Students were given a six-page questionnaire which was designed to elicit both facts and opinions. They were told that it was all entirely voluntary, but their co-operation was encouraged. They were not told to complete the questionnaires in class, as this constitutes an institutional pressure to comply.

Also, in order to avert unnecessary bias, they were not told the precise object of the exercise, although this should not have been too difficult to discern from the nature of the questions themselves.

It should be stated at the outset that the response rates were surprisingly low: at the college 46 per cent and at the polytechnic 34 per cent. Yet there are points of interest about both these figures. (All figures have been rounded up or down for simplicity.) At the college, two groups were involved: students on a Psychology course (response rate 57 per cent) and those on a New Testament studies course (response rate 17 per cent). It is tempting to suspect that if the latter were committed Christians – perhaps of a more conservative persuasion (in the circumstances, a reasonable assumption) – they may have been impatient with what they felt to be irrelevant concerns. At the polytechnic – in contrast to the college – the overwhelming majority of the respondents were mature students i.e. aged 26 and over (74 per cent) although they comprise only about 40 per cent of those taking the course. In this instance, it might be unwise to hazard guesses as to why the younger students were either unwilling to register their views or simply indifferent to the whole exercise.

The sex balance on the courses in the respective institutions was not reflected consistently among the respondents. In the college the vast majority of students were female, and predictably 83 per cent of the respondents were female. Yet at the polytechnic where the balance was only slightly in favour of females, 79 per cent of the respondents were female. These are the facts, but it is doubtful whether we can attribute any particular significance to these facts. There is a mythology that women are more susceptible to metaphysical concerns, but these are suspicions which have yet to be substantiated. Certainly there is no clear evidence that they are *inherently* different from men in this respect.

This disparity in the response rates inevitably begs the question as to what extent they are related to the particular disciplines concerned. Those following science-based disciplines are known to be more sceptical about the study of paranormal phenomena. They are inclined – perhaps unfairly – to reject purported demonstrations of ESP etc. as something which does not accord with the accepted canons of scientific validity, so-called proofs are therefore attributed to coincidence, poor experimental methods and even fraud. In short, scientific 'reception systems' are not usually amenable to intrusive, often unverifiable, disciplines such as parapsychology (Carlton: 1988). But these students are not strictly scientists – that is, unless we allow psychology the status of a science – something we might concede by grace but hardly by law. They are, broadly speaking, arts students who might be expected to be

more sympathetic to the claims of parapsychology. Some research indicates that those with theological interests tend to regard parapsychology
as a companion discipline (Moore: 1977), whereas students of human
behaviour tend to be more sceptical because they are only too well
aware of the high probability of selective perception involved in the
reports of psychic experiences (Moody: 1975).

The first set of questions was primarily factual, and was concerned
with students' general religious orientations. All the college respondents
claimed to be 'believers', though almost 80 per cent agreed that one did
not have to participate in institutionalized religious practices in order to
be 'religious'. Some 58 per cent felt though that people who called
themselves religious should want to worship in this way, and only 21
per cent maintained that those claiming to be religious had an obligation
to share with a religious community. Almost all testified to an active
devotional life. Ninety-two per cent said they prayed, and 80 per cent
further insisted that prayer 'worked' both objectively and subjectively;
some 80 per cent read scriptures and only slightly fewer (75 per cent)
read religious literature. In what might generally be termed their aesthetic or 'spiritual' lives, 92 per cent said they were helped by music, 58
per cent by literature, but rather fewer by art (50 per cent) and film (40
per cent). These were found to be inspirational and enhancing, making
one more accessible to religious ideas. Music particularly was cited as
'relaxing' and 'therapeutic' and therefore an aid to religious receptivity.

In all, there was a very obvious – almost compelling – consensus of
beliefs and practices among these students, but it should also be noted
that there were some apparent inconsistencies. There were respondents
whose practices did not seem to agree with their beliefs, for example,
believers who did not pray or read scriptures and religious literature;
and those who prayed but did not read scriptures. In other cases – as we
shall see – where the beliefs did not seem to be in accord with practices,
some respondents were extremely hazy on a number of philosophical
issues.

The polytechnic students presented a somewhat different profile. Quite
a high proportion (68 per cent) said they were 'believers', 74 per cent
further maintaining that it was not necessary to participate in institutionalized religious practices in order to be 'religious'. But 37 per cent
felt that religious people should want to worship, and only 11 per cent
thought that those claiming to be religious should join with a religious
community. As far as devotional life was concerned, 68 per cent said
that they prayed, though – interestingly – only 48 per cent believed that
prayer worked both objectively and subjectively. Only 27 per cent read
scriptures but – unusually? – twice that number said they read religious

literature. As far as their aesthetic/spiritual lives were concerned, 80 per cent claimed to be helped by music and 84 per cent by literature, but only 32 per cent by art and a mere 21 per cent by film. The reasons given were similar to those given by the college students, and tended to be experiential rather than cognitive in orientation. They were seen to be 'relaxing', 'escapist', 'stimulus' for the emotions; only marginally were they seen as enhancing spiritual awareness.

The second set of questions moved the respondents a little nearer the main point of the project, namely, attitudes to the 'paranormal'. Specifically, they were designed to examine three interrelated themes:

1. Broad cosmological orientations.
2. The 'faith in science' issue.
3. The desirability or otherwise of studying the 'unknown'.

On the first theme, the college students were pretty much agreed (66 per cent) that humans need some 'spiritual vision' and that there is some benevolent power behind the universe (92 per cent). The same number were prepared to take this further and maintain that there is therefore some form of life after death. It followed that only a minority (17 per cent) thought that the universe was entirely governed by chance, although understandably there was some agnosticism on this point. Scientism – 'faith in science' – was not too well represented generally: 92 per cent thought that there were some mysteries in life that science would never explain, in fact, every respondent felt that if the human race is to survive we must all have more 'respect for nature'. Similarly, respondents were doubtful about the possible conquest of disease, 33 per cent favouring the view that science would never solve *all* problems of this kind.

Respondents were generally prepared to entertain the possibility of the novel and the unusual – those things which were probably not amenable to scientific analysis. Eighty per cent accepted the possibility of 'miracles', and only 5 per cent thought that nothing should be believed unless it can actually be proved to be true. Opinion, though, was divided on the issue of actual *investigation* of the paranormal. Just 55 per cent thought this was a legitimate enterprise, while 50 per cent actually expressed the view that it was 'unhealthy' to toy with the unknown (there were even a few unsolicited references on the questionnaires to 'demons' who presumably were thought to be the agents of these unusual – occult? – phenomena).

Again, there were the interesting inconsistencies. Believers who thought that the world was entirely governed by chance; those who carried out

the traditional devotional exercises but did not agree that there was a
benevolent power behind the universe; and there were those who accepted the idea of ultimate benevolence but did not believe in divine
intervention in the form of 'miracles'. And there were even believers
who displayed an acute but uncharacteristic agnosticism on many of
these questions – even to the extent of not giving an answer at all.

On this second set of questions, the polytechnic students displayed a
somewhat different pattern of beliefs. Fifty-three per cent thought that
humans must have some spiritual vision, and a high 84 per cent thought
that there was a benevolent power behind the universe. Although only
47 per cent were prepared to take this further and assert that there
was some form of life after death, and a very small minority (16 per
cent) believed that the universe was entirely governed by chance. Faith
in science was not too well represented among these Humanities students: an overwhelming 95 per cent thought that there were some
mysteries in life that science would never explain, and – as with the
college students – there was complete unanimity on the issue of more
respect for nature to ensure human survival. Less than half (42 per
cent) thought that science would master the fundamental problems
and eventually conquer disease. As far as the paranormal was concerned, 63 per cent were prepared to entertain the possibility of
'miracles', and only 11 per cent thought that nothing should be believed until it was proved to be true. These students were very much
more confident about actual investigation of the paranormal (74 per
cent), and much less nervous about the study of the 'unknown' generally – 89 per cent were in favour of an open mind on these matters.
There were no allusions to satanic agencies.

As with the college students, there were some inconsistencies in their
responses, but they were nothing like as 'obvious' or as numerous.
Obviously where *all* students adopt a religious position, and then appear to deviate from that position, in strange and unpredictable ways,
their responses are thrown into sharper relief than those made by other
students who – as a group – are more heterogeneous and therefore less
unanimous in their views.

The third set of questions was directly related to parapsychological
studies. Students were tested on their beliefs about certain paranormal
phenomena: did they exist? Were they even possible? Did they 'accept'
them?

The results were as shown in Tables 8.1 and 8.2.

It is worth noting two things in particular about the figures in Table
8.1:

Table 8.1 College students

		Very likely (%)	Just possible (%)	Highly unlikely (%)
1.	Extrasensory perception including pre-cognition and telepathy	29	62	9
2.	Out-of-body experiences	25	68	17
3.	Mediumship (the capacity to contact the dead)	12	51	37
4.	Visions/trances	33	62	5
5.	Glossolalia (speaking in tongues)	25	68	17
6.	Xenolalia (speaking in an unlearned foreign language)	10	57	33
7.	Seeing ghosts/apparitions/ experiencing poltergeists etc.	29	61	10
8.	Witnessing extraterrestrial craft/ beings	5	56	39
9.	Psychokinesis (the ability to move objects without physical effort)	12	42	46
10.	Faith-healing	33	62	5
11.	Levitation (the ability to suspend oneself/or be suspended without physical support)	12	33	55

1. Although, in general, 'very likely' statements outweigh 'highly un-likely' statements, the balance is actually fairly even, and that no *great* enthusiasm seems to be evinced for belief in the paranormal.
2. Where there is some support for the likelihood/possibility of para-normal phenomena, it is really an endorsement of already accepted (acceptable?) religious experiences e.g. visions, glossolalia, faith-healing etc., whereas those deemed most *un*acceptable are those which lie outside the normal scope of religious experience e.g. extraterrestrial phenomena, levitation etc.

Again, in Table 8.2 there is a rough equality of opinion. Belief and scepticism seem to be fairly evenly balanced. But although a high per-centage of these students claim to be believers, we find that except for the high values for faith-healing, they are more uncertain about 'reli-gious' phenomena such as visions, glossolalia etc. This may not indicate

Table 8.2   Polytechnic students

	Very likely (%)	Just possible (%)	Highly unlikely (%)
1. Extrasensory perception including pre-cognition and telepathy	37	63	0
2. Out-of-body experiences	21	69	10
3. Mediumship (the capacity to contact the dead)	10	32	58
4. Visions/trances	21	64	15
5. Glossolalia (speaking in tongues)	15	48	37
6. Xenolalia (speaking in an unlearned foreign language)	10	58	32
7. Seeing ghosts/apparitions/ experiencing poltergeists etc.	36	53	11
8. Witnessing extraterrestrial crafts/ beings	11	43	46
9. Psychokinesis (the ability to move objects without physical effort)	20	53	27
10. Faith-healing	26	64	10
11. Levitation (the ability to suspend oneself/or be suspended without physical support)	11	21	68

that they are irreligious but are of a less conservative religious persuasion than their college counterparts.

The fourth section of the questionnaire was concerned with actual claimed *experiences* of the paranormal as opposed to beliefs *about* the paranormal. Students were asked if they had ever had an unusual experience which they would call 'extraordinary' or 'paranormal' and which they could not readily explain in naturalistic terms. Quite a high proportion of students claimed to have had such experiences; 37 per cent of college students and 47 per cent of polytechnic students. Impressionistically, this is the reverse of what might have been expected considering that many of the experiences were of an avowedly 'spiritual' nature, and might therefore be more closely associated with students coming from a 'religious' environment. But actually they are representative of the population as a whole. The researches of Hay and Morrisey (1978) suggest that over a third of people in Great Britain have numinal experiences, that is, they claim to 'having been aware of or influenced by a presence or power ... which was different from their everyday selves'. Greeley and McCready (1975) had also come to similar conclusions in the USA, and both were confirmed by the further researches of Thomas and Cooper (1978) who concluded that 66 per cent had no such experiences, 8 per cent had uncodable experiences, 2 per cent had mystical, and 12 per cent psychic experiences – the basis of differentiation is not clear – and a further 12 per cent had experiences of 'religious consolation'.

'Unusual' experiences are obviously open to a wide range of classifications and interpretations. Donovan (1979) suggests that they can be categorized as

1. Mystical: i.e. brief, inexpressible 'feelings' or 'states of knowledge'.
2. Paranormal: i.e. experiences which seem to conflict with those of the taken for granted physical world, but which are nevertheless expressible in everyday language.
3. Charismatic: i.e. those experiences that could be broadly termed 'religious' and might include healing, glossolalia, visions, etc. This category might also apply to group-generated experiences as well as ostensibly subjective phenomena. Donovan is also prepared to subsume more amorphous qualities such as grace, wisdom, courage etc. within this category.
4. Regenerative: i.e. experiences such as religious conversion which have a lasting, reformative effect.

This typology obviously has its uses, but it also has certain weaknesses. Categories (1) and (2) seem to overlap considerably; some of the more general qualities of (3) appear to be too vague and of questionable significance (e.g. what exactly is the experience of wisdom?); and (4) though a particularly useful *idea*, is not really a category, as such, because it could be seen as the possible outcome of any or all of the other three.

Another way of looking at such phenomena is in terms of contradictory claims to knowledge. Marcello Truzzi (1971) in his examination of what might be generally called 'the occult' maintains that its main characteristic is a concentration on anomalous *objects* (e.g. fairies etc.) and anomalous *processes*, i.e. claims that human experiences or 'fate' can be affected by paranormal means (e.g. witch curses). In other words, Truzzi is concerned with the dissonance between empirical 'truth' and non-empirical claims to 'truth'.

This approach does have certain virtues, not least of comparing and contrasting objective 'reality' and subjective perception. Let us ask again those critical questions that must be asked: What is it that is alleged to be known – what is the nature of the claim itself? Who claims to know it – what is the source of the information? How or why do they know it, and what were the conditions of the experience? How is this belief sustained? Has it changed the subject's world view, and/or does it conduce to any known or accepted world view? In order to gain any real appreciation of any claimed paranormal experience at least some of these questions must permit of satisfactory answers.

Perhaps, therefore, a typology of possible experiences might look something like this:

1. Experiences which are objective and can be objectively explained, i.e. those everyday experiences which can be empirically validated such as breaking a limb or failing an examination.
2. Experiences which can be seen and described objectively, but cannot be explained objectively, that is, the experience is ostensibly objective, but may only be susceptible to subjective interpretations. This could apply to physical phenomena such as, say, the contraction of certain forms of disease which cannot be readily explained, or it could apply to various kinds of paranormal phenomena which appear to be 'real' but which elude scientific parameters.
3. Experiences which are 'purely' subjective, but which lend themselves to possible objective explanations, e.g. certain moods, dispositions, 'appetites' etc., which yield to a variety of reasonably plausible psychological interpretations.
4. Experiences which are intensively subjective and which cannot be objectively explained. This includes all manner of behaviours, especially those involving aesthetic, moral and religious values. These present very special problems: despite the attempt to 'naturalize' values, ultimately values are usually only explicable in terms of themselves.

Paranormal experiences – which can include religious experiences – do not fit exclusively into any one of these types, but may be found in (2), (3) and (4). This is readily apparent from the experiences reported by the respondents who were asked to *recount* their experiences, then try to *account* for those experiences, and also indicate any ways in which those experiences had changed their lives. Their experiences fall into three main categories: those of a specifically religious nature, i.e. experiences interpreted in religious terms; those which would be seen as 'recognizable' paranormal phenomena, e.g. apparitions etc., and those of a vague, intuitive kind which perhaps are too trivial to require any explanation at all. But these categories are only categories; the actual experiences often overlap the boundaries as we can see from specific examples. Among the college students, we have such instances as:

> I have experienced the so-called conversion experience. I was eight years old and I was at a Christian meeting. A man was saying that Jesus was knocking at the door of your heart and all you had to do was open it. I decided to take this step ... and actually felt Jesus taking over my life ... No emotional technique [was] used to bring me to a point of crisis. It was simple truth. Since then I have followed Jesus and he has answered my prayers faithfully ... He controls my life, and that can't be explained in naturalistic terms. God wanted to rule my life, he wanted me to accept his gift of eternal life and salvation. I wanted to accept his gift, and I did and I was rewarded for that decision ...
>
> All the decisions in my life are now handed over to God, and he decides because I know that his choice will be best. Without Jesus my life would be nothing, and there would be no purpose in living.

Or again:

> Experience of the Holy Spirit or Comforter. Timelessness, Unearthly Light. Expanding, vast, spaceless, Peace and Calm ... flowing over me like water. Totally unexpected, not called for ... this occurred twice, in the countryside ... and in prison, 'annihilated by the love of God' as Monica Furlong describes it.

This is seen as an act of 'Providence' and 'mercy' which has changed his life although he still has 'a weakness for the lusts of the flesh' but knows that 'love is far more real and important'.

In another case, no 'real' experience is recounted, but the 'testimony' is still there: 'I've prayed about things and definitely seen answers to my prayers ... God [has changed my life and] makes me feel overcome with joy.'

Other experiences which might be categorized as being more conventionally 'paranormal' also tended to have religious overtones. For example, this case of apparent clairvoyance by a mature woman respondent:

> for several months I felt deeply disturbed about my brother who lived away. I dreamt about him on several occasions. [Others assured me] that all was well [but] six months later I found out that at that exact time he had been going through great difficulties which he had wished to keep secret.

On another occasion: 'I was making a bed and in deep distress [and called upon God, and] immediately I had an experience that I cannot validly put into words but I felt ... tremendous energy ... I then began daily prayer, and have experienced this intensity two more times.' She goes on to say: 'I was an atheist before this experience.'

In another case, a respondent recounted that one night, about 12.30 a.m., she and a friend sat on a sea wall beneath the house of a dead poet who, at one time, was known to row a small boat in the vicinity. She goes on:

> Everything was silent, then suddenly we heard splashes [and] the sound of rowing, we glanced up and there was a white boat and a person sitting in it. The boat was positioned across the estuary near where some [other] friends sat ... we watched the boat for a while, but soon I became frightened ... We ran and asked them ... they had seen or heard nothing even [though] the boat [which had now gone] was near them.

This experience had in no way changed her life. She suspected that it might be explained naturalistically – as a mere product of hyper-imagination.

In yet another case of a mature male respondent, there are – in effect – claims to divinely given paranormal powers which include:

1. Numinous experiences associated with extreme danger, 'a strong sense of a Guardian Angel able to intervene physically to preserve my life'.
2. Clairvoyance experiences both in dreams and in the practice of palmistry, 'a gift which caused me to survive at work through many commercial upheavals'.
3. Visitation experiences in which the subject maintains that he was visited and spoken to by a friend at the time of her death elsewhere.

Again, all these experiences are attributed – either directly or by implication – to a divine facility or a divine intervention which 'was not sought but given'.

There is a spectrum of other reported experiences which range from the vaguely religious to 'feelings' that can hardly be dignified as paranormal. For instance: 'I was at ... choir practice when I heard footsteps behind me; when I turned there was nobody there and nobody else had heard any noise at all.' 'Another time, when I was upset, I felt as if there was somebody else in the room with me who was ... a comforting presence.' There is here the admission of a highly emotional state, but also the belief that these experiences were divinely given to make 'me less afraid of things that I cannot explain as both experiences have been benevolent'.

Other experiences were even more amorphous:

> In a house in a remote island ... in which I was working, if I was alone in the house, I often felt another 'presence'. This took the

form of a feeling – not a vision/apparition/ghost ... it was a friendly
feeling – nothing to be frightened of. I don't know [how to account
for this]. It has made me appreciate that there is more to life than
just what can be 'seen'.

Likewise, another respondent reports:

> On two occasions I have slept at a friend's house ... and awoken
> during the night feeling 'smothered in the darkness'. After a few
> seconds an intense feeling of panic and fright overwhelmed me to
> the point of feeling intensely sick ... I cannot call this experience
> paranormal, but I think that it indicates something ... [as] I am not
> affected in this way when staying in other unfamiliar places.

A similar range of experiences was also found among the polytechnic
students. Some of these were a little nebulous, but not without possible
significance, for example:

> My daughter aged two insisted on looking at a bird in a museum in
> a particular room. It could not be found until we undid a wooden
> door and there was a skeleton of a bird in a glass dome. She had
> never been there before, and could not have seen through the
> wooden door or even under it. This was the first of a few similar
> experiences.

The respondent adds that she tends to be wary of what her daughter
says – 'they are apt to be true ... !'

There was yet another case involving palmistry:

> In 1966 I had my palm read. The palmist said I would soon marry
> (though I had no plans to do so and had not met my future
> husband). The initials D and M were to be significant [and] I
> would have two children without 'breaking my back' ... In 1967 I
> married David Michael ... [and] I had two children by Caesarian
> section without the normal back-breaking labour.

The respondent saw nothing exceptional in this, and simply attributed
it to 'lucky guesses'.

Intuitive experiences of various kinds were particularly common:

> Once when my life was at a very low ebb, I had an experience of
> being 'spoken' to by an inner voice. It was a very calming revitaliz-
> ing experience. It changed by life and my inhibitions about death,
> as if ... there was no death, and with this ... there was a feeling of
> extreme brightness. It was like a rebirth – one had the feeling of
> being whole, clean, pure; like a newborn baby. The overall effect
> cannot be properly described, but I now feel that death is not the
> end. I believe it was some sort of spiritual awakening.

Other experiences straddle the borderline between possible clairvoyance and coincidence. 'I constantly have *déjà vu* – possibly every two

weeks. And I have dreams that came true.' The example then given seems relatively trivial:

> When I was a younger teenager I dreamt that I was sitting on an ancient Greek building with a friend, drinking a bottle of liquid of some sort. Last year I sat on the Acropolis in Athens with [a] friend [who] took a photo of me drinking a bottle of mineral water ... [this] reinforces views previously held [as] I have had many other similar experiences from early childhood to today.

Or to take a similar case: 'Last summer my father (who had been a hairdresser) died after a fairly long illness ... On the day of the funeral service (my 21-year-old daughter) was at home [and] experienced "thoughts" [to which she] "listened".' These 'thoughts' apparently co-incided almost exactly with the remarks of the Rector at the service who perhaps knowing that the deceased had originally wanted to be a priest – referred to hairdressers acting like priests at a confessional. For the respondent, 'It ... proved that something of the individual survives death'.

Other experiences were related which apparently concerned objective phenomena:

> Whilst living in a seventeenth-century cottage many inexplicable occurrences unnerved me to the point where I thought I was going either to leave ... or breakdown. 'Bangings', other noises ... baby – crying from a bedroom ... and many other 'happenings', I felt 'something' wanted me out of the house – I can't explain why. Eventually my husband and I separated [and] I did leave the house. Afterwards, I learnt that three previous tenants had left the property for similar reasons. Also an exorcism had been carried out by a local vicar in 1976 ... I was relieved to find that I hadn't been imagining these phenomena. I can't explain it ... but others put it down to spirits not at rest – two small children in nightwear had been seen by friends of mine.

The respondent asserted that this episode had changed her life, and that having once been a sceptic, she now believed in the 'supernatural'.

As with the college students, some experiences were interpreted in specifically religious terms. There were briefly recounted conversion experiences:

> [I had] a supernatural revelation ... of the Lord Jesus Christ at the moment of conversion. Not just an intellectual understanding or an emotional feeling of peace/elation but a spiritual 'awakening'. It has given my life a purpose, a direction, a hope of a life to come and changed attitudes, habits and outlook.

And claims to divine help: 'Prayers]are] answered every time a request [is] put forward. [Even] the healing of incurable problems.' This respondent maintained that she had been 'carried for a whole day [and] was put down again safely in my home'. It is not clear exactly what this means – whether it is to be taken literally or metaphorically for she adds, 'I then realized who had carried the burden and the weight of the day'. This was attributed to belief in Jesus Christ the Son of God who 'has taught me obedience and faithfulness'.

Faith was sometimes generated by a quite specific experience:

> Despite several operations and investigations during seven years of marriage, I was unable to conceive ... My mother told this to a [Roman Catholic] lady of strong religious conviction. She gave my mother a Catholic medal from the shrine of Our Lady of Walsingham. The instruction was that I was to hold the medal and pray to the Blessed Virgin for a child ... The lady said that she too would pray on my behalf. I had never met this lady, but I did as she instructed me. Seven weeks later my pregnancy was confirmed and I now have an eight-year-old son. Doctors and gynaecologists were unable to explain my pregnancy, which, medically, should have been impossible.
>
> I can't account for this in logical terms. I can only believe that some supernatural power intervened ... I have always believed in God, but now I believe that this God takes care of me, and that my life is mapped out already ... He guides my actions, and whatever happens is preplanned ... Furthermore, I now believe there must be something besides this life, and that my physical death will not be the end of me.

For this respondent faith was not generated and confirmed regardless of the contradictions inherent in the conclusions, that is, the problem of how life can be preordained *and* subject to intervention through prayer. But this is unperceived or disregarded in the light of the apparent 'miracle' of unexpected but joyful motherhood.

Although the majority of respondents made no claims to paranormal experience, the survey showed that most supported the *idea* or possibility of such experiences.

Tables 8.3 and 8.4 show certain significant differences. There is less agnosticism generally among the polytechnic students; at the same time they exhibit less conviction about the religious nature of these experiences and more faith in the capabilities of science to explain them. On the other hand, the college students are more sceptical about naturalistic explanations and more inclined towards the probability of a religious understanding of these phenomena.

Table 8.3 College students

	Strongly agree (%)	Slightly agree (%)	Slightly disagree (%)	Strongly disagree (%)	Don't know (%)
I think these experiences are much more common than we generally realize	16	66	–	7	7
I think these experiences are due to unrealized natural causes	12	41	23	12	12
I think people who have these experiences may have misunderstood what really happened to them	12	33	31	12	12
I think perhaps they are what some people term religious experiences	39	41	7	–	12
I think only specially gifted people have these experiences	–	4	16	72	8
I think things like this could happen to all of us if we looked out for them	4	64	16	12	4
I think science will one day have a complete explanation for such experiences	–	4	12	72	12
I think experiences like this show that there's another reality behind the world we see and feel	65	25	3	–	7
I don't think you have to be religious to have such experiences	62	25	6	–	7

Table 8.4 Polytechnic students

	Strongly agree (%)	Slightly agree (%)	Slightly disagree (%)	Strongly disagree (%)	Don't know (%)
I think these experiences are much more common than we generally realize	38	50	12	–	–
I think these experiences are due to unrealized natural causes	24	46	6	24	–
I think people who have these experiences may have misunderstood what really happened to them	23	35	13	29	–
I think perhaps they are what some people term religious experiences	30	36	6	23	5
I think only specially gifted people have these experiences	–	–	24	60	6
I think things like this could happen to all of us if we looked out for them	16	50	16	12	6
I think science will one day have a complete explanation for such experiences	–	23	43	29	5
I think experiences like this show that there's another reality behind the world we see and feel	46	33	11	5	5
I don't think you have to be religious to have such experiences	60	34	6	–	–

Conclusions

As we have seen, it has been hypothesized that for some an interest in
the paranormal might well be a substitute for religion, and that the
pursuit of possible paranormal experiences could take the place of what
are broadly termed 'religious experiences'. This does not seem to be
borne out of this research among students. Of course, not everyone
would make this distinction. For many, there are simply unusual (=
paranormal?) experiences, and religious experiences are just one form
of these phenomena. This study indicates that this is generally the
position of most of the polytechnic students whereas the college students would appear to favour a clear distinction between them. Religious
experience is to be distinguished from any other kind of experience. It is
characterized by identifiable phenomena, the conversion experience,
answers to prayer etc. The paranormal, on the other hand, is in another
category. It may be discounted altogether, or it may actually carry the
attribution of evil, some even regarding parapsychology as a kind of
dabbling with daemonic forces which are best left undisturbed.
Commonsensically, studies of the paranormal and religious studies would
seem to go together. Parapsychological investigation could be seen as a
possible evidential aid to religious conviction – something which might
provide confirmation for the notion of an other-worldly dimension. But
some see it rather as something separate which should be treated with a
certain reserve – even suspicion. This is possibly evidenced by the
different non-response rates which we have noted within the college
among those taking the New Testament Studies course. We all make
attributions of various kinds – it is difficult to see how we could
harmonize our experiences otherwise. And it is well attested that once
one has made this kind of attribution, confirming evidence, say, sensationalist accounts of bizarre occult practices, is not that difficult to find.
Not uncommonly one develops a guiding fiction for understanding the
intellectually discordant and the emotionally unusual, and once formed
this guiding fiction can be very resistant to change.

   Can paranormal and religious experiences be justly distinguished?
Paranormal experiences are, by definition, unusual, singular and spontaneous. Attempts to replicate them, as per the current vogue for
laboratory testing in parapsychology, ultimately ends in failure and
disappointment. The *idea* of the paranormal has an emotional appeal
but affords little intellectual satisfaction because its claims lend themselves neither to confirmation nor disconfirmation. To this extent it
cannot be effectively distinguished from more narrowly defined religious phenomena. Both are super-empirical. But, in experiential terms,

religious phenomena can be distinguished by virtue of their moral force, and their capacity for personality modification.

In the end, it all comes down to the nature and interpretation of belief. The polytechnic students showed a more open-minded attitude to the possibility of paranormal phenomena in the broader sense; on this the college students tended to be surprisingly dismissive. However, they exhibited a greater predisposition to believe in the narrower religious sense, even if there were sometimes strange inconsistencies between avowed beliefs and actual practices. Beliefs necessarily involve choices, but reality persistently restricts our freedom to choose, so we have to content ourselves with that which is left that we find most satisfying (Pruyser: 1974). The scientific world view tests the limits of our credulity and challenges our capacity for speculation about the 'true' nature of things. But the 'truth' still eludes us; there are still cognitive vacuua. So as William James once suggested (Roth: 1969), it is ultimately faith that creates the fact.

CHAPTER NINE

The Paranormal as an Intellectual Pursuit

The case for and against the legitimacy or validity of parapsychology is both long-standing and rather tortuous. Extreme critics dismiss the entire paranormal 'enterprise' as a gigantic confidence trick, few practitioners doubt that at the outer fringes it does shade into the occult and consequently lays itself open to charges of charlatanism and downright fraud. Such peripheral concerns are what Martin Gardner, a well-known critic, terms the 'fauna' of parapsychology which brings it into disrepute. The more tender-hearted are inclined rather to see parapsychology as a form of misperception – a well-meaning exercise in fatuity. While others – the informed sceptics – see it not as a science and certainly not as a superscience, but more as a kind of pseudo-science; a pretend operation which in its experimental activity apes the methods of real science but without its results. There is little doubt that parapsychologists would like their discipline – if such it can be called – to be accepted by the orthodox scientific community. But except for the sympathetic hearing given by a few practising scientists, there seems to be little hope of this at the present time.

Parapsychologists, by and large, are anxious to distance themselves from what they see as the unashamed materialism of so much natural science. The status of science is such that its materialistic stance is not easily questioned, and its applicatory effectiveness as technology has brought so many benefits to the world that its philosophical underpinnings tend to go unchallenged. Materialism as a doctrine maintains that we should be wary of the so-called subjective experience, and rely instead on that which is amenable to physical investigation. In general, materialism comes in three main guises:

1. With an emphasis on the primacy of *bio-chemical factors* in the study of systems.
2. As *psychological functionalism* which argues that a mental state should be defined in terms of the inputs and outputs of a system – a way of thinking that is particularly amenable to computer technology which, for some, is an analogue of the brain. Complementarily in Sociology and Social Anthropology functionalism is simply a

way of defining an institution or practice in terms of other institutions and practices, so a society or system is said to generate those that it needs – or deserves.

3. *Behaviourism* which certainly in its old-fashioned form argues for a crude stimulus–response model of the human system (see Carlton: 1995, pp. 60–66). Thus mental events are simply brain events – all of which makes interpretation of a thought or action not so much impossible as meaningless. Self-knowledge therefore becomes inexplicable. Feelings, desires, aspirations, hopes and so forth, are relegated to a scientifically unverifiable limbo. The mind is simply a construct; it is the brain that matters and alone is amenable to investigation.

The materialistic creed can be summed up in the words of Victor Stenger: 'whether we like it or not ... we are material beings composed of atoms and molecules, ordered by largely chance processes of self-organisation and evolution to become capable of complex behaviour associated with the notions of life and mind' (Stenger: 1995, p. 18). The problem for this kind of thoroughgoing materialist – at least, from a psychological point of view – is that he will have difficulty in explaining: *intentionality*, which is not understandable simply in terms of bio-chemical factors; *autonomy*, the ineradicable sense of self; and *awareness*, which is the consciousness of our own experience and the interpretive understanding of the experiences of others (see, for example, Madell: 1988). This being so, is the best place to look for empirical evidence of mind to be found in psychical research? Would the PSI phenomenon, for which there is no physical hypothesis, be the final vindication of the non-materialist position (Beloff: 1989)?

It is really a form of reductionism to insist that science – valuable as it is – will ever be able to express all the important facts of human functioning. Physics, in particular, is concerned with impersonal, mechanical forces which are only *in*directly related to the matter of *intention*. As Stephen Braude is keen to point out, the principles and equations of physics have their limitations. Useful as formal systems are for some states of affairs, they are inapplicable to others. So, for example, the properties of objects in curved space do not violate or falsify the principles of Euclidean geometry, they merely reveal that the system only applies to plane surfaces (Braude: 1986, p. 18). Some (for example, Cartwright: 1983) would go as far as to remind us that scientific laws are themselves approximations based on ideal cases involving oversimplified (i.e. single cause) boundary conditions. So much still lies outside the scientific domain.

The intriguing debate concerning what is a science and what is a pseudo-science is related to the question of exactly what constitutes a science, and this, in turn, hinges very much on the question of *plausibility*. Paranormal concerns are so *outré* that they probably require more evidential support than more orthodox scientific investigations. Therefore among parapsychologists there has been a marked tendency, as we have seen, to an increasing reliance on controlled laboratory experiments which, so it is hoped, will give the discipline greater scientific respectability. Any aspiring science is assessed by the recognized standards of scientific conventionality. All disciplines have their own 'reception systems', and the physical sciences are no exception. A reception system constitutes the criteria whereby one disciplines judges an alien or intrusive discipline to be worthy of consideration either for inclusion or simply of credence. Parapsychology, like the 'companion sciences' of psychology and sociology, makes implicit and explicit demands for recognition. But how does it fare?

Those who subscribe to the Rationalistic model of orthodox science which insists on empirical procedures of verification are understandably hesitant – if not actually scornful – about parapsychology in this respect, especially as parapsychologists insist that there are other intangible sources of knowledge. Parapsychologists find that the scientific establishment – by and large – is relatively impervious on this matter. They, on the other hand, are much more attracted to the Indeterminacy model of science which is more open to 'creative hypotheses' than the rigorous procedures of scientific orthodoxy. But whether this is really science or what parapsychologists think a science ought to be, is still a matter of contention (for a fuller discussion, see Carlton: 1995, pp. 66–73).

If we accept the capacity for falsification as one of the key factors in what constitutes a scientific statement, we could look at some phenomena which are purported to be paranormal such as *precognition*. Self-evidently the term denotes knowing something in advance. It is sometimes associated with prophecy and telling the future, and may be an ingredient in the seance experience, although this is usually thought of as being the province of rather suspect 'professionals'. Foreknowledge is often said to come in the form of an 'instinct', a 'feeling' or presentiment, and less commonly as a 'vision'. In short, it is an unusual kind of sensory perception of uncertain provenance which may be triggered by a sight, sound or some sort of impression – and this is just the subjective aspect of precognition. The objective corollary is that what is foreseen actually happens, not in the indefinite future, but quite specifically and unambiguously in the near future so that there can be no doubt as to the applicability of the experience.

The first thing we must ask is whether this is genuine foresight or an inspired speculation. Some prophecies such as those of, say, the famous eighth-century prophets (Amos and Hosea) were much more like reasonably shrewd guesses as to what would happen given the political situation obtaining at the time. It did not take much to anticipate the depredatory intentions of the aggressive Assyrians. What was important to the prophets was the sense that they must interpret the invasion in terms of divine judgement. There is also the all-purpose type prophecy of seers such as Nostradamus which are so generalized as to apply to a number of possible situations. These are not really the sorts of things that parapsychologists study, and they are certainly not what can be irrefutably regarded as precognition.

In parenthesis, there is a further – though indirect – relevant point regarding cause and coincidence. Take the true case of the fervently religious woman whose family was in desperate financial straits, yet was sure that somehow her faith would pull them through. A substantial bill arrived which was about to take them over the edge when, within no time at all, they received a cheque – a completely unanticipated rebate – for exactly the same amount as the bill. Was it coincidence, as most might suppose, or was it a reward for religious fidelity? The example may seem trivial, but it crops up time and time again concerning the problem of answers – or believed answers – to prayer. In this case, it was regarded as irrefutable evidence of divine blessing for those concerned, whereas for the observer it might be seen as just one of those fortuitous conjunctions of events. After all, for many there seem to be no certain answers to prayer, any more than for most, dreams do not come true.

Yet, having said this, there are some very odd occurrences. Jenny Randles, well known as a researcher into the paranormal, cites an instance from her own experience (Randles: 1996). One morning in March 1968, she awoke having had a dream about a paper mill, situated near a bridge, which was on fire. She noted the dream on her writing pad, and within 24 hours while on a sponsored walk this 'curious and precise scene [was] duplicated in reality'. The odds on such a coincidence are extremely high, so understandably for Mrs Randles precognition was the most reasonable explanation. As she points out, if this sort of thing was a very rare phenomenon, the sceptics would have a good case, but research has shown that precognition is probably the most common of all paranormal events.

Some particularly interesting examples of ostensible precognition have been related concerning: (1) the attempted assassination of Ronald Reagan, (2) the assassination of Anwar Sadat, and (3) the *Achille Lauro* incident (reported by Hearne: 1982). The percipient in all these cases was Barbara Garwell, a middle-aged housewife from the north of England. She had only an elementary education, is a practising Catholic and is self-confessedly superstitious. Cattell Personality Tests – admittedly a limited indicator – suggested that she was rather conservative and 'somewhat neurotic'. Independent testimony came from two sisters and a friend who provided confirmation of these dream accounts before the events actually occurred:

Case 1: three weeks before the attempt on President Reagan's life in March 1981, the percipient had a dream of a pock-marked actor (possibly Trevor Howard) getting out of a car and being shot by a uniformed German SS man. Reagan was, of course, a one-time actor, and John Hinckley his would-be assassin was a former member of a neo-Nazi group. However, the connection between the dream and the reality seems rather tenuous.

Case 2: again the percipient had a dream three weeks before President Sadat was killed in October 1981. The dream 'depicted' a stadium with a row of seated men in pin-striped suits. The men were said to be 'coffee coloured', and there was a sense that the setting was somewhere in the Middle East. Two soldiers were seen to go up to these men and shoot them with automatic weapons. This 'scene' was very close to the actual events, indeed the conjunction seems quite remarkable.

Case 3: yet again, a dream was reported three weeks before the incident concerned. The dream depicted a ship at sea, and two coffins were being lowered into the water. In the actual *Achille Lauro* incident two people died of heart attacks during a fire on board (another woman died who went overboard). But given that the percipient had two friends who were also going on a sea cruise, one of whom was not in good health, suggests that the dream may well have related to them, and not to the unfortunate victims on the *Achille Lauro*.

In the vast majority of cases of ostensible precognition, it is impossible completely to rule out the possibility of chance, coincidence or reasonable anticipation. Furthermore, there must be a vast number of instances where the 'prediction' goes unrealized. The entire phenomenon is difficult to test because there is a spontaneity about precognition which hardly lends itself to the colourless monotony of the laboratory experiment. In the three cases we have considered the claim is certainly unproven, although the Sadat incident does suggest that there was a genuine premonition. Nevertheless, critics are not convinced. They are quick to detect any possibility of a hoax, and this is just what happened in relation to the attempted assassination of Ronald Reagan. Four days after the incident American television broadcast a tape which was said to have been made three months before by Tamara Rand a well-known Los Angeles psychic. On the tape Rand 'predicted' that the President would be shot by a man answering the description of the would-be killer. Rand also gave the assassin's initials and foretold the approximate date of the shooting. On investigation it transpired that the tape had been prepared in Las Vegas 24 hours *after* the shooting, whereupon the networks shamefacedly admitted that it was 'probably a hoax'. Most of the television executives concerned had been genuinely bamboozled, but those who were complicit were duly exposed and one seriously contemplated suicide. Rand, surprisingly, did not really suffer from the exposé, and many saw it as a temporary aberration on her part. It remains a wonder that this sort of thing could happen in the first place. Are the public just too ready to accept the paranormal at face value (Frazier and Randi: 1986)?

However, as we have already seen, *one* genuine instance is enough to prove that there is such a thing as ESP. The alternative explanation that in modern society we have less time for fantasy, and that making rational judgements is considered far more important than 'trusting our feelings' (Randles: 1996, p. 187) is surely open to question. Indeed, it might be argued that although commerce and industry are based upon rational-legal principles, so much of modern culture is experientially orientated.

Sceptics are keen to point out that if ESP including precognition, telepathy and clairvoyance really works, why are not psychics making fortunes on the lottery, the stock exchange or some other lucrative form of gambling? Popular experiments have been done in this area, but – in the UK at lest – so far all have failed. Indeed, all sorts of 'mystics' have surfaced to provide the gullible with mathematical formulae, zodiacal signs and other esoteric nostrums for bringing good fortune, but to little avail. Yet there have been instances when people have *dreamed* of a series of lottery numbers and met with some success.

Debunking the paranormal has become something of a field sport for a number of writers and journalists. And there is no doubt that to some extent parapsychologists and camp-following psychics have contributed to their own suspect image by giving too many 'hostages to fortune'. This has been particularly so in the realms of spiritist/mediumistic activity and clairvoyance (see for example, Harris: 1986). The whole subject area has also been brought into some disrepute by the uninformed vaporizings of certain well-known personalities in the entertainment world who catch the public's attention simply because they are celebrities. New Age fauna, in particular, flourish because of the appeal of sensationalism and an ignorance of the work of serious researchers (see Gardner: 1988). It is perhaps little wonder therefore that interested and informed sceptics are proving such a thorn in the side of parapsychologists. The long-standing challenge of magician, James Randi, a founding member of the Committee for Scientific Investigation in Claims of the Paranormal (CSICOP) to pay $10 000 to anyone who can convincingly demonstrate any paranormal, occult or supernatural event under controlled conditions has not been successfully taken up. It is understood that through the Internet this has been boosted to $500 000 – but so far it has remained unclaimed. Randi, who has been involved in several court cases with Uri Geller, has set up an educational foundation in order to fund research that will look specifically at claims regarding the paranormal.

Magicians, in particular, are past masters at exposing misperception and fraud. From Harry Houdini, the escapologist, to 'The Amazing Randi' magicians and illusionists who, in keeping with professional honour, are loathe to reveal the secrets of their trade to outsiders, are only too willing to expose those whom they are convinced are deceiving the public. They have challenged the demonstrations of some of the most revered figures in the modern history of the paranormal including the PK 'expert' Nina Kulagina, a whole host of acclaimed mediums, and several more contemporary characters such as Uri Geller and Ted Serios who confounded many experts with his seeming ability to reproduce 'thought pictures' on film. But it should be noted that in very many of these cases, the magicians in question were only able to show how the paranormal effects *could* have been achieved, not whether that was how they actually *were* achieved.

Something else which has done nothing but potential harm to parapsychology are the well-meaning, quasi-scientific banalities of some of the research. Some years ago Francis Crick, Nobel prize-winner (with James Watson) for his work on the structure of DNA, wrote:

> The most striking thing about the work of the last thirty years on ESP has been its complete failure to produce any technique whatsoever which is scientifically acceptable ... Not one truly reproducible experiment has been devised although the record is thick with fakes and sloppy experimentation ... We must conclude either that the phenomenon does not exist or that it is too difficult to study by present methods. (Crick: 1973)

Extreme as this may seem to some, there is undoubtedly a great deal in what Crick says. The 'trade' is replete with spurious findings. For example, it is said to be possible to formulate certain kinds of testable hypotheses linking PSI with particular modes of behaviour. How is this done? Two researchers using the idea of 'cohesion' as an independent variable, hypothesized that 'PSI occurrences are more frequent between individuals whose relationships have been cooperative than they are between individuals who have been competitive'. Furthermore, they say that 'PSI occurrences are more frequent in egalitarian than in authoritarian groups'. This leads to a third unremarkable hypothesis that 'PSI occurrences are more frequent between people who like each other than between people who do not' (LeShan and Margenau: 1980). And so it goes on. Mind you, it is readily admitted that it is not easy to test these hypotheses as certain 'correction factors' must be introduced for bias and so forth. What is not so readily conceded is how highly dubious such an exercise was in the first place. Surely these enthusiasts are clutching at consolatory straws. Scientific authenticity is not achieved by having the mundane masquerading as academic truths.

Social Science too has made its own quizzical contribution to the study of the paranormal. In a now well-known text (Collins and Pinch: 1982), the psychic trade in general and the SPR in particular are questioned about their irrational absurdities. The text (*Frames of Meaning*) raises the age-old philosophical problem of objectivity, and concludes that there may be no such thing as *the* 'truth' only what is deemed to be true by social consensus. In other words, there are many frames of meaning, several rival paradigms, some of which will become dominant in their time and will then be superseded by others. The whole approach is extremely relativistic and, in a special sense, idealist in its orientation. For the sociologists in question rationality is what society considers is rationality. There will always be incommensurable logics, different ways of seeing and interpreting the world, and the paradigm that is accepted will be that which society finds most acceptable at the time. Truth is social truth, and social truth is subject to negotiation. Natural science is now the dominant paradigm, and because scientific authority has been socially sanctioned, the paranormal is automatically excluded.

This thesis has to be set against the work of more sympathetic social scientists. For example, the psychologist, Hans Eysenck, not the kind of person to receive pseudo-scientists gladly, had an open mind about parapsychology. Many years ago he wrote:

> Unless there is a gigantic conspiracy involving [many] University departments all over the world, and several hundred highly respected scientists in various fields, many of them originally hostile to the claims of psychical researchers, the only conclusion the unbiased observer can come to must be that there does exist a

small number of people who obtain knowledge existing either in other people's minds, or in the outer world, by means as yet unknown to science. (Eysenck: 1957, pp. 131–2)

Recently, the whole research enterprise was given a considerable boost by reports from Princeton University that experiments had produced 'startling evidence that the human mind can exert paranormal control over objects ... [and has] confounded hardened sceptics' (*Sunday Telegraph*, 16 November 1997). These tests have been carried out by Professor Robert Jahn and others using electronic random number generators, and have apparently demonstrated to their satisfaction that PK does exist. The carefully controlled experiments which have been conducted over a period of 12 years with more than a 100 subjects have shown that thought alone can produce scores well above expectation. The Jahn team insists that the chances of this happening fortuitously are impossibly remote. Princeton now has the largest datasets on what they regard as the most systematic experiments of this kind ever performed.

Should one thus be impressed by modern experimental methods which try to test the reality of ESP and PK? Critics are still unsure. Parapsychologists, are now especially interested in altered states of consciousness, in dreams, distance-viewing and the like, and employ modern techniques such as the Ganzfeld (really a sensory deprivation device for inducing possible paranormal experiences), computer-based random number/event generators, and other devices which smack of technological modernity but which still do not produce the 'proof' that researchers are looking for. After all, extraordinary claims require extraordinary evidence. Sceptics argue that it is all delusion, and that too many are suffering from what Paul Kurtz has called the 'transcendental temptation', a kind of yearning for the magical, a hunger for 'deeper mysteries' (Kurtz: 1986). He argues that this urge lies deep in the human psyche and subverts critical judgement. Thus it leads us to accept unsubstantiated myths and with them both religious and paranormal belief-systems.

A similar proclivity is more than hinted at in one of astrophysicist Carl Sagan's last books. In this text (Sagan: 1996) which is effectively a *cri de coeur* on behalf of science, he argues – contrary to some popular objections – that scientific thinking is necessary to safeguard our democratic institutions. He points to the widespread ignorance of scientific thought throughout the ages. In doing so, he ranges widely over some of the subjects of our present discussion such as witchcraft and similar crazes, and pours scorn on many present-day 'demons' such as the fashionable occult, spiritism, alien abduction and the like. But he is not out to promote crude scientific materialism, and refutes the allegation that science destroys spirituality. Like Albert Einstein, he recognizes that we are merely on the fringes of understanding what the world is all about. As Einstein himself once said, 'All our science, measured against reality, is primitive, and childlike – and yet it is the most precious thing we have'.

Excursus: The Phenomena of Hauntings and Apparitions

This brief discussion is not just about the objective reality of ghost and poltergeist phenomena (which should perhaps be distinguished) but is also concerned with the *subjective belief* in such occurrences which is interesting in itself. If apparitions of various kinds are entirely subjective and only exist in the minds of those who perceive them, as many – perhaps most – suppose, then one would expect their forms to differ with both the culture and historical epoch in which they appear. For example, there is some evidence to suggest that the eighteenth-century 'Age of Reason' was not a good time for ghosts, and that for a while the phenomenon went into eclipse. Research indicates that variations do occur, but there are certain invariant features, and these indicate that the phenomena may be, at least, partly independent of the percipients.

Stories of apparitions, like so many psychic phenomena, have been with us since early history. And many more recent reports come from absolutely reputable sources. But even so, such sources may still be mistaken for a whole variety of reasons. Again, we are back with the problem of possible or actual misperception. The early – though still influential – psychologist, William James, suggested some useful distinctions between illusion, delusion and hallucination. He classified an *illusion* as false perception, and gave the example of the 'movement' experienced by a passenger on a train leaving the station when all stationary objects visible through the window gave him the sensation of moving in the opposite direction. A *delusion*, on the other hand, he regarded as a false opinion about a matter of fact such as when a mentally deranged person thinks he or she is someone other than he or she is. This too can involve perception, but does not have to. In contrast, a *hallucination* is a mistaken mental image, and many would class ghosts as coming within this category.

Among the many research reports issued on the question of apparitions, one of the most notable was that produced by an American sociologist, Professor Hornell Hart, and his associate, entitled the 'International Project for Research on ESP Projection'. This was extensively debated and published as 'Six Theories about Apparitions' (*Proceedings of the SPR*, 1953–56, Vol. 50, pp. 153–239) and can be summarized as five alternative hypotheses:

1.   Apparitions are mental hallucinations created by percipients in response to directly or indirectly received telepathic impulses.
2.   Apparitions are idea-patterns produced currently or very recently

by the subconscious levels of the percipient with or without the assistance of the apparition (appearer).

3. Apparitions are 'etheric images' created currently or in the past by 'some mental act'.

4. The occultist hypothesis which holds that apparitions consist of the astral or etheric bodies of the appearers (which have a time as well as a physical dimension) complete with clothing and accessories.

5. The spiritualist hypothesis that apparitions are indeed manifestations of the spirits of the departed.

(For a fuller discussion see MacKenzie: 1983, ch. 2).

The 'trade' tends to distinguish between hauntings and apparitions. Hauntings seem to be characterized by some degree of persistence, perhaps over a considerable period such as those said to occur in certain old Cambridge colleges. Apparitions, by contrast, seem to be one-off affairs. At least, this is how the terms are used, although in practice there has to be a certain amount of blurring at the margins. Poltergeists, on the other hand, are regarded as a separate category; they are not 'seen', but are evidenced by the disturbance they cause. Some years ago a pair of very reputable researchers studied the characteristics of 500 reported hauntings, with and without apparitions, which were compiled from already published sources (Gauld and Cornell: 1979). These were therefore both apparition and poltergeist cases, and were analysed by features (house-centred, nocturnal, voices, cold breezes and so forth), and were grouped into clusters. Most of the cases were either in the nineteenth century (38 per cent) or the twentieth century (30 per cent), and mainly they were taken from European countries. This was compared with a more recent study by Carlos Alvarado and Nancy Zingrone (1995) which hypothesized that cases *with* apparitions would display a higher frequency of features, and might therefore indicate intelligence and intention. These predictions were not confirmed although, within this group, there was a higher frequency of disturbance phenomena.

A haunting case which has become the subject of much controversy among the paranormal-oriented community is the Borley Rectory phenomenon. This case has been reviewed and re-reviewed in the pages of the appropriate literature, and is still without resolution. Borley Rectory in Essex has been cited as 'Britain's most haunted house'. This reputation was founded largely on the work of one of Britain's most suspect psychic investigators, Harry Price, sometimes – not always complimentarily – known as 'the ghost buster'. Price, as his sobriquet suggests, was something of a sensation-seeker (it did little for his reputation as a researcher when he claimed to have discovered a mongoose that appeared from time to time in the Isle of Man which could speak six languages!). He was mainly responsible for promoting the Borley image in a successful book published in 1940. Yet, as one writer asserts, what actually happened at Borley 'looks like an inextricable tangle of fact, fantasy and possible fraud ... the whole affair typifies not only the perennial difficulties of research ... but also the fury that can be generated among investigators' (Haynes: 1982, p. 147).

Borley Rectory was built in 1863, and as early as 1886 there were stories going round that it was haunted. Its original incumbent was followed by his son, also a clergyman, who claimed that he had seen an apparition of his mother in the garden. His four sisters too said that they had seen an image of a nun, and it was his successor, the Reverend Eric Smith, who became so worried by various phenomena that he contacted – of all publications – the *Daily Mirror* which, in turn, got in touch with Harry Price (not to be confused with Professor H.H. Price, a distinguished scholar and member of the SPR). The next occupants of the house, the Foysters, also began to report strange phenomena, knockings, bells ringing and even 'spirit writings'. Price again visited the rectory, and suspected this time that it was possibly a fraud perpetrated by Mrs Foyster. Once she heard of this she denied everything and refused permission for further visits, although there is now some evidence that she was given to fantasy and deceit (Wood: 1992). Two years after the Foysters moved out in 1935, Price moved in for a year and advertised for investigators to come and see what they made of things. The phenomena continued, but in 1939 the place burned down, in accordance – so it is said – with the 'spirit's' prediction.

Price died in 1948 and remains to this day an enigmatic figure (Banks: 1996). Later, in the 1950s, three members of the SPR published a well-researched investigation of the matter. They came to the conclusion that Price may have faked much of the evidence, but in what was an altogether damming report, there was a grudging admission that there just might have been *some* truth behind Price's claims. It became such an issue within the hallowed halls of the SPR that another examination of the evidence was conducted in 1965 by Robert Hastings. His conclusions, which were published four years later, largely exonerated Price of fraud. The case has rumbled on with articles, for and against, still being written from time to time but without any unambiguous resolution.

Despite all kinds of well-attested evidence to the contrary, there is a great deal of informed scepticism about hauntings. Indeed, some of the writers closely associated with CSICOP have actually spoken of 'fighting the war against superstition' (Baker and Nickell: 1992, p. 11). Yet even the most virulent critics are patently fascinated with the paranormal if only to debunk the claims of its 'believers'. They have actually referred to joining the paranormalists as a 'disease of the mind for which there is neither an antidote nor a cure' (ibid.: p. 64). Even as they make derogatory remarks, critics are often still keen to show parapsychologists how it should be done. Some write as though all one needs are the right investigatory techniques, and all would be clear. But it is not difficult to infer from their work that there is a vestigial suspicion that there might just be something there, after all. Opponents are therefore often divided in their thinking between those who appeal for critical open-minded investigation, and those who feel that the whole enterprise should be summarily dismissed as worthless.

Scepticism is heightened when oft-cited evidence is underminded. When it comes to buttressing their arguments, parapsychologists refer to their cache of favourite cases, particularly so when it comes to hauntings and apparitions. Though, to be fair, some of the harshest critics are the parapsychologists themselves. One of the most famous ghost stories in the archives is that of the apparitions said to have been witnessed by two ladies in the park at Trianon in France. On 10 August 1901 a Miss Moberly and a Miss Jourdain claimed to have seen a 'sketching lady' whom they identified as Marie Antoinette. The Queen last visited the park in 1789, the same year as the outbreak of the French Revolution which eventually claimed the lives of her and her husband, Louis XVI. Afterwards, the ladies gave slightly different versions of their 'adventures', and took the trouble to research their subject which has since been written up in books, journals and magazines. It has, needless to say, been treated with some reserve by the professionals, one writer going so far as to suggest that we 'relegate the Ghost of the Trianon to the limbo of those fictional ghosts which so thrilled our Victorian and Edwardian ancestors but which carry little conviction today' (Coleman: 1988).

Another case that appeared to be well authenticated, mainly because of the unimpeachable credentials of the percipient, concerns the ghost of C.S. Lewis, the academic and writer. The clergyman and author, Dr J.B. Phillips, claimed to have 'seen' C.S. Lewis, with whom he had been slightly acquainted, twice after his death in November 1963. But his dating of the incidents is uncertain, there is some doubt in his accounts as to which month and even which *year* they took place. Some of us would have liked to believe that here at last was an unassailable case, but alas ...

However, despite all the doubts and reservations, there is a residue of cases that still defies adequate explanation. Admittedly, many of these are anecdotal and have never been – perhaps cannot be – properly investigated, but they are nevertheless intriguing and involve both pre-cognition and retrocognition. Take for instance, the purportedly true incident recounted by Anthony Hippisley Coxe which he refers to as his favourite ghost story (Hippisley Coxe: 1973, p. 12). It begins, un-exceptionally, with a navy lieutenant who, having spent much of his life overseas, decided to retire and settle down with his wife in the country. While he was away, his wife had frequently dreamed of her ideal home, and this became something of a family joke. As they set off to visit one particular property on the house agent's list, his wife was able to describe the route, although neither had been there before. And when they approached the house she immediately recognized it as the house in her dreams. As the agent showed them over the house, the wife was able to make all kinds of comments on the history of the property which turned out to be entirely correct including the fact that the house was said to be haunted. The couple bought the house, and some time afterwards the wife met the agent who asked her if she liked her new home. She said that she and the children were delighted, but they were sorry not to have seen the ghost, whereupon the agent replied, 'I didn't think they would, *you* are the ghost – I've seen you here many times'. (As a postscript to this I might add that I know a person who had a similar experience of this kind. She dreamt of the house and village where she was due to take a holiday, but on finding that it was exactly like her dream, thought that it was all just too creepy to stay, and went on elsewhere.)

Attempts have been made to investigate experimentally whether or not it was possible to 'facilitate' apparitions. One such experiment which again demonstrates how parapsychologists try to give a pseudo-scientific gloss to their work was carried out at the University of Nevada. Seven subjects were required to gaze into a mirror in a dimly lit room while 'aspects of the local environment and physiological parameters were monitored' in the hope that they would experience something unusual. But nothing lifelike happened, except 'mild apparitional expe-riences'. These turned out to be no more than 'feeling the presence of deceased persons and animals'. There were, however, some equally mild physiological changes detected, and it was thus unsurprisingly surmised that there was some interaction between mental states and the physical environment. The researchers admitted that they still could not deter-mine whether phantasms were fact or fantasy. The answer, they concluded with some understatement, 'appears to be more complicated than they had originally thought' (*JSPR*, 61, (843), pp. 65–7, 1996).

The close cousin of the ghost is, of course, the poltergeist. The activity of the poltergeist is said to be person centred rather than place

centred, as with a haunting. It is also an activity which tends to continue only briefly, whereas ghosts may make themselves known over a
period of time (Randles: 1996, p. 162) – but the literature suggests that
this can only be a vague generalization. Poltergeists must though come
into a different category from ghosts, because unlike apparitions they
do seem to leave clear physical evidence of their presence. The problem
for researchers is what exactly causes the reported disturbances? Are we
dealing with some post-mortal phenomenon, or a paranormal (PK)
effect of some psychological condition, or simply the antics of
mischevious children? In theory, of course, it could be various combina-
tions of all three such as in the famous Enfield case (Playfair: 1980).

Poltergeist activity – or what has been construed as poltergeist or
daemonic activity – has been with us for a very long time. It was not at
all unusual, given the nature of much poltergeist activity, to attribute
such acts to malevolent spirits. Such an interpretation can obviously be
linked to the common belief in vengeful ancestors in some tribal societies and, of course, to witchcraft itself. Poltergeist hauntings have been
reported with varying degrees of reliability and exorcisms of 'evil spirits'
still take place and appear to work, but what precisely happens in these
cases is still not known. It is said that on some occasions poltergeist
activity ceases simply on the command of the percipient. It is even
reported that some poltergeists will play 'games' with the percipients, as
in one case in South Wales where 'the alleged poltergeist apparently
synchronized its own use of missiles with those thrown by witnesses'
(reported by Fontana: 1996, pp. 385–402).

Because the evidence of disturbances is reasonably clear, parapsychologists – once they have eliminated the possibility of human agencies
– are often prepared to admit that some form of human PK might be at
work (which would still be classified as paranormal), but would be very
hesitant about attributing these phenomena to discarnate agencies. What
many eminent professionals are especially loathe to do is to see this
often otherwise inexplicable activity as evidence of the survival hypothesis (note the somewhat acrimonious debate in JSPR, 53, (800), 1985,
pp. 87–100).

Not only are there refluent themes in parapsychological literature,
but there are also many oft-repeated cases. Sometimes they are rehashed
for now popular book collections, at other times re-reviewed to prove
some particular point. It is therefore refreshing for the non-professional
observer to discover a survey of some 200 previously unpublished cases
of apparitional experiences of 'our own time' (Rae-Ellis: 1990). The
problem yet again is that so many have no supporting testimony – but
then this is usually in the nature of things. Such phenomena rarely wait

to be announced. Many of these cases have impressed critics enough for them to be pronounced genuine, or probably so, certainly by the criteria laid down in Tyrell's classic text (Tyrell: 1953). Concerning poltergeists, the 'score' is similar. An acknowledged researcher, William Roll, estimates in a survey of 116 cases that about one-third are genuine, i.e. due to psychokinetic energy (hence paranormal), about one-third fraudulent, and the remaining third he regards as yet unexplained and perhaps inexplicable, which takes us back whence we began. Perhaps the late J.B.S. Haldane, a biologist, was right when he said that his suspicion was that 'the universe is not only stranger than we suppose, but stranger than we *can* suppose' (quoted in Boslough: 1993, p. 35).

Postscript: The Paranormal and the Quest for Meaning

It is probably true to say that all of us – at one time or another – experience a strange *sense of finitude*. A kind of wonder tinged with despondency about our place in the cosmos; an incomprehension about our role in the order of things. Our first reaction may be to assert that it makes no real difference. Even those of us who are most aware of our incapacities and constraints are reluctant to see them as limiting factors. We can resort to well-tried functional alternatives, faith in science, political systems and the like, but ultimately we may see these 'solutions' as mere delusions. Much as we try, we are ultimately defeated by our own limitations.

We can, of course, try to hide from those limitations. Freud, for example, maintained that some people avoid neuroses by allying themselves with religion which for them becomes a source of personal consolation. Similarly the American psychologist, Abraham Maslow, also noted that some individuals adopted a religious frame of reference to satisfy their 'security needs'. There is little doubt that some people can find a sense of consolation – some might add, refuge – in religious and similar communities. But does this mean – contra Maslow – that they defer or even deny personal development?

Acceptance of our limitations, on the other hand, often brings with it the search for a sense of purpose. In religious terms, this means an attempt to link oneself to an ultimate principle, an eternal *raison d'être*. Personal meaning is achieved through faith and commitment. Alternatively, acceptance can have a humanistic focus, in which case we are compelled to make our own meanings. Truth is not only there to be discovered, it is also humanly constructed and imposed on the ongoing flux of experience. We endow the world with values, and life only has the purpose we give it. There is, however, another possibility – a kind of compromise position. We can choose from a menu of secular alternatives, a 'way of salvation' that appeals to the emotions and the intellect. For some – a tiny minority – this is to take comfort from an engagement with the paranormal. This can involve belief in phenomena outside the normal parameters of human experience, yet not necessarily of supramundane origin, but which are actually part of the mundane world which we do not as yet understand. To this extent they can be accurately described as paranormal.

This division was reflected in a 1998 poll conducted for the *Daily Mail* in which 1 000 respondents were each interviewed for two hours. The results indicated a decline in religious belief, but showed that 63 per cent 'believed in the paranormal, that is, phenomena that cannot be explained by science'. Some 64 per cent said they believed in psychic powers, 38 per cent in ghosts, rather fewer in poltergeists, and 29 per cent in alien visitations. Opinions are hopelessly divided on the question of why people are drawn to such ideas, especially as it is claimed by some researchers (for example, Professor Wiseman of the University of Hertfordshire) that *fewer* people now claim to have had any *personal* experience of the paranormal. Almost certainly this fascination with the paranormal has been fostered by the media, especially television, which presents these phenomena as a form of entertainment. Only very rarely are programmes presented which give them even a hint that the subject has been approached with any degree of intellectual rigour. Was it not G.K. Chesterton who once suggested that the opposite of believing in something was not to believe in nothing, but to believe in *anything*?

So where can the study of the paranormal go from here? The beliefs themselves – or variants of them – will continue to exist; it is very doubtful if science will ever be able to explain everything. Perhaps, as Emile Durkheim once suggested, life cannot wait so belief is likely to pass science and complete it prematurely. No, it is the *study* of the paranormal that is in question. Has parapsychology any future, especially in its institutional forms? Debate is healthy, but the acrimony that one sometimes detects among the ranks of the *cognoscenti* hardly bodes well for the 'trade'. The divisions, as we have seen, take many forms. The old guard (survivalist) school versus the more agnostic new guard; the narrow experimentalists versus the experientialists (those who would put more emphasis on spontaneous experience); the human agency ESP/PK supporters versus the discarnate agency advocates.

As long ago as 1987 in an address given to the SPR, one of its most active though disenchanted members, Dr Susan Blackmore, was arguing that psychical research had failed to resolve its many controversies, and had been unable to establish itself as a respected area of scientific enquiry. She went on to contend that people were still asking the same fundamental questions that puzzled the society a hundred years ago, and she laid much of the blame on the vain search for the elusive concept of PSI which she felt directly and indirectly affected research into many other substantive areas of parapsychology (Blackmore: 1988). A year or so later, Dr Blackmore reported on a survey she had done of 38 leading parapsychologists and sceptics which, she claimed, again showed how belief in PSI had decreased especially among those who had actually 'worked in the field'. The respondents were chosen on the basis of recent publications, and even the sceptics admitted that better research and more convincing theory might persuade them otherwise (Blackmore: 1989).

Similar doubts had already been raised by one of Britain's most eminent parapsychologists, Professor D.J. West, who deplored the fact that so many learned journals were either unwilling or actually opposed to publishing any articles on psychical research. In reviewing the losses and gains of parapsychology he admitted that despite its refined experimental techniques the discipline was not greatly advanced. At the same time, he conceded that many researchers were now less than convinced of the validity of the 'dramatic marvels' (mediumistic displays and so forth) of former days (West: 1987). Today, parapsychology is more restrictive in its concerns, and to some extent those concerns have changed over time. But has it gained in precision as some of its practitioners claim? Some professionals, as we have seen, take the view that the paranormal incidents/behaviour are essentially unpredictable and transient, and outside laboratory control. Others see them as special gifts or manifestations associated with specific conditions or particular people – a kind of you-cannot-all-be-Serios approach. If so, possibly these conditions can be reproduced so as to test the phenomena in question, as in seances or in specially constructed experiments. But has parapsychology profited from moving away from the possibility of a spiritual dimension in its pursuit of the paranormal? Is the will to believe in something 'beyond' just a self-comforting myth, or is it based upon some inexplicable yet persistent sense of the eternal which all peoples seem to have, and which some parapsychologists try to corroborate and identify.

It is known that both the Russians and the Americans have spent vast sums in testing – or trying to test – certain paranormal phenomena. The Central Intelligence Agency (CIA), for instance, has been particularly interested in 'remote viewing' experiments (see Morehouse: 1996). There have been some very exciting results reported from the Stanford Research Institute where some time ago one subject claimed that he could see a 'ring' around Jupiter similar to those surrounding Saturn. He was laughed out of court by the astronomical élite, but two years later the spacecraft Voyager 1 established it as fact. Another account to emerge from the CIA files was that of Police Commissioner Price who 'saw' a Soviet nuclear research centre, and described a 60-ft diameter globe as part of a beam weapon device. Three years later an American spy satellite was able to confirm the existence of the research laboratory and also the huge globe which was its main component (*JSPR*, **61**, (847), pp. 391–7, 1997).

Yet impressionistically convincing as such incidents may seem, they too are not without their critics. This has become a bone of contention especially in connection with the related and fascinating matter of 'psychic sleuths'. Particularly open to question is Colin Wilson's claim that there are those who can merely be shown a crime-related object (a piece of clothing, a comb or whatever) and use their 'extraordinary psychic powers to solve a crime' (Wilson: 1984). Again this issue turns on two questions: have any persons purported to have extrasensory powers actually been successful in solving cases? And is some kind of ESP the best explanation for what has occurred? The standard sceptical explanation for alleged successes in this field is that the sensitives are only able to offer vague highly generalized accounts of, say, where the body of a person assumed to have been murdered is now hidden. Then once the situation has been discerned, there is a retroactive interpretation which favours the psychic. The Centre for Scientific Anomalies Research (CSAR) project in Michigan reported in 1984 that no conclusive evidence could be adduced for the psychic sleuth phenomenon, although some investigators wished to reserve judgement on a few cases. Even less promising was the series of tests carried out earlier by the Los Angeles Police Department's Behavioural Science Section. Here controlled experiments were conducted with 12 psychics who were asked to look at the evidence from four crimes. Little useful information came out of this, and investigators concluded that so-called sensitives were no better than the police in making plausible guesses (Hoebens and Truzzi: 1987).

Sadly, for those who would like to be able to endorse psychic sleuthing practices, there have been reports which have turned out to be either spurious or misleading. The classic text on such cases (Tabori: 1974) relates details of a number of incidents in which fraud was exposed. More recently there have been other collections of cases of a suspect nature. One such case is that of Dutch psychic, Marinus Dykshoorn who was said to have solved an incident of theft in Germany while still in Holland. He was said also to have identified the thief and given the precise location of the booty. It was reported by the media as a spectacular achievement, but subsequently the German police flatly denied the story and insisted that the case had been solved by normal police methods (Hoebens and Truzzi: 1987). Professionals in crime detection are very divided on this issue, yet despite the uncertainties of psychic detection, some police departments have shown a lively interest in the technique. Marcello Truzzi, himself an eminent academic and interested sceptic, admits to having correspondence with police who have commended the work of psychics especially in long ongoing homicide cases. Extraordinary achievements have been reported in all sorts of areas of experience (such as the American doctor who could identify a piece of music simply by looking at the grooves on the record – a feat later verified by the quizzical James Randi). But whether these are attributable to *extra*sensory powers or to, as yet, little understood *sensory* powers is still uncertain.

In a more recent investigation, J. Nickell, a former magician now turned academic, organized a task force of 11 researchers from different disciplines to look into the whole issue of psychic sleuthing. They looked at the work and claims of a number of well-known American psychics, but came to no affirmative conclusions (Nickell: 1994). The first British attempt to evaluate the same phenomenon was carried out in 1994 by R. Wiseman, D. West and R. Stemman (*JSPR*, 61, (842), pp. 34–45, 1996). It was a small-scale study in which they investigated three psychics, and used three students as a control group. The subjects were asked to comment on three solved cases of homicide. They were given objects relating to the crimes and then presented with question-naires containing 18 statements and asked to select six which they believed (or sensed) to be true of each crime. The results showed that the psychics' scores were no better than those of the students, and that neither group performed above chance levels. Curiously, when each group was 'debriefed' and told about the true nature of each crime, the students readily admitted that they had done rather badly, but the psychics were defensive, and rationalized that they had not done so badly at all.

Further large-scale work carried out in the USA came to similar conclusions. A survey of police departments in the 50 largest cities in America revealed that 65 per cent never use psychics, and that where they are used they have tended to hinder rather than help the investiga-tions (Sweat and Durm: 1993). The investigators were keen to counter sensationalist claims in popular magazines which implied that psychic sleuthing was the new big thing in the art of detection (for example, articles in *McCall's* October 1987 'Clairvoyant Crime Busters' and in February 1993 'Can Psychics See what Detectives can't?'). Almost all the Departmental Chiefs interviewed who had used or had been contacted by psychics were extremely doubtful about their usefulness, but had often resorted to 'sleuthing' of this kind either as a last resort or at the request of the families of the victims concerned. Such responses have been echoed by other investigators. During the Atlanta child murders, one psychic, Dorothy Allison, is said to have just 'ridden around in a big limousine ... for three days' and then gone home. During that time she gave the police 42 names of a possible killer – all of them wrong

(Gordon: 1987). In fact in the Atlanta child murders (1979–81) some hundreds of psychics offered their services, but none came up with anything closely resembling the right answers. Perhaps psychic sleuthing should always be the last investigative tool. In another well-documented case, a psychic named John Catchings was involved, but it is reported that 'All in all ... Catchings' visit was a disappointment. He provided nothing specific, only a few impressions which he admitted reservations about' (Stowers: 1986, p. 195). Catchings, however, claimed that in his career as a psychic he had located 12 bodies and brought about the arrest of 13 people, although he also admitted that this was done in conjunction with the use of 'common sense'. More to the point, some law enforcement officers said that they felt his contributions had been 'significant'.

Other cases have yielded similar results. The established psychic Peter Hurkos who, it was claimed, had 'solved' the terrible Boston Strangler case in which 13 women were killed between June 1962 and January 1964 by Albert DeSalvo (found stabbed to death in his prison cell in November 1973) has been shown to have done no such thing. Nor were the claims made for him by Norma Lee Browning (*The Psychic World of Peter Hurkos*) over the Sharon Tate killings in August 1969 any better. The information given to the police by Hurkos concerning these murders committed by the 'Manson family' was said to be not merely useless but hopelessly incorrect. Interestingly, on very rare occasions, the self-proclaimed psychic will prove to be the chief suspect. In a case of a sexual attack on a woman in Staten Island, New York, a man who said he had 'psychic visions' volunteered information to the police that only the offender could have known, and – rightly or wrongly – he was convicted of attempted murder.

Obviously the case for or against parapsychology cannot stand or fall simply on the issue of psychic detection, but this can act as one yardstick whereby we might determine something of the future of the discipline. Is it something worth pursuing, or is it all just a waste of time? It seems fairly clear that on the question of the validity or otherwise of psychic detection the jury is still out. There seems to be some evidence both ways, although by and large the critics appear to have the stronger case. It could, of course, be true that where psychics have given information to the police which is only generally or marginally relevant, the psychic may rationalize after the case has been solved that their contribution has been of some significance. This happened in the case of the notorious serial killer, Ted Bundy, in Florida. A psychic named Ann Gehman claimed to have helped the police with information, but this led neither to the location of a victim nor to the arrest of Bundy himself (he was actually apprehended by chance in much the same circumstances as Peter Sutcliffe, the 'Yorkshire Ripper', by a routine police check on a car). In this kind of situation it is always possible for the psychic to chalk up the giving of highly generalized information as one more success (Rowe: 1993).

It will be seen that much of the critical evidence concerning psychic detection and sundry other paranormal activity emanates from CSICOP which is itself associated with the *Skeptical Enquirer* and Prometheus Books. The investigations of their contributions are not Molotov cocktail attacks, but scholarly – if sometimes a little snide – attempts to get at the truth. They look not only at the details of particular claims, but also question the intellectual underpinnings of the whole parapsychological enterprise. There is the implication, however, in some critical literature that 'believers' are somewhat ingenuous, and are prepared to accept at face value any apparently confirmatory evidence no matter how uncertain it may be. This is much too sweeping as a judgement. A relatively recent study of 60 subjects (mostly students) at the University of Adelaide to test this found that although there was a definite correlation between superstitiousness and modest intellectual ability, there was no correlation between low intellectual ability and belief in the paranormal (Thalbourne and Nofi: 1997).

A parallel problem for 'believers', especially those who are academics, is the reluctance of their fellows to accord them – or at least their beliefs – any scientific credibility. But then the orthodox scientific community can be very dismissive of any views that are not in keeping with scientific orthodoxy. Note, for instance, the case of Dr Dean Radin who was recently dismissed from his post at the University of Nevada largely because his work of a parapsychological nature in the university's Consciousness Research Laboratory did not meet with the approval of his academic superiors. This applies as much to fellow scientists as those on the heterodox fringes of academia. Materialism is as much a faith as any other ideology. The two sides should be prepared to examine their common ground. Such confrontational posturings do little for either cause. Those who feel that the very idea of paranormal phenomena is nonsense and see any kind of development in this area as a 'pernicious virus' (*Independent*, 26 December 1996) should perhaps heed the prediction of Professor H.H. Price that it is the timidity of our hypotheses not their apparent extravagance that will evoke the derision of posterity.

Bibliography

Alcock, J. (1981), 'Psychology and Near Death Experiences', in K. Frazier (ed.), *Paranormal Borderlands of Science*, Buffalo, NY, Prometheus Books.

Almeider, R. (1992), *Death and Personal Survival: The Evidence for Life after Death*, Lanham, MD, Rowman & Littlefield.

Alsop, S. (1989), *Whispers of Immortality*, London, Regency Press.

Alvarado, C. (1985), 'Review of Miracles (D.S. Rogo)', *JSPR*, 53.

Alvarado, C. (1986), 'ESP During Spontaneous Out-Of-Body Experiences', *JSPR*, 53, (804), 393–7.

Alvarado, C. and Zingrone, N. (1995), *JSPR*, 60, (841).

Alvarado, C. and Zingrone, N. (1997), 'Out-of-Body Experiences and Sensations of "Shocks" to the Body', *JSPR*, 61, (846), 304–13.

Badham, P. (1984), 'The Concept of the Soul', *The Christian Parapsychologist*, 5.

Baker, R. and Nickell, J. (1992), *Missing Pieces: How to Investigate Ghosts, UFOs, Psychics and Other Mysteries*, Buffalo, NY, Prometheus Books.

Banks, I. (1996), *The Enigma of Borley Rectory*, Chippenham, Foulsham.

Barber, T., Spanos, X. and Chaves, J. (1997), *Hypnosis, Imagining, and Human Potentialities*, Elmsford, NY, Pergamon.

Bastedo, R. (1981), 'An Empirical Test of Popular Astrology', in K. Frazier (ed.), *Paranormal Borderlands of Science*, Buffalo, NY, Prometheus Books.

Bayer, R. (1973), 'Parapsychology in Turkey', in A. Angoff and B. Shapin (eds), *Parapsychology Today: a Geographic View*, New York, Parapsychology Foundation.

Beloff, J. (1976), 'On Trying to Make Sense of the Paranormal', *Proceedings of the SPR*, 56, 173–97.

Beloff, J. (1989), 'The Refutation of Materialism', *JSPR*, 55, (814), 284–97.

Benor, D. (1990), 'A Psychiatrist Examines Feats of Healing', *JSPR*, 56, (821).

Berger, P. (1969), *The Social Reality of Religion*, London, Faber.

Berger, P. (1972), *A Rumour of Angels*, Harmondsworth, Penguin.

Bernal, M. (1991), *Black Athena*, London, Vintage Books.

Beutler, J. (1988), 'Paranormal Healing and Hypertension', *British Medical Journal (BMJ)*, 296, 1491–4.

Blackmore, S. (1981), *Beyond the Body: An Investigation of Out-of-Body Experiences*, London, Heinemann.

Blackmore, S. (1982a), 'Have you ever had an OBE?', *JSPR*, **52**, (791), 292–303.

Blackmore, S. (1982b), Review of J.L. Mitchell's *Out-of-Body Experiences*, *JSPR*, **51**.

Blackmore, S. (1984), 'A Postal Survey of OBEs and other Experiences', *JSPR*, **52**, (796), 225–44.

Blackmore, S. (1988), *JSPR*, **55**, (811), 49–59.

Blackmore, S. (1989), *JSPR*, **55**, (814), 251–62.

Blackmore, S. (1993), *Dying to Live: Science and the Near Death Experience*, London, Grafton Books.

Blackmore, S. and Woofitt, R. (1990), 'Out-of-Body Experiences in Young Children', *JSPR*, **56**, (819), 155–8.

Boslough, J. (1993), *Masters of Time*, London, Phoenix Books.

Brandon, R. (1983), *The Spiritualists: The Passion for the Occult in the 19th and 20th centuries*, London, Weidenfeld & Nicholson.

Braude, S. (1986), *The Limits of Influence: Psychokinesis and the Philosophy of Science*, London, Routledge & Kegan Paul.

Braude, S., Davis, G. and Wood, R. (1979), 'Experiments with Matthew Manning', *JSPR*, **50**, (782), 199–223.

Briggs, R. (1996), *Witches and Neighbours: The Social and Cultural Context of European Witchcraft*, London, HarperCollins.

Broad, C.D. (1953), *Religion, Philosophy and Psychical Research*, London, Routledge & Kegan Paul.

Broad, C.D. (1958), *Personal Identity and Survival*, London, SPR.

Budden, A. (1994), *Allergies and Aliens – The Visitation Experience – an Environmental Health Issue*, London, Discovery Times Press.

Burkert, W. (1985), *Greek Religion*, Oxford, Blackwell.

Byrd, R. (1988), 'Positive therapeutic effects of intecessory prayer in a coronory care population', *BMJ*, **296**, 1491–4.

Carcopino, J. (1970), *Daily Life in Ancient Rome*, London, Purnell.

Cardozo, R. (1970), 'A Modern Witch Craze', in M. Marwick (ed.), *Readings in Witchcraft and Sorcery*, Harmondsworth, Penguin.

Carlton, E. (1973), *Patterns of Belief*, London, Allen & Unwin.

Carlton, E. (1987), 'Parapsychology as a Religious Surrogate', *JSPR*, **54**, (807).

Carlton, E. (1988), 'Science, Pseudo-Science or Suprascience: A Look at the Anomalous Status of Parapsychology', *Self and Society*, **16**, (3).

Carlton, E. (1994), *Massacres: An Historical Perspective*, London, Scolar Press.

Carlton, E. (1995), *Values and the Social Sciences*, London, Duckworth.

Carlton, E. (1996), *The Few and the Many: A Typology of Elites*, Aldershot, Scolar Press.

Cartwright, N. (1983), *How the Laws of Physics Lie*, New York, Oxford University Press.

Cassirer, M. (1996), *Medium on Trial: The Story of Helen Duncan and the Witchcraft Act*, Stansted, PN Publishing.

Cavendish, R. (ed.) (1976), *Encyclopedia of the Unexplained*, London, Routledge & Kegan Paul.

Cerullo, J. (1982), *The Secularisation of the Soul: Psychical Research in Modern Britain*, Philadelphia, University of Philadelphia Press.

Chauvin, R. (1986), 'A PK Experiment with Mice', *JSPR*, **52**, (804), 348–51.

Christie-Murray, D. (1978), *Voices from the Gods: Speaking with Tongues*, London, Routledge & Kegan Paul.

Clark, W. (1958), *The Psychology of Religion*, New York, Macmillan.

Cockell, J. (1993), *Yesterday's Children: The Extraordinary Search for my Past Life Family*, London, Piatkus Books.

Cole, J. (1981), 'Anthropology Beyond the Fringe', in K. Frazier (ed.), *Paranormal Borderlands of Science*, Buffalo, NY, Prometheus Books.

Coleman, M. (ed.) (1988), *The Ghosts of the Trianon*, Wellingborough, Aquarian Press.

Collins, H. and Pinch, T. (1982), *Frames of Meaning, The Social Construction of Extraordinary Science*, London, Routledge & Kegan Paul.

Covensky, M. (1966), *The Ancient Near Eastern Tradition*, New York, Harper & Row.

Cox, W. (1974), 'Note on some experiments with Uri Geller', *Journal of Parapsychology*, **38**, 408–11.

Crick, F. (1973), *Of Molecules and Men*, London, Picador.

Cross, T. (1993), 'The Missing Fingers Case: Corroborated Evidence of Survival', *JSPR*, **59**, (831), 109–13.

Crow, W. (1972), *A History of Magic, Witchcraft and Occultism*, London, Abacus.

Darling, D. (1995), *After Life: In Search of Cosmic Consciousness*, London, Fourth Estate.

David, R. (1982), *The Ancient Egyptians*, London, Routledge & Kegan Paul.

Davidoff, L. (1980), *Introduction to Psychology*, New York, McGraw-Hill.

Davies, P. (1995), *Superforce* (rev. edn), Harmondsworth, Penguin.

Dawkins, R. (1998), *Unweaving the Rainbow: Science, Delusion and the Appetite for Wonder*, Harmondsworth, Penguin.

Donovan, P. (1979), *Interpreting Religious Experience*, London, Cox & Wyman.

Ducasse, C. (1951), *Nature, Mind and Death*, La Salle, Open Court Publishing.

Durkheim, E. (1968), *Elementary Forms of the Religious Life*, London, Allen & Unwin.

Eccles, J. (1953), *The Neurophysical Basis of Mind*, Oxford, Clarendon Press.

Edge, H. (1986), 'Survival and other Philosophical Questions', in H. Edge, R. Morris, J. Palmer and J. Rush (eds), *Foundations of Parapsychology*, London, Routledge & Kegan Paul.

Edge, H., Morris, R., Palmer, J. and Rush, J. (eds) (1986), *Foundations of Parapsychology*, London, Routledge & Kegan Paul.

Edwards, P. (ed.) (1992), *Immortality*, New York, Macmillan.

Edwards, P. (1996), *Reincarnation: a Critical Examination*, Buffalo, NY, Prometheus Books.

Eisenbud, J. (1969), *The World of Ted Serios*, New York, Paperback Library.

El-Guindi, F. (1977), *Religion in Culture*, London, W.M. Brown.

Evans, H. (1983), *The Evidence for UFOs*, Wellingborough, Aquarian Press.

Evans, H. (1984), *Visions, Apparitions, Alien Visitors*, Wellingborough, Aquarian Press.

Evans, H. (1994), Review of 'Unusual Personal Experiences: An Analysis of the Data from Three National Surveys', *JSPR*, 59, (834), 379–81.

Evans-Pritchard, E. (1937), *Witchcraft, Oracles and Magic among the Azande*, London, Clarendon Press.

Eysenck, H. (1957), *Sense and Nonsense in Psychology*, Harmondsworth, Penguin.

Eysenck, H. and Sargent, C. (1983), *Explaining the Unexplained*, London, Prion Books.

Falding, H. (1972), *The Sociology of Religion*, New York, McGraw-Hill.

Farina, A. (1976), *Abnormal Psychology*, Englewood Cliffs, NJ, Prentice-Hall.

Feder, K. (1986), '"American Genesis" A New Chapter in "Cult" Archaeology', in K. Frazier (ed.), *Science Confronts the Paranormal*, Buffalo, NY, Prometheus Books.

Fell, B. (1977), *America BC*, New York, Quadrangle Books.

Flaceliere, R. (1965), *Greek Oracles*, London, Elek.

Fontana, D. (1996), *JSPR*, 57, (823), 385–402.

Fontana, D. (1998), 'Psychical Research and the Millennium: New Light on the Nature of Man', *Proceedings of the SPR*, October.

Frazier, K. (ed.) (1981), *Paranormal Borderlands of Science*, Buffalo, NY, Prometheus Books.

Frazier, K. and Randi, J. (1986), 'Prediction after the Fact: Lessons of the Tamara Rand Hoax', in K. Frazier (ed.), *Science Confronts the Paranormal*, Buffalo, NY, Prometheus Books.

Gabbard, G. and Twemlow, S. (1984), *With the Eyes of the Mind: An Empirical Analysis of Out-of-Body States*, New York, Praeger.

Gallup, G. (1982), *Adventures in Immortality: A Look Beyond the Threshold of Death*, London, Souvenir Press.

Gardner, G. (1968), *Witchcraft Today*, London, Jarrolds.

Gardner, M. (1988), *The New Age: Notes of a Fringe Watcher*, Buffalo, NY, Prometheus Books.

Gauld, A. (1982), *Mediumship and Survival*, London, Heinemann.

Gauld, A. and Cornell, A. (1979), *Poltergeists*, Boston, Routledge & Kegan Paul.

Geertz, C. (1966), 'Religion as a Cultural System', in M. Banton (ed.), *Anthropological Approaches to the Study of Religion*, London, Tavistock, ASA Monographs.

Good, T. (1987), *Above Top Secret*, London, Sidgwick & Jackson.

Good, T. (ed.) (1990), *The UFO Report 1991*, London, Sidgwick & Jackson.

Good, T. (1998), *Alien Base*, London, Century Books.

Goodman, J. (1977), *Psychic Archaeology: Time Machine to the Past*, New York, Berkley.

Goodman, J. (1981), *American Genesis*, New York, Berkley.

Gordon, C. (1971), *Before Columbus*, New York, Crown Books.

Gordon, H. (1987), *Extrasensory Deception*, Buffalo, NY, Prometheus Books.

Grant, F. (1957), *Ancient Roman Religion*, New York, Bobbs-Merrill.

Grattan-Guinness, J. (1985), Review of James McLenon's, *Deviant Sciences: The Case of Parapsychology*, JSPR, 53, (800).

Greeley, A. and McCready, W. (1975), 'Are we a Nation of Mystics?', *New York Times Magazine*, 26 January.

Gregory, A. (1977), 'Anatomy of a Fraud: Harry Price and the Medium Rudi Schneider', *Annals of Science*, 34, (449).

Gregory, A. (1981), 'Psychical Research as a Social Activity', JSPR, 51.

Gregory, A. (1982a), Review of H.M. Collins and T.J. Pinch's *Frames of Meaning*, JSPR, 51.

Gregory, A. (1982b), 'London Experiments with Matthew Manning', *Proceedings of the SPR*, 56, part 212, October.

Gregory, A. (1983a), Review of J.J. Cerullo's *The Secularisation of the Soul*, *JSPR*, **52**.

Gregory, A. (1983b), Unpublished letter to *Nature*, 30 January, Gregory Papers, SPR Archives.

Grey, M. (1985), *Return from Death: An Exploration of the Near Death Experience*, London, Routledge & Kegan Paul.

Haining, P. (1972), *Anatomy of Witchcraft*, London, Souvenir Press.

Haraldsson, E. and Wiseman, R. (1995a), 'Investigating Macro-PK in India: Swami Premananda', *JSPR*, **60**, (839).

Haraldsson, E. and Wiseman, R. (1995b), 'Reactions to and Assessment of a Videotape on S'ytha Sai Baba', *JSPR*, **60**, (839).

Haraldsson, E. and Wiseman, R. (1996), 'Two Investigations of Ostensible Macro-PK in India', *JSPR*, **61**, (843), 109–13.

Harris, M. (1986), *Sorry You've been Duped: Classic Mysteries of the Paranormal*, London, Weidenfeld & Nicholson.

Harrison, G. (1992), 'Witchcraft in Salem', Westminster Conference, London.

Hay, D. and Morrisey, A. (1978), 'Reports of Estatic, Paranormal or Religious Experience in Great Britain and the United States – a Comparison of Trends', *Journal of the Society for the Study of Religion*, **18**.

Haynes, R. (1982), *The Society for Psychical Research: A History 1882–1982*, London, MacDonald.

Heaney, J. (1984), *The Sacred and the Psychic: Parapsychology and Christian Theology*, New York, Paulist Press.

Hearne, K. (1982), *JSPR*, **51**, (791).

Hill, F. (1966), *A Delusion of Satan: The Full Story of the Salem Witch Trials*, London, Hamish Hamilton.

Hill, M. (1973), *The Sociology of Religion*, London, Heinemann.

Hippisley Coxe, A. (1973), *Haunted Britain*, London, Hutchinson.

Hoebbens, P.H. and Truzzi, M. (1987), 'Reflection of Psychic Sleuths', in P. Kurtz (ed.), *A Skeptic's Handbook of Parapsychology*, Buffalo, NY, Prometheus Books.

Holm, N. (1982), *Religious Studies*, London, Almquist & Wiskell.

Hopkins, B. (1987), *Intruders*, New York, Random House.

Hopkins, B. (1981), *Missing Time*, New York, Marek.

Hovelmann, G. (1985), 'Evidence for Survival from Near-Death Experiences. A Critical Appraisal', in P. Kurtz (ed.), *A Skeptic's Handbook of Parapsychology*, Buffalo, NY, Prometheus Books.

Howard, R. (1997), *Charismania*, London, Mowbrays.

Hoyle, F. (1983), *The Intelligent Universe*, London, Michael Joseph.

Hynek, A. (1974), *The UFO Experience*, London, Corgi.

Inglis, B. (1977), *Natural and Supernatural: A History of the Paranormal*, London, Hodder & Stoughton.

Inglis, B. (1983), *JSPR*, 52, (795), 209–12.

Inglis, B. (1989), *Trance: A Natural History of Altered States of Mind*, London, Grafton Books.

Irwin, H. (1980), 'Out of the Body Down Under', *JSPR*, 50, (785), 448–59.

Irwin, H. (1985), *Flight of the Mind: A Psychological Study of Out-of-Body Experiences*, Metuchen, NY, Scarecrow Press.

James, W. (1958), *The Varieties of Religious Experience*, New York, New American Library.

Janin, P. (1986), 'The Tychoscope: A Possible New Tool for Parapsychological Experience', *JSPR*, 53 (804).

Johnson, M. (1984), 'A Technique for Testing the PSI-Field Theory with Some Implications for Survival Research Part II, The Survival Issue', *JSPR*, 52.

Keene, M.L. (1976), *The Psychic Mafia*, New York, Dell Books.

Keesing, R. and Keesing, F. (1971), *New Perspectives in Cultural Anthropology*, New York, Holt Rinehart & Winston.

Keil, H., Herbert, B., Pratt, J. and Ullman, M. (1976), 'Directly Observable PK Effects', *Proceedings of the SPR*, 56, Part 210, January.

Kelly, I. and Saklofske (1986), 'Alternative Explanations in Science: the Extroversion-Intraversion Astrological Effect', in K. Frazier (ed.), *Science Confronts the Paranormal*, Buffalo, NY, Prometheus Books.

Kildahl, J. (1972), *The Psychology of Speaking in Tongues*, New York, Harper & Row.

King, F. (1970), *Ritual Magic in England*, London, Spearman.

Kirk, G. (1974), *The Nature of Greek Myths*, Harmondsworth, Penguin.

Klass, P. (1988), *UFO Abductions: A Dangerous Game*, Buffalo, NY, Promethus Books.

Koestler, A. (1956), *Reflections on Hanging*, London, Gollancz.

Koestler, A. (1972), *The Roots of Coincidence*, London, Hutchinson.

Koestler, A. (1973), *The Challenge of Chance*, London, Hutchinson.

Koestler, A. (1980), *Bricks to Babel*, London, Hutchinson.

Krippner, J. (1980), 'A Suggested Typology of Folk Healing and Its Relevance to Parapsychological Investigation', *JSPR*, 50, (786).

Kübler-Ross, E. (1975), *Death: The Final Stage of Growth*, Englewood Cliffs, NJ, Prentice-Hall.

Kurtz, P. (1986), *The Transcendental Temptation*, Buffalo, NY, Prometheus Books.

Kurtz, P., Zelen, M. and Abell, G. (1981), 'Results of US Test of the

"Mars Effect"', in K. Frazier (ed.), *Paranormal Borderlands of Science*, Buffalo, NY, Prometheus Books.

Leland, C. (1899), *Aradia, or the Gospel of the Witches*, London.

LeShan, L. and Margenau, H. (1980), 'An Approach to a Science of Psychical Research', *JSPR*, 50, (783).

Levack, B. (1995), *The Witchhunt in Early Modern Europe*, London, Longman.

Lorimer, D. (1984), *Survival? Body, Mind, and Death in the Light of Psychic Experience*, London, Routledge & Kegan Paul.

Lundahl, C. (ed.) (1982), *A Collection of Near-Death Research Readings*, Chicago, Nelson-Hall.

MacKenzie, A. (1983), *Hauntings and Apparitions*, London, Paladin.

Madell, G. (1988), *Mind and Materialism*, Edinburgh, Edinburgh University Press.

Manning, M. (1974), *The Link*.

Manning, M. (1977), *In the Minds of Millions*.

Manning, M. (1978), *The Strangers*.

Martin, B. (1981), *Abnormal Psychology*, London, Holt, Rinehart & Winston.

Marwick, M. (ed.) (1970), *Readings in Witchcraft and Sorcery*, Harmondsworth, Penguin.

Matlock, J. (1986), Review of D.S. Rogo's *The Search for Yesterday*, *JSPR*, 53.

Mayer, P. (1970), 'Witches', in M. Marwick (ed.), *Readings in Witchcraft and Sorcery*, Harmondsworth, Penguin.

Mayo, J., White, O. and Eysenck, H. (1978), 'An Empirical Study of the Relation between Astrological Factors and Personality', *Journal of Social Psychology*, 105, 229–36.

McClenon, J. (1984), *Deviant Science: The Case for Parapsychology*, Philadelphia, University of Philadelphia Press.

McCreery, C. and Claridge, G. (1995), 'Out-of-the-Body Experiences and Personality', *JSPR*, 60, (838), 129–48.

McGervey, J. (1981), 'A Statistical Test of Sun-sign Astrology', in K. Frazier (ed.), *Paranormal Borderlands of Science*, Buffalo, NY, Prometheus Books.

Meadow, M.J. and Kahoe, R. (1984), *Psychology of Religion*, New York, Harper & Row.

Merton, R.K. (1949), *Social Theory and Social Structure*, London, Free Press.

Mes, G. (1975), *Faith Healing and Religion*, New York, Philosophical Library.

Millar, R. (1995), 'Bonfire of Insanity', *Sunday Times Magazine*, 29 January.

Mitchell, B. (ed.) (1971), *The Philosophy of Religion*, Oxford, Oxford University Press.

Mitchell, J.E. (1982), *Out-of-Body Experiences: A Handbook*, London, McFarland & Co.

Moody, R. (1975), *Life after Life*, Covington, GA, Mockingbird Books.

Moore, B. (1981), *The Philosophical Possibilities Beyond Death*, Springfield, Il, Charles Thomas.

Moore, E. (1977), *Try the Spirits: Christianity and Psychical Research*, Oxford, Oxford University Press.

Morehouse, D. (1996), *Psychic Warrior*, London, Michael Joseph.

Murray, M. (1921), *The Witch Cults in Modern Europe*, Oxford, Oxford University Press.

Murray, M. (1960), *The God of Witches*, New York, Doubleday.

Nelson, G. (1968), 'The Concept of Cult', *Sociological Review*, November.

Nelson, G. (1969), *Spiritualism and Society*, London, Routledge & Kegan Paul.

Nickell, J. (1994), *Psychic Sleuths: ESP and Sensational Cases*, Buffalo, NY, Prometheus Books.

Nottingham, E. (1964), *Religion and Society*, London, Free Press.

Noyes, R. and Kletti, R. (1977), 'Depersonalization in Response to Life-Threatening Danger', *Comparative Psychiatry*, 18, 181–94.

Ophuls, W. (1975), *Readings in Sociology*, Guildford, CT, Dushkin.

Ornstein, R. (1977), *The Psychology of Consciousness*, New York, Harcourt Brace.

Palmer, J. (1978), 'The Out-of-Body Experience: a Psychological Theory', *Parapsychology Review*, 9, 19–22.

Parrinder, G. (1970), *Witchcraft, European and African*, London, Faber.

Pasricha, S. (1990), *Claims of Reincarnation: an Empirical Study of Cases in India*, New Delhi, Harman Publishing.

Perry, M. (1979), Review of D. Christie-Murray's *Voices from the Gods*, *JSPR*, 50.

Playfair, G. (1980), *This House is Haunted*, London, Souvenir Press.

Pruyser, P. (1974), *Between Belief and Unbelief*, New York, Harper & Row.

Rae-Ellis, V. (1990), *The Ghost Stories of our own Time*, London, Faber & Faber.

Randi, J. (1995), *The Supernatural A–Z: the Truth and the Lies*, London, Headline.

Randles, J. (1981), *UFO Study*, London, Robert Hale.

Randles, J. (1983), *UFO Reality: A Critical Look at the Physical Evidence*, London, Robert Hale.

Randles, J. (1996), *The Paranormal Source Book*, London, Piatkus.

Rees, M. (1997), *Before the Beginning*, London, Simon & Schuster.

Rhine, J.B. (1947), *The Reach of the Mind*, New York, William Morrow.

Ring, K. (1992), *The Omega Project*, New York, Morrow.

Robbins, R. (1964), *Encyclopedia of Witchcraft and Demonology*, London, Neville.

Robertson, R. (1970), *The Sociological Interpretation of Religion*, London, Blackwell.

Rogo, D.S. (1980), 'Theories about PK: A Critical Evaluation', *JSPR*, 50, (784), 359–78.

Rogo, D.S. (1971), *JSPR*, 46, (750).

Rogo, D.S. (1982), *Miracles: A Parascientific Enquiry into Wondrous Phenomena*, New York, Dial Press.

Rogo, D.S. (1984), *JSPR*, 52, (797), 322.

Rogo, D.S. (1985), *The Search for Yesterday: A Critical Examination of the Evidence for Reincarnation*, New York, Prentice-Hall.

Rogo, D.S. (1989), *JSPR*, 55, (816), 432.

Roll, W. (1974), 'Survival Research: Problems and Possibilities', in J. White (ed.), *Psychic Exploration*, New York, Putnams.

Roth, J. (ed.) (1969), *The Moral Philosophy of William James*, London, Crowell.

Rowe, W. (1993), 'Psychic Detective: A Critical Examination', *Skeptical Enquirer*, 17, Winter.

Rush, J. (1977), 'Problems and Methods in Psychokenesis Research', *Parapsychological Research*, 1, 15–78.

Rush, J. (1986a), 'Findings from Experimental PK Research', in H. Edge, R. Morris, J. Palmer and J. Rush (eds), *Foundations of Parapsychology*, London, Routledge & Kegan Paul.

Rush, J. (1986b), 'Spontaneous PSI Phenomena', in H. Edge, R. Morris, J. Palmer and J. Rush (eds), *Foundations of Parapsychology*, London, Routledge & Kegan Paul.

Rush, J. (1986c), 'Parapsychology: A Historical Perspective', in H. Edge, R. Morris, J. Palmer and J. Rush (eds), *Foundations of Parapsychology*, London, Routledge & Kegan Paul.

Sabom, M. (1982), *Recollections of Death*, New York, Harper & Row.

Sagan, C. (1974), *The Cosmic Connection*, London, Coronet Books.

Sagan, C. (1996), *The Demon Haunted World*, London, Headline Books.

Saklani, A. (1992), 'Follow up Studies of PK Effects on Plant Growth', *JSPR*, 58, (827), 258–65.

Sargent, C. (1986), *The Astrology of Rising Signs*, London, Rider & Co.

Samarin, W. (1972), 'Glossolalia', *Psychology Today*, 6 (3), 48–50, 78–9.

Schmeidler, G. (1983), 'Interpreting Reports of Out-of-Body Experiences', *JSPR*, 52, (794), 102–4.

Schmidt, H. and Terry, J. (1977), 'Search for a Relationship between Brain Waves and PK Performance', in J. Morris et al. (eds), *Research in Parapsychology 1976*, Metuchen, NY, Scarecrow Press.

Schnabel, J. (1994), *Dark White: Aliens, Abductions and the UFO Obsession*, London, Hamish Hamilton.

Seigal, R. (1977), 'Hallucinations', *Scientific American*, 132–40.

Shorter, A. (1978), *The Egyptian Gods*, London, Routledge & Kegan Paul.

Showalter, E. (1997), *Hystories: Hysterical Epidemics and Modern Culture*, London, Picador.

Smyth, F. (1970), *Modern Witchcraft*, London, MacDonald.

Von Soden, W. (1994), *The Ancient Orient*, Grand Rapids, MI, Eerdmans.

Spedding, F. (1975), 'Concepts of Survival', *JSPR*, 48, (763).

Spencer, J. (1989), *Perspectives: A Radical Examination of the Alien Abduction Theory*, London, MacDonald.

Spiro, M. (1966), 'Religion: Problems of Definition and Explanation', in M. Banton (ed.), *Anthropological Approaches to the Study of Religion*, London, Tavistock, ASA Monographs.

Stafford-Clark, D. (1967), *What Freud Really Said*, Harmondsworth, Penguin.

Stanford, R. and Fox, C. (1975), 'An Effect of Release Effort in a Psychokinetic Task', in J. Morris et al. (eds), *Research in Parapsychology 1974*, Metuchen, NY, Scarecrow Press.

Steiger, B. (1976), *Project Blue Book*, New York, Ballantine.

Stemman, R. (1979), 'Surviving as a Psychic', *Alpha*, September–October.

Stenger, V. (1995), *The Unconscious Quantum: Metaphysics in Modern Physics and Cosmology*, Buffalo, NY, Prometheus Books.

Stevenson, I. (1974), *Twenty Cases Suggestive of Reincarnation*, rev. 2nd edn, Charlottesville, University of Virginia Press.

Stevenson, I. (1983), *JSPR*, 52, (793), 1–30.

Story, R. (1976), *The Space Gods Revealed*, London, New English Library.

Stowers, C. (1986), *Careless Whispers: The Lake Waco Murders*, New York, Pocket Books.

Strieber, W. (1988), *Transformation*, New York, Morrow.

Sturrock, P. (1987), 'A Brief History of the Society for Scientific Exploration', *Journal of Scientific Exploration*, 1, (1), 1–2.

Summers, M. (1965), *A History of Witchcraft and Demonology*, first published in 1926, London, Routledge & Kegan Paul.

Sweat, J. and Durm, M. (1993), *Skeptical Enquirer*, 17, Winter.

Tabori, P. (1974), *Crime and the Occult*, New York, Taplinger.

Tart, C. and Palmer, J. (1979), 'Some PSI Experiments with Matthew Manning', *JSPR*, 50, (782), 224–8.

Taylor, J. (1980), *Science and Supernatural*, London, Temple Smith.

Taylor, N. (1963), *Narcotics: Nature's Dangerous Gift*, New York, Delta Books.

Thalbourne, M. and Nofi, O. (1997), *JSPR*, 61, (847).

Thomas E. and Cooper, P. (1978), 'Measurement and Incidence of Mystical Experiences', *Journal of the Society for the Study of Religion*, 17.

Thouless, R. (1978), 'Theories about Survival', paper presented to the Second International SPR Conference, Cambridge, March.

Thouless, R. (1979), 'Theories about Survival', *JSPR*, 50, (779), 1–8.

Thouless, R. (1984), 'Do we Survive Death?', *Proceedings of the SPR*, 57.

Truzzi, M. (1971), 'Definitions and Dimensions of the Occult', *Journal of Popular Culture*, Winter.

Truzzi, M. (1974), 'Towards a Sociology of the Occult: Notes on Modern Witchcraft', in J. Zaretsky and M. Leone (eds), *Religious Movements in Contemporary America*, Princeton, NJ, Princeton University Press.

Tyrell, G.N. (1953), *Apparitions*, London, Duckworth.

Vallee, J. (1977), *UFOs: The Psychic Solution*, London, Panther.

Vallee, J. (1990), *Dimensions: A Casebook of Alien Contact*, London, Sphere Books.

Wallace, R. and Benson, H. (1972), 'The Physiology of Meditation', *Scientific American*, 226, 84–90.

Watson, L. (1976), *The Romeo Error*, London, Coronet.

Weatherhead, L. (1951), *Psychology, Religion and Healing*, New York, Abbingdon-Cokesbury.

Weber, M. (1965), *The Sociology of Religion*, London, Methuen.

West, D.J. (1987), *JSPR*, 54, (806), 1–15.

Williams, G. (1989), *A Life Beyond Death*, London, Robert Hale.

Wilson, B. (1961), *Sects and Society*, London, Heinemann.

Wilson, C. (1973), *The Occult*, London, Mayflower Books.

Wilson, C. (1984), *The Psychic Detectives*, London, Pan Books.

Wilson, C. and Grant, J. (1981), *A Directory of Possibilities*, Exeter, Webb & Bower.

Wilson, I. (1981), *Mind out of Time*, London, Gollancz.

Wilson, I. (1987), *The After Death Experience*, London, Sidgwick & Jackson.

Wood, R. (1992), *The Widow of Borley: A Psychical Investigation*, London, Duckworth.

Worsley, P. (1968), *The Trumpet Shall Sound*, 2nd edn, New York, Shocken.

Index